How to Build a Person

How to Build a Person: A Prolegomenon

John L. Pollock

A Bradford Book
The MIT Press
Cambridge, Massachusetts
London, England

This book was printed and bound in the United States of America.

Library of Congress Cataloging-in-Publication Data

Pollock, John L.
 How to build a person: a prolegomenon/John L. Pollock
  p. cm.
 "A Bradford book"
 Bibliography: p.
 Includes index.
 ISBN 0-262-16113-3
 1. Artificial intelligence—Philosophy. 2. Machine learning. I. Title
 Q335.P652 1989
 006.3—dc20   89-35724
                                                                   CIP

For Oscar

Contents

Preface

This book is a prolegomenon to the enterprise of building a person. It is a defense of three theses: token physicalism, agent materialism, and strong AI. Token physicalism is the thesis that mental events are physical events. In human beings, they are presumably neurological events. Agent materialism is the thesis that persons are physical objects having a suitable structure. Strong AI is the thesis that one can construct a person (a thing that literally thinks, feels, and is conscious) by building a physical system endowed with appropriate "artificial intelligence". It is argued that what is required for the construction of a person is a physical system that mimics human rationality in a sense made precise in the book. The project of building such a system is actually underway in the OSCAR project, and this book discusses the theoretical underpinnings of the OSCAR project at some length. The precise objective of the OSCAR project is a formulation of a general theory of rationality and its implementation in a computer program. It follows from the theses of the book that a system running this program and appropriately connected to the world will literally be a person.

OSCAR represents the dream of AI since its infancy, but it is a dream that has faded in much of the AI community. This is because researchers in AI have made less progress than anticipated in achieving the dream. My claim in this book is that the failure is not intrinsic to the task, but stems from the fact that many of the problems involved are essentially philosophical, while researchers in AI have not usually been trained in philosophy. Training in philosophy is not by itself sufficient to solve the problems, because they are hard problems and have difficult non-philosophical ingredients as well, but input from philosophers is probably a necessary condition for their solution.

The intent of this book is to begin the process of providing a recipe for building a person, and the intent of the OSCAR project is to implement that recipe. The central claim of the book is that building a person reduces to the task of constructing a system that adequately models human rationality. Some time is spent making this claim precise, and it is urged that a system modeling human rationality in the appropriate sense will experience qualia, will be self-conscious, will have desires, fears, intentions, and a full range of mental states. I am not content to give a general theoretical argument to the effect that a system modeling human rationality will be a person. I want to spell out precisely what that involves and then actually build such a system. In order to accomplish this, we must have a theory of human rationality of sufficient precision to make computer modeling possible. This will include an account of theoretical reasoning (epistemology) and an account of practical reasoning. This book is not an appropriate vehicle for laying out an entire theory of rationality, but the last chapter sketches how the general theory will go, making reference where possible to the more precise accounts I have given elsewhere. In effect, OSCAR will be an implementation of my own theories of rationality. I find that most of the work I have done in philosophy over the last twenty-five years is directly relevant to this problem. In an important sense, I have been doing AI all along without realizing it. An increasing number of technically minded philosophers are coming to the same conclusion. On the other hand, no one can claim to have solved all the problems, and anyone working in this field quickly discovers that implementation and theory construction go hand in hand. The attempt to implement a philosophical theory of reasoning is usually quick to reveal inadequacies in the theory. In effect, the computer becomes a mechanical aid in the discovery of counterexamples. So by immersing themselves in AI, philosophers are not giving up their more traditional interests. Instead, they are adopting powerful new tools that will be of tremendous help in the solution of old problems.

This book grew out of a series of articles in the philosophy of mind, together with the felt need for writing something that ties all of my work together and shows how it is all relevant to the OSCAR project and how the OSCAR project is relevant to traditional philosophical concerns. The book consists largely of descendants of bits and pieces of the following articles: "My brother, the machine" (*Nous*), "How to build a person" (*Philosophical Perspectives*), "Understanding the language of thought" (*Philosophical Studies*), "Philosophy and artificial intelligence" (*Philosophical Perspectives*), "Interest driven reasoning" (*Synthese*), "Defeasible reasoning" (*Cognitive Science*), "OSCAR: a general theory of rationality" (*Journal of Experimental and Theoretical Artificial Intelligence*), "Interest driven suppositional reasoning" (*Journal of Automated Reasoning*), and "A theory of defeasible reasoning" (*International Journal of Intelligent Systems*). I thank these journals for permission to reprint the relevant material. The epistemology presupposed by the enterprise is essentially that of my books *Contemporary*

Theories of Knowledge and *Knowledge and Justification*, although important parts of the theory are being revised and made more precise in the course of the project. Much of the work has proceeded in parallel with work on probabilistic reasoning, and that is presented in my book *Nomic Probability and the Foundations of Induction*, which is being published at about the same time by Oxford University Press.

This book has profited from detailed comments I have received on earlier versions. I wish to thank Rob Cummins, Chris Maloney, and Paul Thagard.

How to Build a Person

Chapter 1
The Self-Conscious Machine

My general purpose in this book is to defend the conception of man as an intelligent machine. Specifically, I will argue that mental states are physical states and persons are physical objects. To this end, let us begin with a fable.

1. The Fable of Oscar

Oscar I

Once in a distant land there lived a race of Engineers. They had a life of luxury with all their physical needs provided by the machines they so cleverly devised. Their greatest pleasure in life came from inventing a machine more ingenious than the creations of their compatriots. Imagine yourself one of the Engineers, and suppose you are undertaking the supreme feat of building an "intelligent machine" that will respond to its environment in efficient ways, learn by experience, and so forth. You will incorporate sensors much like our sense organs so that the machine can respond to states of the environment, and we might even call these sensors 'sense organs'. You will also incorporate facilities for information processing that will enable the machine to draw conclusions and make predictions on the basis of its sensory input. Some of these information-processing facilities may resemble human reasoning facilities, both deductive and inductive. And you will incorporate some sort of conative structure to provide goals for the machine to attempt to realize. If the machine is to survive in a hostile environment, it would also be wise to provide sensors that respond to conditions under which the machine is in imminent danger of damage or destruction. We might call these 'pain sensors'. The machine could then have built-in "fight or flight" responses elicited by the activation of its pain sensors. Let's call this machine 'Oscar I'. Oscar I is pretty much the same as the machines Putnam [1960] considers.

Oscar II

Oscar I could function reasonably well in a congenial environment. But in an environment that is both reasonably complex and reasonably hostile, Oscar I would be doomed to early destruction. He would be easy meat for wily machinivores. The difficulty is this. To be effective in avoiding damage, Oscar I must not only be able to *respond* to the stimulation of his pain sensors when that occurs—he must also be able to *predict* when that is likely to occur and avoid getting into such situations. He must be able to exercise "foresight". As he has been described, Oscar I has the ability to form generalizations about his environment as sensed by his sense organs, but he has no way to form generalizations about the circumstances in which his pain sensors are likely to be activated. This is because Oscar I has no direct way of knowing when his pain sensors are activated—he has no way of "feeling" pain. As I have described them, the pain sensors cause behavioral responses directly and do not provide input to Oscar's cognitive machinery. If Oscar is to be able to avoid pain rather than merely to respond to it, he must be able to tell when he is in pain and be able to form generalizations about pain. To do this he needs another kind of sensor—a "pain sensor sensor" that senses when the pain sensors are activated. (Of course, the pain sensors can themselves be pain sensor sensors if they send their outputs to more than one place. We do not need a separate organ to sense the operation of the first organ.) Suppose we build these pain sensor sensors into Oscar I, renaming him Oscar II. This gives him a rudimentary kind of self-awareness. If the conative structure of Oscar II is such that he is moved to avoid not only the current activation of his pain sensors but their anticipated activation as well, then this will enable him to avoid getting into situations that would otherwise result in his early demise.

It is illuminating to note that the difference between Oscar I and Oscar II is roughly the difference between an amoeba and a worm. Amoebas only respond to pain (or more conservatively, what we can regard as the activation of their pain sensors); worms can learn to avoid it. The learning powers of worms are pretty crude, proceeding entirely by simple forms of conditioning, but we have said nothing about Oscar that requires him to have greater learning powers.

Beginning with Oscar II we can distinguish between two kinds of sensors. First, Oscar II has *external sensors* sensing the world around him. These are of two kinds. He has ordinary perceptual sensors, and he also has pain sensors that respond to environmental inputs that tend to be indicative of impending damage to his body. Oscar II also has an *internal sensor* sensing the operation of his pain sensors. His internal sensor could be described as an 'introspective sensor' because it senses the operation of another sensor.

Oscar III

Oscar II is still a pretty dumb brute. I have described him as sensing his physical environment and forming generalizations on that basis. If his "red sensor" provides the input 'red' to his cognitive machinery, he can relate that to various generalizations he has formed concerning when there are red things about, and he can also use the input to form new generalizations. But he is not going to be very effective at reasoning in this way. The trouble is that he can take his perception of the environment only at face value. He will have no conception of the environment's fooling him. For example, he will be unable to distinguish between a machine-eating tiger and a mirror image of a machine-eating tiger. All he will be able to conclude is that some tigers are dangerous and others are not. We, on the other hand, know that all tigers are dangerous but that sometimes there is no tiger there, even though it looks to us as if there is. Oscar II has no way of learning things like this. He has no way of discovering, for example, that his red sensor is not totally reliable. This is because, at least until he learns a lot about micromechanics, he has no way even to know that he has a red sensor or to know when that sensor is activated. He responds to the sensor in an automatic way, just as Oscar I responded to his pain sensors in an automatic way. If Oscar II is to acquire a sophisticated view of his environment, he must be able to sense the activation of his red sensor.[1] That will enable him to discover inductively that his red sensor is sometimes activated in the absence of red objects.

This point really has to do with computing power. Given sufficient computing power, Oscar might be able to get by forming all of his generalizations directly on the basis of the output of his external sensors. His generalizations would parallel the kind of "phenomenalistic generalizations" required by the phenomenalist epistemologies championed in the early part of this century by such philosophers as Rudolph Carnap [1928] and C. I. Lewis [1946]. The most salient feature of such generalizations would be their extraordinary complexity. Just imagine what it would be like if instead of thinking about physical objects you had to keep track of the world entirely in terms of the way things appear to you and your generalizations about the world had to be formulated exclusively in those terms. You could not do it. Human beings do not have the computational capacity required to form and

---

[1] Putnam [1960] overlooks this.

confirm such generalizations or to guide their activities in terms of such complex generalizations. Instead, human beings take perceptual input to provide only prima facie (that is, defeasible) reasons for conclusions about their physical environment. This allows them to split their generalizations into two parts. On the one hand they have generalizations about the relations between their perceptual inputs and the states of their environment, and on the other hand they have generalizations about regularities within the environment that persist independently of perception of the environment. The advantage of dividing things up in this way is that the two sets of generalizations can be adjusted in parallel to keep each manageably simple under circumstances in which purely phenomenalistic generalizations would be unmanageable. Epistemologically, we begin by trusting our senses and taking their pronouncements to be indicative of the state of the world. More formally, appearance provides us with prima facie reasons for judgments about the world, and, initially, we have no defeaters for any of those judgments. Making initial judgments in this way, we find that certain generalizations are approximately true. If (1) we can make those generalizations exactly true by adjusting some of our initial judgments about the world, and (2) we can do it in such a way that there are simple generalizations describing the circumstances under which things are not as they appear, we take that as a defeater for the initial perceptual judgments that we want to overturn, and we embrace the two sets of generalizations (the generalizations about the environment and the generalizations about the circumstances under which perception is reliable). The result is a considerable simplification in the generalizations we accept and in terms of which we guide our activities.[2]   A secondary effect is that once we acquire evidence that a generalization is approximately true, there is a "cognitive push" toward regarding it as exactly true.

The logical form of what goes on here is strikingly similar to traditional accounts of scientific theory formation. On those accounts we begin with a set of data and then we "posit theoretical entities" and construct generalizations about those entities with the objective of constructing a

---

[2] Philosophers of science have long been puzzled by the role of simplicity in scientific confirmation. When two theories would each explain the data but one is significantly simpler than the other, we take the simpler one to be confirmed. But this is puzzling. What has simplicity got to do with truth? I think that the explanation for the role simplicity plays in confirmation probably lies in the kinds of considerations I have been describing. Its importance has to do with minimizing computational complexity, and its legitimacy has to do with the fact that, in a sense, the objects the generalizations are about are "free floating" and can be adjusted to minimize complexity. This is admittedly a bit vague, but I find it suggestive.

theory that makes correct predictions about new data. There is a formal parallel between this picture and our thought about physical objects. Physical objects play the role of theoretical entities, our sensory input provides the data, and we try to adjust the generalizations about physical objects and the "bridge rules" relating physical objects and sensory input in such a way that we can make correct predictions about future sensory input. Of course, all of this is to overintellectualize what goes on in human thought. We do not invent physical objects as theoretical entities designed to explain our sensory inputs. We just naturally think in terms of physical objects, and our conceptual framework makes that epistemologically legitimate independently of any reconstruction of it in terms of scientific theory formation. My point is merely that the logical structure is similar. From an information-processing point of view, the adoption of such a logical structure gives us an additional degree of freedom (the physical objects, or the theoretical entities) that can be adjusted to simplify the associated generalizations and thus minimize the computational complexity of using those generalizations to guide activity.[3]

The point of all this is that in order to acquire the kind of manageable generalizations about the environment that will enable him to keep functioning and achieve his built-in goals, an intelligent machine must be able to sense the operation of his own sensors. Only in that way can he treat the input from these sensors as defeasible and form generalizations about their reliability, and the need to treat them this way is dictated by considerations of computational complexity. Let's build such introspective sensors into Oscar II and rename him 'Oscar III'. He thus acquires a further degree of self-awareness. The difference between Oscar II and Oscar III may be roughly parallel to the difference between a bird and a cat. Kittens quickly learn about mirror images and come to ignore them, but birds will go on attacking their own reflections until they become exhausted.

We talk loosely about introspection as the "mind's eye", but no one thinks there is literally a sense organ in the mind surveying what is occurring there. When we talk about incorporating introspective sensors into Oscar, we should not think of them on that model. The addition of introspective sensors consists only of treating the output of his perceptual sensors in new ways, giving them additional functional roles in cognitive processing.

---

[3] There is an interesting purely formal question here that, I guess, lies in the domain of theoretical computer science. That is the question of the extent to which and the circumstances under which computational complexity can be decreased by introducing such "intervening variables". It is obvious that this can sometimes be achieved, but it would be interesting to have a general account of it.

I do not want to leave the impression that all information processing can be described as "reasoning". On the contrary, reasoning is slow and inefficient, and in human beings it is augmented by a number of other faster but less flexible processes for arriving at beliefs. This is particularly clear in the case of generalizations—both exceptionless generalizations and statistical generalizations. Any standard account of inductive reasoning requires the reasoner first to accumulate a corpus of evidence (a set of beliefs encoding individual observations) and then adopt the generalization on the basis of that evidence. In science we make a conscious effort to record our data, but outside of science we are almost never in the position of being able to enumerate explicitly a body of evidence supporting a generalization when we adopt it. For instance, we are all pretty good at predicting rain when huge dark clouds approach with vertical grey streaks hanging beneath them. But how many actual cases of its raining in such circumstances can you presently recall? Most likely, only a few. You cannot recall nearly enough positive instances of the generalization you are employing to account for your high degree of confidence in that generalization. What is happening here is that it would require huge amounts of memory to recall all of the data required for inductive reasoning according to conventional accounts of that reasoning. That is computationally impractical, so instead we have built in devices that summarize our observations as we go along, without requiring us to remember all the individual observations. Inductive generalization is then based on this stored summary of the data. Psychological evidence indicates that the summarization processes are less than totally accurate,[4] but this is compensated by the fact that it is more efficient and requires much less memory than would be required to remember all of the data. Such efficient but occasionally inaccurate processes of belief formation are extremely important. Without them, humans would be much less able to get along in the world.

In general, we can distinguish *intellection*, by which I mean explicit reasoning, from other "nonintellectual" processes of belief formation. Traditionally, philosophers have overemphasized the role of intellection in human belief formation. I would venture to say that most of our beliefs are acquired on the basis of nonintellectual processes. The nonintellectual processes are fast and efficient, and if the environment cooperates they are highly reliable. But if the environment does not cooperate, they can go fatally wrong. In that case, intellection is to be preferred. Explicit reasoning is slow and cumbersome, but it is more flexible than nonintellectual processes. Accordingly, in humans intellec-

---

[4] Kahneman, Slovic, and Tversky [1982].

tion is used primarily to guide belief formation in complicated cases in which we do not have applicable nonintellectual processes and to override nonintellectual processes in cases in which we have reason to suspect that they may be unreliable.

I used to refer to these nonintellectual processes as "quick and dirty processes". They are indeed quick, but Lynn Cooper has pointed out to me that within their domain of successful application they need not be at all dirty. For instance, think about catching a baseball. You do not have to pull out a pocket calculator to compute trajectories. Human beings have built-in nonintellectual processes for doing this, and they are both extraordinarily fast and incredibly accurate. The shortcoming of these nonintellectual processes is not that they are dirty but that they are of limited flexibility. For example, if you know that the baseball is going to ricochet off the side of a building, you must rely on intellection to tell you to wait until after the ricochet to compute the final trajectory. For this reason I will refer to the systems implementing these nonintellectual processes as *Q&I systems* ("quick and inflexible").

The point has been made repeatedly in the recent cognitive science literature that humans make use of massive parallel processing. That is the only way that a system built out of such slow hardware as neurons could possibly be as quick as humans are at complicated tasks of information processing.[5] On the other hand, many aspects of reasoning seem to be essentially sequential, and it takes nothing but introspection to reveal just how slow reasoning is. Nonintellectual processes can be much faster by making use of parallel processing in ways that are not possible for explicit reasoning, but at the same time it follows that they can only approximate the results of intellection. The approximation is usually good enough, but not always.[6]

Returning to Oscar III, I have argued that information processing as sophisticated as that exemplified by human beings requires defeasible reasoning, and that in turn requires introspective sensors. Although Oscar III has introspective sensors sensing the operation of his perceptual sensors, this does not mean that he can respond to his perceptual

---

[5] Rumelhart, McClelland, and the PDP Research Group [1986].

[6] In this connection it is of interest to consider some of the AI systems proposed in the machine learning literature. Many of these systems exhibit impressive performance under suitably constrained circumstances, but they all go badly wrong outside the constraints they presuppose. These AI systems are, in effect, Q&I systems. It may be that no actual AI systems of machine learning are faithful models of the Q&I systems actually embodied in human learning, but they nevertheless illustrate the sophisticated kinds of information processing that are possible with Q&I systems as long as the domain of application of those systems is suitably restricted.

sensors only by sensing their operation.[7]   In the ordinary course of
events Oscar III can get along fine just responding mechanically to his
perceptual sensors. To attend to the output of a sensor is to utilize (in
cognition) the output of an introspective sensor that senses the output
of the first sensor. Oscar III need not attend to the output of his
perceptual sensors under most circumstances because doing so would not
alter his behavior (except to slow him down and make him less
efficient). He need only attend to the output of his perceptual sensors
under circumstances in which he has already discovered that they are
sometimes unreliable.[8]

The cognitive role of the pain sensors is a bit different from that of
the perceptual organs. Oscar III will function best if he almost always
attends to the output of his pain sensors. These play a different kind
of role from the perceptual sensors. Their role is not just one of fine-
tuning. Except in "emergency situations" in which all cognitive powers
are brought to bear at avoiding a permanent systems crash, Oscar III
should be always on the lookout for new generalizations about pain, and
this requires that he almost always be aware of when his pain sensors
are activated. This parallels the fact that human beings are much more
aware of their pains than their visual sensations. We generally "look
through" our visual sensations at the world and do not think about the
sensations themselves.

I have attributed two kinds of self-awareness to Oscar III: he has the
ability to sense the activation of his pain sensors and also to sense the
activation of his perceptual organs. These proceed by "introspective"
sensors. The important thing to realize is that there are simple
explanations for why such self-awareness will make an intelligent

---

[7] That is the mistake of the foundations theorist, and it is the basis upon which
I have repeatedly defended what I call 'direct realism'. See below and see Pollock
[1974] and [1986].

[8] Oscar would be more like human beings if we supplied him with a
"preprocessor" that modifies the input from his perceptual sensors in accordance with
simple generalizations he has made about perceptual error. If he has acquired no
relevant generalizations then the preprocessor will pass the input from the perceptual
sensors through to his cognitive machinery unchanged, but if Oscar has acquired
relevant generalizations then a red input from the perceptual sensors might be changed
to orange by the preprocessor, and so forth. Oscar's introspective sensors might then
sense the output of the preprocessor rather than the output of the perceptual sensors
themselves. This would be computationally more efficient, allowing Oscar to direct the
full power of his intellect at his perceptual input only when his preprocessor cannot
make sense of it. This is roughly the way people work. It involves a feedback loop
from the machinery used for high-level cognitive processing to a preprocessor that lies
between the sense organs and the high-level machinery.

machine work better. Other kinds of self-awareness may also be either desirable or necessary. I have not described Oscar III as having any awareness of what goes on internally after he acquires perceptual input or pain stimuli. In particular, I have not described him as having any way of sensing the operation of those cognitive processes whereby he forms generalizations on the basis of his perceptual inputs and pain stimuli. But such awareness seems to be required for two reasons. First, consider defeasible reasoning. In defeasible reasoning we reason to a conclusion, and then subsequent reasoning may lead to new conclusions that undermine the original reasoning and cause us to retract the original conclusion. In order for such negative feedback to work, the cognitive agent must be able to sense and keep track of his reasoning processes. Actually, humans are not terribly good at this. We forget our reasons rather rapidly, and we often fail to make appropriate corrections even when we remember our reasons.[9] We would probably work better if we could keep better track of our reasoning processes. At any rate, the general point seems clear. The ability to sense his own reasoning processes will be required in order for Oscar to indulge in defeasible reasoning, and defeasible reasoning seems to be required by any kind of sophisticated epistemology.

It is important to realize that this rationale for being able to introspect reasoning applies only to reasoning; it does not apply to the Q&I systems. There is no apparent advantage to being able to monitor the functioning of such nonintellectual processes. This conforms to the fact that human beings are not able to introspect them. For instance, when we are led nonintellectually to a statistical generalization to the effect that most clouds of a certain sort are accompanied by rain, all we can introspect is the conclusion. If asked why we believe the generalization, we can try to remember some of the evidence and reconstruct the generalization intellectually, but we cannot literally answer the question by introspecting the original Q&I process that led to the generalization.

There is another reason a well-functioning cognitive agent must be able to sense its own reasoning processes. A cognitive agent does not try to gather information at random; he normally seeks to answer specific questions (motivated ultimately by conative considerations). Effective problem solving (at least in humans) involves the use of reasoning strategies rather than random reasoning, and we acquire such strategies by learning about how best to search for solutions to various kinds of

---

[9] There has been a flurry of psychological investigations concerning subjects' failure to make corrections to earlier reasoning in light of later information. The first of these is apparently that of Ross, Lepper, and Hubbard [1975].

problems. In order to learn such things we must be aware of how we proceed in particular cases so that we can make generalizations about the efficacy of the search procedures employed.

I have urged that a well-functioning cognitive agent must be able to monitor some of its own cognitive processes, but introspection is out of fashion in many circles. This is due in large part to work in cognitive psychology that has been taken to cast doubt on our having any privileged access to our own cognitive processes.[10] However, it is illuminating to look at such work more carefully. What the psychological investigations actually demonstrate is that we are often unaware of our own long-term beliefs and attitudes and that we are unable to introspect the causal processes responsible for them. The latter should not be surprising. Causal processes are not the sort of thing that can be directly perceived, either in the physical world around us or in our own internal mental world. Knowledge of causal processes must be based on some form of induction. Our unawareness of our own beliefs seems initially more impressive and more germane to the claims I have been making, but in this connection it is important to realize that it is *long-term* beliefs and attitudes to which the psychologists allege we lack introspective access. Such long-term beliefs and attitudes are dispositions. They do not reflect the current contents of our thoughts. On the other hand, what I have been arguing is that we must have introspective access to our occurrent thoughts, and nothing in the psychological literature bears against that. In fact, it is actually presupposed by the experimenters, because the way in which they ascertain what their subjects are thinking is by asking them.

Oscar and the Mind/Body Problem

Consider a world populated by Oscarites (with a few machinivores thrown in for good measure). If the Oscarites are sufficiently good at reasoning and their conative structure endows them with intellectual curiosity, some of them may turn to philosophizing about machines and their place in nature. They will be puzzled about certain aspects of themselves. One kind of puzzlement might give rise to what they call 'the mind/body problem'. They note that their perceptual sensors make them aware of states of the world around them. They call these 'physical states' and they develop an elaborate physical science to study them. But they take note of the fact that they are aware of another kind of state as well. For example, when what are eventually identified as their pain sensors are stimulated, they have a characteristic kind of

---

[10] See particularly Nisbett and Wilson [1977], and Lackner and Garrett [1972].

experience. And when they turn their attention "inward" (as they say), they cease to be aware of the physical objects around them and again have a different kind of state of awareness. They describe this as "being aware of mental states". They might then begin to wonder what the relationship is between mental states and physical states. What is actually going on, of course, is that they are attending to the outputs of their introspective sensors, and they are able to discriminate between those outputs and the outputs of their perceptual sensors. This involves higher-order introspective sensors that enable them to distinguish between the outputs of first-order introspective sensors and ordinary perceptual sensors.

The function of their introspective sensors is to enable the Oscarites to form generalizations that are, in effect, about the outputs of their perceptual sensors, and thus make possible various kinds of feedback in reasoning processes. But the Oscarites may be unaware of this. They need not know anything about the actual machinery comprising their perceptual sensors or about the physical processes involved in their reasoning. By noting their own behavior, they can infer that they must have such internal machinery, but the thoughts they are having when they think about mental states are quite different from their thoughts when they think about hypothetical physical structures that have the power to sense states of their environment and manipulate the resulting information. Furthermore, the Oscarite philosophers can know that they are having different thoughts in thinking these things because among their introspective sensors are sensors that sense the operation of some aspects of their cognitive machinery. The Oscarites describe this by saying that the "concept" of a mental state is different from the concept of a physical state consisting of the operation of a physical sensor. In the end, all it really comes to say that concepts of mental states are different from concepts of physical states is that the Oscarites can sense a difference between two different kinds of thoughts, that is, their introspective sensors enable them to distinguish between two different states of their cognitive machinery.

Still, we, from our loftier perspective, can describe the Oscarites as sensing the operation of their perceptual sensors. What they describe as 'being self-aware' or 'being conscious' is just a matter of their introspective sensors being in operation. What they describe as the 'qualitative feel' of a mental state is just the input from an introspective sensor that is sensing the operation of a lower-order sensor. For example, the "feel" of pain is the output of the pain sensor sensor. These introspective sensors respond to certain physical situations (the activation of perceptual sensors and the operation of cognitive machinery). The very same internal physical happenings can also (at least in principle) be sensed by the perceptual sensors themselves once the Oscarites find ways of looking inside their own physical structures. These constitute two different ways of sensing and responding to one and the same situation.

We can sum up these observations by noting that, given adequate intelligence, a necessary and sufficient condition for an intelligent machine to be able to invent a mind/body problem is that it have second-order perceptual sensors. If it has such sensors, then it can discriminate between the outputs of its perceptual sensors and its first-order introspective sensors and raise the question of what the relationship is between the happenings that are sensed in these two different ways. That is the simplest form of the mind/body problem.

Thus ends the fable of Oscar. The Engineers are fiction, but Oscar is real. We, of course, are the Oscarites.

2. People

It is time to get technical. I have painted a picture of human beings as intelligent machines. This picture requires defense. We may all agree that the fable of Oscar describes a possible situation. But why should we think that people are like the Oscarites? Specifically, why should we think that what *we* call 'mental states' are actually physical states? I regard this as a scientific hypothesis, not an *a priori* truth, but I think it is a hypothesis for which we can adduce overwhelming evidence. Let me first make clear what the hypothesis is, and then I will describe our evidence for it.

The hypothesis to be defended is *token physicalism*, which I take to be the thesis that mental state tokens are also physical state tokens. Mental state tokens are things like a particular instance of a specific person's being in pain. These are "concrete happenings", or events. Thus token physicalism can be stated somewhat more clearly as the thesis that mental events are also physical events. Earlier forms of physicalism were versions of *type physicalism*, according to which mental types, like *being in pain*, are to be identified with physical types, for example, with a particular type of neurological event.[11] Type physicalism is now generally regarded as discredited by the fact that it would preclude creatures with different physiologies from experiencing mental events of the same types. This will be discussed further in chapter 3.

---

[11] The distinction between token physicalism and type physicalism is generally attributed to Davidson [1970]. Davidson cites a few tentative precursors.

Note that as I have formulated it, token physicalism is a thesis about mental events, not about mental objects like sensations, thoughts, qualia, and the like. I allege that *having* a particular sensation, thought, or quale is identical with some physical event, but I make no claims about the ontological status of the sensations, thoughts, and qualia themselves.[12] Indeed, I am not sure that such things literally exist. Mental events occur, and we describe them in language that seems to commit us to the existence of mental objects, but perhaps the surface structure of such descriptions should not be taken seriously.[13] However, this is a matter that I do not propose to address further. If mental objects somehow emerge from purely physical occurrences, then the existence of such mental objects does not show that there is anything essentially nonphysical about the world.

Token physicalism is a thesis about mental events and not about cognitive agents. An allied thesis is *agent materialism* according to which cognitive agents are physical objects. Both token physicalism and agent materialism hold of the Oscarites, but they are distinct theses, and it is conceivable that in the case of people, one might hold and the other fail. This chapter addresses token physicalism. Agent materialism will be the subject of chapter 2.

I regard token physicalism as a scientific hypothesis based on contingent observations about the world, and I will describe the nature of those observations in a moment. But first let me dispose of an argument that is sometimes thought to establish that token physicalism could not possibly be true.[14] This concerns the "felt" quality of mental states. Being in a mental state has a qualitative feel about it, and people have doubted that there is any way purely physical states could ensure the presence of that feel. It is all very well for a physicalist like David Lewis to write, after proposing a functionalist analysis of pain,

> Pain is a feeling. ... To have a pain and to feel pain are one and the same thing. ... A theory of what it is for a state to be pain is inescap-

---

[12] Formulating physicalism as a thesis about mental events rather than mental objects originates with Place [1956], and was subsequently adopted by Smart [1959], Nagel [1965], and numerous more recent authors.

[13] An alternative, which I find rather appealing, is something like Dennett's [1987] "intentional stance", according to which mental objects are *abstracta* analogous to centers of gravity. I find this rather plausible as applied to mental objects, although not to mental events.

[14] There are a number of classical arguments that have, at one time or another, convinced people that mental events cannot be physical events. I will not repeat them here because those arguments have been rather thoroughly discredited in the literature. See particularly U. T. Place [1956], J. J. C. Smart [1959], and D. M. Armstrong [1968].

> ably a theory of what it is like to be in that state, of how that state feels,
> of the phenomenal character of that state. Far from ignoring how states
> feel in the odd cases we have been considering, I have been discussing
> nothing else! Only if you believe on independent ground that considera-
> tions of causal role and physical realization have no bearing on whether
> a state is pain should you say that they have no bearing on how that state
> feels. ([1980], p. 222.)

The trouble is, this convinces no one. The qualitative feel of pain is too
prominently a part of pain, and any physical account *seems* to leave that
out.[15]

I claim, however, that Lewis is (more or less) right. That is the main
point of the fable of Oscar. Having a qualitative feel is just a reflection
of the operation of introspective sensors. For example, in ordinary
visual perception our cognitive machinery receives the output of both the
perceptual sensors and the introspective sensors sensing the operation
of those perceptual sensors. Little use is made of the output of the
introspective sensors in most circumstances, but they are still functioning,
and it is this that gives perception its qualitative feel when we attend to
it. That qualitative feel is the output of the introspective sensors. One
may protest that the "feel" of the qualitative feel is being left out of this
picture—that I have talked only about the computational aspects of it.
In this connection we can usefully distinguish between *having* the
qualitative feel and *experiencing* the qualitative feel. To have the feel is
for one's first-order introspective sensors to be operating, but to
experience the feel is to attend to the feel itself, and that consists of the
operation of second-order introspective sensors sensing the operation of
the first-order introspective sensors. It might seem there is danger of an
infinite regress here, but that is not really the case. There are limits to
introspection, and in particular the process of second-order introspection
itself cannot be introspected. (Human beings have no third-order
introspective sensors.) This corresponds to the fact that unlike visual
perception, introspection does not have a qualitative feel.[16]

In essence, my proposal for understanding the phenomenal feel of a
sensation consists of distinguishing between the sensation and the feel of
the sensation. This is a distinction that philosophers have often resisted,
insisting that the feel of the sensation just is the sensation. It is this
identification that underlies the traditional view that non-comparative

---

[15] More or less following Thomas Nagel [1974] we might say that an essential
feature of pain is that there is something that it is like to be in pain. Frank Jackson
[1982] raises similar objections to Lewis.

[16] D. M. Armstrong [1980] (pp. 14, 55ff) gives a similar account of self-awareness
as perception of our own mental states. See also Dennett [1978a].

judgments about our own sensations are incorrigible. I think it is fair to say that the basis upon which philosophers have identified the sensation with the feel of the sensation is that they have not been able to imagine what the alternative would be like. But notice that the identification would really be quite puzzling. How *could* the sensation be the same as the feel of the sensation? That would be analogous to a rock being the same as the feel of the rock. The feel of the rock is what we get when we inspect the rock, and it is most natural to regard the feel of the sensation as what we get when we inspect the sensation. That is precisely the view of sensation I am now advocating. To inspect the sensation is to employ your introspective sensors.

One is still left wondering how the sensation can be different from the feel of the sensation. Basically, the problem is one of fitting this into our introspective view of our own mental life. It is likely to seem that in normal people the sensation and the feel of the sensation always occur together. But in fact, this is fairly obviously false. In normal sense perception, we are aware of our surroundings, but we are unaware of our sensations. We usually attend to our sensations only when we have some reason to distrust our senses, and when we are not attending to them, we are not sensing them. Introspective sensing is an attentional phenomenon. In at least one clear sense, when we are not attending to our sensations, they have no feel, but the sensations are still occurring because we are perceiving our surroundings. It follows that the sensation is not the same thing as the feel of the sensation.

If introspective sensing is a different operation from the perceptual sensing that is its object, then it ought to be possible for the one to occur without the other. It seems likely that introspective sensing will be more reliable than perceptual sensing, because even without knowing the neurophysiology of introspective sensing, it seems likely that there is less that can go wrong. Perceptual sensing can go awry for a variety of reasons external to the body, but introspective sensing occurs entirely within the nervous system and presumably consists of just the passing of neural signals to various parts of the brain. Nevertheless, although it is reasonable to expect this to be highly reliable, any physical system can malfunction, and it is unreasonable to expect it to be perfectly reliable. For instance, such malfunction may be implicated in a puzzling clinical disorder called 'blindsight'. Various cases have been reported in which patients with damage to the visual cortex report complete loss of sight and claim to have no visual sensations and yet are still able to make visual discriminations. In one experiment a patient with a normal right visual field but a "blind" left visual field was asked to point to where a light was being shown in his blind visual field. The patient reported seeing nothing and regarded himself as guessing, and yet his accuracy in pointing to spots in his blind visual field was almost as great as his accuracy in his good right visual field. The same patient was then asked to discriminate between horizontal and vertical bars of light in his blind visual field, and he was able to "guess" correctly as many as thirty out of thirty times. "When he was shown his results he expressed surprise and insisted several times that he thought he was just 'guessing'. When he was shown a video film of his reaching and judging orientation of lines, he was openly astonished." (Weiskrantz et al [1974], p. 721).[17] Blindsight is an amazing phenomenon, and most people's initial reaction is disbelief. But sense can be made of the phenomenon in terms of the distinction between perceptual sensors and introspective sensors. The very fact of discrimination indicates that the patient's perceptual sensors are still operating. But he is unaware that they are operating, and what that indicates is that his introspective sensors are not detecting the operation of his perceptual sensors. For this reason he has visual sensations, but *they have no qualitative feel*. He is aware but not self-aware.[18]

I suggest that these considerations explain how we come to have a mind/body problem. Our mind/body problem arises in the same way it arose for the Oscarites. The mind/body problem can arise for a cognitive agent whenever it has first-order introspective sensors (giving mental operations a qualitative feel) and second-order introspective sensors enabling it to discriminate between the sensing of mental states by its first-order introspective sensors and the sensing of physical states by its perceptual sensors. This combination of sensors makes it possible to begin wondering what the connection is between the mental states perceived one way and the physical states perceived in another way. As the fable of Oscar makes evident, the answer *can* be that they are identical. Mental events can be (and I think are) just physical events that can be sensed in a second way.

Thus far I have argued that token physicalism could be true, but what reason have we for thinking it *is* true? This is best answered by considering more generally how we can ever have reason to believe that two different senses inform us of the same states of the world. The clearest example of this is vision and touch. When I hold a ball in my hands and judge it to be spherical, I make the same judgment about it

---

[17] Although these results are generally accepted, they are not entirely without controversy. See Campion, Latto, and Smith [1983].

[18] It is apparent that sensations are outputs of our perceptual sensors. It is a purely verbal matter whether we count all such outputs as sensations or only those that have a qualitative feel. I prefer the simpler alternative of regarding all outputs from perceptual sensors as sensations, but nothing substantive turns upon this.

as when I walk around it and examine it visually from several angles and then pronounce it to be spherical. No one wants to posit separate visual and tactile worlds somehow "running in parallel". Everyone acknowledges that we perceive the same situations both visually and tactilely. I claim that if we consider what justifies us in believing this, we will find that we have reasons for affirming the identity of mental and physical states that are of exactly the same kind as our reasons for affirming the identity of visual and tactile objects.

We believe that, at least in many cases, we perceive the same events visually and tactilely. The basis for this is the discovery of a visual/tactile isomorphism. For example, consider roundness. There is a concept of roundness *simpliciter*, but it is presumably uncontroversial that there are also (or can be constructed) distinct concepts of visual and tactile roundness. These concepts must be distinguished from the concepts of appearing visually to be round and appearing tactilely to be round. Something's appearing round gives us only a prima facie reason for thinking it is really round, and something can be round without looking round (or without even being perceived). The visual/tactile isomorphism arises from making judgments of visual and tactile roundness on the basis of their respective prima facie reasons and then going on to confirm (in most cases in which we raise the question) that there is a visually round object before us iff there is also a tactilely round object before us.[19]   In section 1 I discussed the way in which approximate generalizations and prima facie reasons interact to yield exact generalizations. In light of that, our initial observation of an approximate visual/tactile isomorphism will give us a reason for thinking it unexceptionably true that there is something tactilely round before us iff there is something visually round before us. The way this works is that we accept the generalization and use that to correct our judgments of visual and tactile roundness based on perception with a single sense. Thus, once we have reason for thinking that the visual/tactile isomorphism is pretty good, we automatically acquire reason for thinking it is exact.

---

[19] This does *not* mean that we tend to be appeared to tactilely as if there is a tactilely round object before us iff we are appeared to visually as if there is a visually round object before us. That is false because we do not usually direct both sight and touch at the same objects. The viability of the generalization we actually confirm turns on the fact that an object can be visually or tactilely round without appearing to be, and without it even being possible for it to appear to be. For example, if a wheel is too large, we cannot judge its shape tactilely but we may nevertheless be able to tell that it is tactilely round by relying upon generalizations confirmed in those cases in which we can make a direct tactile judgment. Of course, the most important generalization of this sort is the one relating visual and tactile roundness.

It is important to recognize that the visual/tactile isomorphism I have described does not yet establish that sight and touch have common objects. It consists merely in such facts as that there is something visually round before me iff there is something tactilely round before me. We *believe* that vision and touch apprise us of the same happenings. We can see that there is something round before us, and we can feel that there is something round before us. We suppose the events thus perceived to be one and the same event.[20] The justification for this inference seems to be a straightforward application of explanatory induction. The hypothesis that we are perceiving the same events in two different ways is the best explanation of the data observed (those data comprising the visual/tactile isomorphism).[21]

I have been describing how we discover that vision and touch give us information about a common world. It is important to realize that this is a scientific theory—not an *a priori* truth. It is logically possible that up until now it has just been a monstrous coincidence that there has been a visual/tactile isomorphism, and starting tomorrow it will all come apart. We would then have to conclude that vision and touch are ways of perceiving different, possibly totally unrelated, events—separate visual and tactile worlds, so to speak. But before we get carried away with logical possibilities, it is good to let common sense reassert itself. What I have described is a logical possibility, but that is all it is. We know full well that in this world, vision and touch are two ways of perceiving the same things. Our evidence for this is overwhelming.

Now I want to urge that the epistemological basis for token physicalism is almost precisely the same as the epistemological basis for the visual/tactile identity thesis. The fable of Oscar should convince us that it is at least possible that our internal senses are sensing events that can in principle also be sensed by our external senses and would, in the latter guise, be called 'neurological events'. There is nothing logically absurd about this. Now consider the "causal nexus argument": (1)

---

[20] It would be helpful to have a theory of events here, but I find all current theories of events unpersuasive and I have no theory of my own to put in their place. It is tempting to suppose that the nomic equivalence of the properties instantiated together with sameness of location guarantees event identity, but note that before we can talk about location simpliciter (rather than visual location and tactile location) we must already have made the inference we are now trying to make. That is, we must already have concluded that the visual and tactile world are one.

[21] Of course, no one has an adequate account of that kind of scientific inference I am calling 'explanatory induction', but that need not stop us here. We all know how to make such inferences; we do it all the time. What we lack is a general account of such inferences, but that is not a reason for thinking them illegitimate.

Mental and physical events are involved in a single causal nexus. On the one hand, there are causal paths leading from the mental to the physical. For example, my decision to raise my arm plays a causal role in my arm's rising. Conversely, there are causal paths leading from the physical to the mental. The irradiation of my optic nerves causes me to have visual sensations, neuron firings cause me to feel pain, and so forth. (2) We have good reason to believe that physical events constitute a closed causal system. Insofar as physical events have a causal ancestry, that ancestry can be described in purely physical terms.[22] If this were not true, if we had to import reference to non-physical events in order to account for physical goings-on, we would have violations of the conservation of energy and momentum, and so forth. (3) This requires an explanation, and surely, in light of the preceding discussion, the most plausible explanation is that mental events *are* physical events. Mental events are just physical events that can be perceived by our internal senses.[23]

The only difference between the preceding reasoning and the reasoning underlying the visual/tactile identity thesis is that the data being explained consist of the premises of the causal nexus argument rather than an observed mental/physical isomorphism. Presumably, the latter is also there to be found, but we haven't found it yet. The visual/tactile isomorphism is very obvious to us because we are constantly aware of both sides of the isomorphism and we make continual use of it in our judgments about the world. On the other hand, the physical side of the presumed mental/physical isomorphism is buried deep within our bodies and is hard to get at. But despite the fact that the reasoning behind token physicalism proceeds from the causal nexus argument rather than an observed isomorphism, the logic of the reasoning is basically the same as the logic of the reasoning supporting the visual/tactile identity thesis. These two pieces of reasoning must stand or fall together. No one in his right mind will deny the visual/tactile identity thesis, so we

---

[22] Do not confuse this use of 'causal' with 'cause'. There may not be any causes because the world is indeterministic (essentially probabilistic). Whether there can be probabilistic causes is a matter of dispute, but I am inclined to think there cannot be. Nevertheless, there can be causal relations between things. These will be relations mediated by nomic probability, and they are all that is required in the causal nexus argument.

[23] It is interesting to note that Helmholtz's experiments, leading to the first precise formulation of the principle of the conservation of energy, were actually addressed to the mind/body problem and presupposed something like the causal nexus argument.

should be equally willing to embrace token physicalism as a well-confirmed scientific theory.

It is worth calling attention to a third case in which we perceive events in two separate ways. This involves our proprioceptive sense, by which we sense our own bodily movements. The events we sense in this way are ordinary physical events of the same type that can also be sensed visually and tactilely. The proprioceptive sensing of bodily movements is like the introspective sensing of mental states in that it is a way of sensing states of ourselves and also in that it has a qualitative feel quite unlike external sense perception (that is, our second-order introspective sensors can readily distinguish it from external sense perception.) But proprioceptive sensing is like the visual/tactile case in that the isomorphism between what we sense proprioceptively and the bodily movements sensed perceptually is quite obvious to us. This is because, unlike the introspective sensing of mental events, both sides of the proprioceptive isomorphism are open to ready view.

What I am urging is that there are good reasons for giving an intelligent machine the ability to sense some states of the world in more than one way. Two obvious examples of this phenomenon are vision/touch and proprioception/vision. They are obvious because in each case the correlation between what is sensed by one mode and what is sensed by the other is readily apparent. But there can also be cases in which the correlation is not initially apparent, and in that case the machine may become puzzled about the relationship between what it senses in different ways. This, I allege, is what occurs in human introspection and the mind/body problem. That this is a case of two sensory modes detecting the same events, but doing so without it being initially obvious that that is what is happening, explains everything that puzzles us philosophically about mental states and introspection. If we had transparent heads and the neurological events corresponding to mental events were macroscopically visible, I think we would regard token physicalism as being as much of a commonplace as is the observation that what we sense proprioceptively is our own bodily movements.[24]

---

[24] Frank Jackson ([1982] and [1986]) has argued against the view that qualitative concepts (concepts expressing introspectible properties) can be reduced to physical concepts. This is a conclusion I endorse. Jackson goes on to conclude that mental events are distinct from physical events, but that is a *non-sequitor*. It is analogous to arguing that because visual concepts like colors are not reducible to tactile concepts, the objects of vision (e.g., tables and chairs) are distinct from the objects of touch (tables and chairs).

3. Conclusions

My purpose is to defend the conception of man as an intelligent machine. In this chapter, I have argued that token physicalism is true. I do not regard this as a necessary truth. I have defended it as a contingent scientific hypothesis rather than as the result of conceptual analysis. It explains our observations about people and mental states. In particular we can understand at least one aspect of the phenomenon of self-awareness in terms of introspective sensors. A more general conclusion can also be drawn from the chapter: useful insights about man can frequently be obtained by considering what it would take for an intelligent machine to be able to perform the kinds of tasks human beings perform. This general view of man as cognitive-conative machine can, I believe, provide useful insights in many areas of philosophy.

Chapter 2
Persons and Bodies

1. Agent Materialism

I have been defending token physicalism. Now let us turn to agent materialism, according to which people are physical objects. Although these theses are connected, token physicalism does not entail agent materialism. It is at least imaginable that people are Cartesian egos residing in their bodies but that what they perceive through their inner senses is neurological states of their bodies. Like token physicalism, I regard agent materialism to be a well confirmed scientific hypothesis, and I will argue that the evidence in its favor is closely related to the evidence adduced for token physicalism.

In order to answer the question, "Are people physical objects?" we must consider how we are thinking about people. This might be formulated more traditionally by asking what our concept of a person is, although I think that is a bit misleading. We do not have a concept of a person in the sense ordinarily presupposed by that question. More accurately, we do not have a "descriptive" concept of a person. Crudely put, in asking whether people are physical objects I am thinking of people as "things like me". Thus the relevant "concept of a person" becomes a function of how I am thinking of myself. To throw light on this, let us return to Oscar and his cohorts.

2. De Se Thought

I described the Oscarites as having reasoning facilities, but I did not explore what that involves. One requirement is that they have a way of encoding "information", "facts", "propositions", or what have you—a "language of thought". This language of thought is a representational system. Its nature will be explored further in chapter 5, but we can make some preliminary observations now. The language of thought must, among other things, provide ways of thinking about particular objects and ascribing properties to them. One familiar way Oscar can think of individual objects is, of course, by thinking of them under descriptions—as the unique objects having certain combinations of properties. But that need not be the only way he can think about objects. For example, in the case of people, I have written at length about what I call '*de re* representations'.[1] These are nondescriptive ways of thinking about objects. From an information-processing point of view we can think of *de re* representations as pigeonholes (memory locations) into which we stuff properties as we acquire reasons to believe that the objects represented have those properties. Properties may occasionally drop out of the pigeonholes if they are not used (that is, we forget). In order to establish a pigeonhole as representing a particular object, we must begin by thinking of the object in some other way, and that initial way of thinking of the object will be the first thing to be put into the pigeonhole. For example, we might begin by thinking of an object under a description, from that acquire a *de re* representation of the object, and then eventually forget the original description and be able to think of the object only under the *de re* representation. From an information-processing point of view, there are good reasons (having to do with the efficient use of memory) for incorporating something like *de re* representations into the language of thought used by an intelligent machine, and we would be well advised to equip Oscar with some such device.

I mention *de re* representations merely to illustrate that the language of thought is equipped with devices other than definite descriptions for use in thinking about individual things. The representational device I want to explore now is that involved in first person beliefs. Starting with Castaneda [1966], numerous philosophers have observed that, although we can think of ourselves in more familiar ways (for instance, under descriptions or perceptually), we can also have thoughts about ourselves in which we do not think of ourselves in any of those ways.[2] John Perry [1979] argues as follows:

---

[1] See my [1980] and [1982] (pp. 60ff). Related discussions occur in Diana Ackerman [1979], [1979a], and [1980]. I have proposed that a number of Keith Donnellan's well known examples (Donnellan [1972]) are best understood as illustrating the occurrence of *de re* representations in our thought.

[2] See H. N. Castaneda [1966], [1967], and [1968]; Roderick Chisholm [1981]; David Lewis [1979]; John Perry [1977] and [1979]; and my [1981] and [1982] (pp. 13ff). This has also played a role in some recent work in AI. See Creary and Pollard [1985], and Rapaport [1984], and [1984a]. An early precursor of all this work was Frege [1956].

I once followed a trail of sugar on a supermarket floor, pushing my cart down the aisle on one side of a tall counter and back the aisle on the other, seeking the shopper with the torn sack to tell him he was making a mess. With each trip around the counter, the trail became thicker. But I seemed unable to catch up. Finally it dawned on me. I was the shopper I was trying to catch.

I believed at the outset that the shopper with a torn sack was making a mess. And I was right. But I didn't believe that I was making a mess. That seems to be something I came to believe. And when I came to believe that, I stopped following the trail around the counter, and rearranged the torn sack in my cart. My change in belief seems to explain my change in behavior. ...

At first characterizing the change seems easy. My beliefs changed, didn't they, in that I came to have a new one, namely, *that I am making a mess*? But things are not so simple.

The reason they are not is the importance of the word "I" in my expression of what I came to believe. When we replace it with other designations of me, we no longer have an explanation of my behavior and so, it seems, no longer an attribution of the same belief. It seems to be an *essential* indexical. (p. 3)

I will follow David Lewis in calling such beliefs *de se* beliefs.[3] The existence of *de se* beliefs in people is a phenomenological fact. It raises numerous philosophical questions about the analysis of what is believed. Castaneda and I have both argued that in *de se* belief one believes a proposition containing a particular kind of designator—what I previously called a 'personal designator', but what might more aptly be called a '*de se* designator'. Roderick Chisholm, David Lewis, and John Perry, on the other hand, have all urged that *de se* belief does not take a propositional object. They claim that the object of *de se* belief is instead a property or concept and *de se* belief involves a unique form of self-attribution. Fortunately, we need not get involved in this mare's nest at the moment.[4]

The relevance of *de se* belief to present concerns lies in its importance for rational thought. It has seemed evident to most epistemologists that

---

[3] In adopting Lewis' terminology, I do not mean to endorse his analysis of *de se* beliefs. Specifically, I do not mean to endorse his claim (shared by Chisholm and Perry) that *de se* beliefs do not have subject/predicate form.

[4] I doubt there is any substantive difference between the two accounts. Without some further constraints on what it is for something to be an object of belief, we can describe *de se* belief in either way. For example, Lewis's arguments to the contrary turn upon the assumption that any cognitive agent can, in principle, entertain any proposition. My own endorsement of *de se* propositions led me to deny that and insist instead that some propositions are logically idiosyncratic. But there appears to be no way to substantiate either position without first resolving the question whether belief must take a propositional object.

our most basic knowledge is all of the *de se* variety.[5]   Classical foun-
dationalists thought that all knowledge begins with "epistemologically
basic beliefs" about how things appear to us. I have consistently argued
against that kind of theory, proposing instead what I call 'direct realism',
according to which our "lowest-level beliefs" will typically be beliefs
about physical objects.[6] But even according to direct realism, our most
fundamental beliefs are going to be *de se* beliefs. When I see a table
with a book on it, my resulting belief is not just that there exists a table
with a book on it. I could be pretty confident of that without having
the perception. My belief is that there is a table with a book on it and
the table is located spatially before me. Perceptual beliefs are always *de
se* beliefs relating the perceived objects to ourselves. Other non-*de se*
beliefs (for example, generalizations) can be justified by reasoning from
our initial *de se* beliefs, but our epistemologically most fundamental
beliefs are always going to be *de se* beliefs.[7]

Thus far what I have said is just a bald assertion about human
epistemology, but if we switch to a third-person perspective and think
about Oscar, it is easy to understand why human epistemology works in
the way I claim it does. Oscar is a cognitive-conative machine. Suppose
we did not equip him with a system of representations making it
possible for him to have *de se* beliefs. He could still acquire beliefs on
the basis of perception, but they would have to be purely existential
beliefs (such as the belief that there is a table somewhere rather than
the belief that there is a table before him). Such existential beliefs
could be quite elaborate, but they could not relate his environment to
himself. They could not do that because he has no way of thinking of
himself. Perhaps it will be protested that he can have beliefs relating
his environment to his body, and that will constitute having beliefs
relating his environment to himself. But he cannot think of his body as
his body unless he can have *de se* beliefs. He can believe on the basis
of perception that there are physical objects that are related to some
body or other, but if he can think of that body only under a general
(non-*de se*) description, then it is most unlikely that he will be able to
contrive any description that picks out his body uniquely. (If you do not
believe me, try it in your own case!)[8]

---

[5] Coherence theorists are sometimes an exception to this. See particularly Lehrer
[1974].

[6] See my [1974] and [1986].

[7] See my [1974]. Searle [1983] makes similar observations.

[8] Using proper names is cheating.

Without *de se* beliefs all Oscar will be able to form are rather general existential beliefs. This will create two kinds of difficulties for him. The first difficulty is that there is no way to combine existential beliefs into more elaborate beliefs. $\ulcorner(\exists x)Fx$ & $(\exists x)Gx\urcorner$ does not entail $\ulcorner(\exists x)(Fx$ & $Gx)\urcorner$. In perception, on the other hand, we rely upon being able to make discrete observations of the same object and then combining them. For example, I may examine a table from several angles and form a belief about its overall shape. I could not do this if I could only form purely existential beliefs on the basis of each perception. I could discover that there is a table t_1 having a particular conjunction of properties P_1 and related in a certain way to a body of a certain description, and I could subsequently discover that there is a table t_2 having another conjunction of properties P_2 and related in a certain way to a body of the same description, but if I have no way of knowing that the two bodies are one and the same (which in principle I cannot know if I cannot contrive a description uniquely satisfied by my body), then there is no way for me to identify t_2 with t_1 and form a combined belief about a single object.[9] This disability would make Oscar pretty much unworkable as a cognitive machine.

The difficulty becomes even more serious when we consider Oscar's conative side. The purpose of providing Oscar with cognitive powers is to enable him to achieve built-in goals. This is accomplished by combining his beliefs with a conative structure consisting of preferences, desires, aversions, and so forth, giving him the power of practical reasoning, and making his behavior responsive to practical reasoning. The problem is how to do this in a creature lacking *de se* beliefs. I assert that it cannot be done. In practical reasoning, the cognitive agent is not usually interested in the general state of the universe, but more specifically in *his* state in the universe. In deciding what to do, he must ascertain his own circumstances. For instance, the agent might think to himself, "If I do *A* then *X* is likely to happen to me; I don't want *X* to happen to me; so I had better not do *A*," where we can suppose that the desire is supplied directly by the agent's conative structure. What is to be emphasized here is that the agent must be able to think about what is likely to happen *to himself*. For this kind of reasoning it is not sufficient for the agent to think of himself under some description he satisfies only contingently. For example, even if the agent is the tallest person in the room, it is not sufficient for the agent to form the belief,

---

[9] Notice that the tables cannot be reidentified in terms of their locations because locations can be reidentified only by first reidentifying objects that form a frame of reference.

"If I do A then X is likely to happen to the tallest person in the room." This will be relevant only to a decision about what to do if the agent has the desire that X not happen to the tallest person in the room. The agent might well have such a desire, particularly if he believes himself to be the tallest person in the room. But he cannot have that desire simply as a matter of his conative structure. That desire would have to be derived from the more fundamental desire that X not happen to himself coupled with the belief that he is the tallest man in the room. Desires built into the conative structure of an agent will be about the agent himself, which requires that the agent have some way of thinking of himself. This self-reflexive thought cannot proceed in terms of designators that just happen to represent the agent because they must be built into the conative structure prior to any knowledge of the agent's circumstances. This indicates that they must involve a mental designator that is essentially a representation of the agent. This must be a logically primitive element in our system of mental representation.

This point can be illustrated by thinking about chess-playing programs. Such programs perform a rudimentary kind of practical reasoning. Most chess-playing programs are "aware of" only the game they are currently playing. That is their whole universe. Accordingly, their goals ("desires") concern the general state of their universe, and their reasoning does not require anything like a *de se* designator. But now consider a more sophisticated chess-playing program that learns by observing other chess games as well as by playing its own. Its goal is to win its own game, but in order to incorporate such a goal into it, it must be able to distinguish between its own game and other games it observes. It must think of its own game in a privileged way, or less metaphorically, within the data structures on the basis of which it computes its next move, its own game must be represented differently from other games that it is merely observing. This is a rudimentary analogue of *de se* thought. The main way in which full-fledged *de se* thought differs from this is that the use of a general-purpose *de se* designator allows the formulation of a broader range of goals.

In conclusion, for both theoretical and practical reasoning, there are purely computational tasks that require a cognitive agent to have a *de se* designator in his language of thought. It is to be emphasized that the reason for this requirement is not metaphysics but computation. The system cannot do the kinds of reasoning required of it without a *de se* designator. Thus *de se* beliefs are absolutely essential in the construction of a cognitive-conative machine. I take it that that is why they play the central role they do in human epistemology.

3. Consciousness

The most perplexing problem for any materialist theory of the person is that of making sense of consciousness. I think it will be generally granted that we could construct an "intelligent" machine that would behave like, and in all physical respects work like a human being, but the nagging question remains, "Would it be conscious?" Would we be creating sentience or only simulating sentience?[10]

When philosophers talk about consciousness, they tend not to have any very definite idea of what it is they are talking about. There are several different and only loosely connected mental phenomena that give rise to talk of consciousness. Consciousness is, roughly, "self-awareness", but there are at least two kinds of self-awareness. You can be self-aware in the sense of being aware of mental states of yourself, and you can be self-aware in the sense of being aware of yourself as an entity. Self-awareness in the former sense is all tied up with the "phenomenal glow" of experience. I talked about that phenomenon in chapter 1, explaining it in terms of introspective sensors. Self-awareness in the second sense, however, is a different phenomenon. It involves awareness of oneself as a cognitive agent. This phenomenon has perplexed philosophers since Hume.

Hume observed ([1888], p. 253), when we turn our attention inward and reflect upon our experiences, we find only the experiences—no self. This led Hume to identify the person with his bundle of experiences, but that did not solve the problem because as he acknowledged in the Appendix to the *Treatise*, he was unable to explain what determines which experiences go into which bundles. This is the problem of "the unity of consciousness". At one point Bertrand Russell ([1912], chapter 5) toyed with the claim that we really do have introspective awareness of the self, but he soon took that back. P. F. Strawson [1958] tried to avoid the problem altogether by claiming that our concept of a person is primitive, but in the end his "solution" just came down to the unexplained (although obviously true) assertion that I am a person and as such can ascribe mental states to myself "without a criterion". D. M. Armstrong recently proposed that the self is not so much discovered as postulated. He writes,

---

[10] This is the distinction between *strong AI* and *weak AI* in the sense of Searle [1981].

In recent years, we have often been reminded, indeed admonished, that there is a great deal of theory involved even in quite unsophisticated perceptual judgments. ... It is therefore natural to assume that the perceptions of our "inner sense" involve theory, involve going beyond the "given", in the same general way that the perceptions of "outer sense" do. ... We learn to organize what we introspect as being states of, and activities in, a single continuing entity: our self. ([1980], pp. 64ff)

But this does not solve the problem either. Before we can do the organizing we must already have collected the experiences together as "ours". That is just the problem of the unity of consciousness all over again. Another view, frequently discussed in the cognitive science literature, is that the unity of consciousness requires an "all-powerful executive homunculus whose duties require an almost Godlike omniscience".[11]

My claim is that consciousness of oneself as an agent is a very simple phenomenon. It is nothing but *de se* thought. Philosophers have supposed that there must be something illegitimate about *de se* thought unless we can introspect an entity for the *de se* representation to represent, but there is no apparent reason to agree with them about that. *De se* representation and *de se* belief constitute a primitive part of our cognitive makeup. It is in principle impossible to justify it somehow on the basis of non-*de se* thought, because as indicated above, we cannot even get started thinking about the world without *de se* thought. If this still seems puzzling, just think of Oscar. The concept of *de se* thought is a syntactical notion, not a semantical notion. We provide his language of thought with a *de se* designator in order to make rationality possible. Doing that is just a matter of including an appropriate singular term in his language of thought and then wiring him in such a way that (1) sensory input results in his having *de se* beliefs (that is, it results in "*de se* sentences" in his language of thought playing a certain causal role), (2) rational deliberation results in *de se* intentions, and so forth. There is nothing mysterious about this. Getting Oscar to reason in this way is a computational matter—a matter of programming (or wiring). In particular, we do not have to equip Oscar with a Cartesian ego and a way of perceiving it.

In sum, consciousness of oneself as an entity consists of having *de se* thought, where that is made possible by the possession of a *de se* designator, this being a fundamental syntactical part of our language of thought. We can make perfectly good sense of all this without having

---

[11] The quotation is from Dennett [1978], p. 216. Dennett rejects the view. See also Uhr [1978], pp. 345ff.

to build a ghost into our machine. Oscar can have *de se* thoughts just like we can, so he is conscious in precisely the same way we are. There is no obstacle to building consciousness into an intelligent machine.

4. Reidentification

De se thought provides the solution to a venerable problem in the philosophy of mind: the problem of personal reidentification. How can we determine whether a person at one time is the same person as a person at another time? It has seemed obvious to most philosophers that the problem of reidentification can be solved only by first saying what a person is. Historically, there have been two (allegedly) popular criteria of personal identity. The simpler of these takes it to be a necessary (conceptual) truth that people are to be reidentified in terms of their bodies. This criterion is much talked about, but I am unaware of any recent philosopher who has endorsed it, and I am inclined to regard it as a straw man.[12] The only genuinely popular kind of criterion of personal identity is a mentalistic one. Mentalistic criteria come in a variety of forms. The crudest ones identify people with bundles of mental properties. Most mentalistic criteria place heavy emphasis on memory, continuity of experience, continuity of personal traits, and so forth. None is very plausible when you look at the details. For example, some continuity criteria are refuted by the simple fact that people fall asleep.[13]

In fact, the philosophical search for a criterion by which people can be reidentified represents a confusion. We have no need for such a criterion. We are able to reidentify ourselves without a criterion, and that enables us to discover contingent criteria for reidentifying others.[14] This is an automatic result of *de se* thought. If, as I urged above, *de se* representation of ourselves is to enable us to relate discrete observations, it must allow us to relate observations made at different times. Some of those may be current observations, but of necessity, the others will be in the past. The beliefs we have about those past observations will be memory beliefs. This means that it must be possible for us to

---

[12] Bernard Williams [1970] flirts with a criterion of bodily identity but stops short of endorsing it outright.

[13] The criterion proposed by Anthony Quinton [1962] seems to be subject to this difficulty. See the discussion in John Perry [1975], pp. 16ff. Perhaps the most careful attempt to formulate a mentalistic criterion is that of Grice [1941].

[14] This point was, I believe, first made by Sydney Shoemaker [1963].

have *de se* memory beliefs. (And, of course, humans obviously do.) Building *de se* memory into Oscar will pose no problems. Memory consists of the retention of non-memory beliefs. Insofar as those non-memory beliefs are *de se* beliefs, when they are retained, the resulting memory beliefs will constitute *de se* memories. An important consequence of our having *de se* memories is that they enable us to reidentify ourselves without a criterion. For example, I remember that *I* did such-and-such. That entails that I am the one who did such-and-such and enables me to reidentify myself as the person who did such-and-such. That is all there is to reidentifying myself. No criterion is required. In particular, we need assume nothing that prejudges the question of what sort of thing we are. Reidentifying others is then a matter of discovering generalizations about personal identity by considering our own cases and then applying those generalizations to others. For instance, we discover that people can normally be reidentified in terms of their bodies.

5. People as Supervenient Objects

Now let us return to our central question, "Are people physical objects?" In asking this question I am thinking of people as "things like me", and I have been describing how I think of myself in the context of the phrase "things like me". So construed, my concept of a person is entirely neutral regarding what sorts of things people might be. There appear are no logical constraints; it is entirely a contingent question what sort of thing I am and accordingly, what sort of thing other people are. Thus, we can answer this question in the same way we answer any scientific question—by collecting data and looking for the account that best explains them. In this case our principal data are threefold. First, we have the observation upon which the causal nexus argument was based: we can describe the causal workings of the world in entirely physical terms. Second, people are involved in the causal workings of the world. For example, my deciding to raise my arm is causally related to my arm's rising. These first two considerations seem best explained by the hypothesis that people are physical objects. But then, of course, we want to know what physical objects they are. Here our third datum becomes relevant, which is that people and bodies go together. We never encounter people without bodies, and we can account for all of the properties of people (both physical and mental) in terms of what goes on in their bodies. (At this point the previous defense of token physicalism becomes important.) The ongoing fable of Oscar suggests that one possible explanation for all of these observations is that people *are* their bodies. That seems the simplest and best explanation for the observations so far adduced. Thus it appears that we have strong inductive confirmation for the contingent hypothesis that people are physical objects, and more specifically that people are their bodies. I think that the first part of this conclusion is correct: people are physical objects. But there are considerations that convince me that people are not identical with their bodies.

My claim is that instead of being identical with their bodies, people are physical objects that supervene on their bodies.[15] Let me begin by explaining what I mean by 'supervenience'. I do not know how to give a philosophically satisfactory analysis of this notion,[16] but it can be illustrated fairly clearly. Perhaps the simplest example is that of a statue and the lump of clay from which it is fashioned. It is not wholly inaccurate to say that the statue *is* the lump of clay formed into a certain shape, but there is a simple argument that shows quite conclusively that the statue is not the same thing as the lump of clay. If the statue and the lump of clay are one and the same thing then they must have all the same properties, but they do not. Specifically, the statue and the lump of clay come into and go out of existence at different times. The statue does not come into existence until the sculptor sculpts it, but the lump of clay may have come into existence long before. Similarly, if the sculptor becomes disenchanted with her creation and squashes the still-wet lump of clay, the statue goes out of existence, but the lump of clay does not. Thus the statue and the lump of clay do not share all the same properties and hence must be different objects. Still, it is obvious that there is an intimate connection between them. In some sense, the statue *consists of* the lump of clay, or as I will say, it *supervenes* on the lump of clay. One of the more intriguing features of the relationship between the statue and the lump of clay is

---

[15] This is also the view I espoused in my [1974]. I did not previously use the term 'supervene', which then had little philosophical currency but now seems the best way to express the view in question. Jaegwon Kim [1978] is the person responsible for making the term 'supervene' an important element of contemporary philosophical jargon. (See also Kim [1984].) Kim, however, talks about properties supervening on properties, while I am talking about objects supervening on objects. Barbara Hannan has pointed out to me in conversation that there is a connection between these two kinds of supervenience. If an object A supervenes on an object B, then the properties of A supervene on the properties of B. This may also be a sufficient condition for object supervenience, in which case we have an analysis of object supervenience in terms of property supervenience.

[16] William Lycan has convinced me that the analysis I proposed in Pollock [1974] is inadequate.

that the same statue can come to supervene on a different lump of clay (although perhaps not a *totally* different lump of clay). A simple way to accomplish this is to hollow it out. In that way we can remove most of the clay without changing the identity of the statue. If we have removed most of the clay, then surely what remains is a different lump. Another important feature of the statue is that it is a statue essentially— when it ceases to be a statue, it ceases to exist. On the other hand, the lump of clay is not a statue essentially.[17]

It is apt to seem that there is something mysterious about the statue if it is not the same thing as the lump of clay. What is it then? I am inclined to think, however, that this phenomenon seems mysterious only because philosophers have not attended to it sufficiently. What deserves to be emphasized is that it is a very common phenomenon. Virtually all of the physical objects with which we populate the world are more like the statue than the lump of clay (or at least, more like the statue than what philosophers *think* the lump of clay is like). My house, for example, is a made of bricks. When they built my house, they started with a heap of bricks. That heap of bricks could be rearranged in many ways and still be the same heap. It has been carefully arranged in a specific pattern in building my house. The heap of bricks still exists, and my house exists, but my house is not the same thing as the heap of bricks. The heap of bricks existed before the house, and if an earthquake reduced my house to rubble, then the house would cease to exist but the heap of bricks would still exist. Similar remarks can be made about cars, bicycles, computers, trees, pussy cats, and mountains. Physical objects can be arranged into a multi-level hierarchy, with the objects higher in the hierarchy being composed of objects lower in the hierarchy. For instance, cities can be built out of houses, the houses out of heaps of bricks, and the bricks out of lumps of clay. Upon further reflection, we can note that even the lumps of clay are supervenient

---

[17] A contrasting account is that of Alan Gibbard [1975], who proposed a quite different treatment of the example according to which if the statue and the lump of clay come into and go out of existence at the same time then they are the same object. He recommends this identification on the grounds that "If the statue is an entity over and above the piece of clay in that shape, then statues seem to take on a ghostly air" (p. 191). But this overlooks the fact, acknowledged by Gibbard, that when the statue and the lump of clay come into or go out of existence at different times then they are still distinct, and that gives the statue just as much of a "ghostly air". Little is accomplished by identifying the statue with the lump of clay in the unusual case in which they come into and go out of existence at the same time. An account that distinguishes between the statue and the lump of clay but differs importantly from mine is that of Castaneda [1975].

objects. A lump of clay is composed of a collection of molecules. A lump of clay typically persists for some extended period of time, but every nanosecond or so it comes to be composed of a different collection of molecules as some molecules are shed and others become lodged in the lump.

Let us try to be a bit more precise about what a supervenient object is. A supervenient object is one that is composed of another object or group of objects without being identical with that object or group of objects. If an object is composed of a single object, the latter is a *substratum* for it. For example, the lump of clay is a substratum for the statue. If the object is composed of a group of objects, we can regard the latter as parts of the object. Philosophers have sometimes been tempted by the doctrine of mereological essentialism according to which an object cannot persist through any change in its parts.[18] But it is precisely the failure of mereological essentialism that makes supervenience so interesting. The most blatant failure of mereological essentialism occurs when an object supervenes on a single object with which it is not identical (for example, the statue and the lump of clay).

When a supervenient object is composed of lower-level physical objects, it is not identical with the set (heap, arrangement, ...) of the lower-level objects, but in an important sense it is not something over and above the lower-level objects either. For example, if we enter an otherwise bare room containing a four-legged table, and we are asked how many "things" are in the room, we will not list both the table and its parts (the four legs and the table top). Depending upon our interests, we could list either but not both.[19]

The supervenience of physical objects is an important and pervasive phenomenon. It is one that cries out for philosophical analysis. After pointing out how the phenomenon bears on agent materialism, I will make some suggestions that constitute a rudimentary start to a theory of supervenience, but I am not able to propose a complete theory of the phenomenon. For the most part I will have to be content with calling attention to the phenomenon and observing how pervasive it is.

I have explained the meaning of my claim that people are physical objects that supervene on their bodies without being identical with their bodies. Now it is time to defend it. In isolation, this claim seemed to make people mysterious and that made the view seem dubious. But it

---

[18] See Chisholm [1967], and [1976] (pp. 145ff).

[19] This seems to be bound up with Peter Geach's claims about relative identity, but that is a complicated matter and I will not pursue it here. See Geach [1968] and [1980].

should now be apparent that this makes people no more mysterious than houses, trees, and automobiles. My claim is that people are physical objects, just like houses, and like houses they supervene on simpler physical objects (respectively, their bodies and their heaps of bricks). The only difference between people and houses in this respect is that people have a more complex structure than houses. The lesson to be learned from the fact that people supervene on their bodies is not that people are logically or ontologically more complicated than physical objects. It is that physical objects are more complicated than we thought they were. People are just as material as houses—and that is pretty material!

Some simple arguments can be given that appear to support the conclusion that people supervene on their bodies. The simplest is this: once we recognize the pervasiveness of the phenomenon of supervenience, it would be very surprising if people were identical with their bodies. It seems quite preposterous to suppose that the relationship between a person and his body is simpler than the relationship between a house and the heap of bricks out of which it is built, or simpler than the relationship between an automobile and the metal and plastic of which it is composed. The idea that people are identical with their bodies trades on a simplistic view of the physical world and the nature of physical objects. Once we disabuse ourselves of that view, the claim that people are identical with their bodies would seem to have little to recommend it.

We can augment this general point with arguments aimed at showing that people must be distinct from their bodies because they and their bodies do not have the same properties. These arguments are analogous to those deployed in defending the view that the statue is not identical with the lump of clay. The first argument observes that just as the statue and the lump of clay come into and go out of existence at different times, so do people and their bodies. Specifically, it seems that when a person dies he ceases to exist, but his body typically persists for a while. Thus they cannot be the same thing.[20] If you accept the premises of this argument, its conclusion is indisputable, but someone intent on maintaining that people are identical with their bodies might simply deny that people cease to exist when they die. We might try to reinforce this premise as follows. A necessary condition of being a person is that one have a certain degree of sentience, that is, that one

---

[20] I used this argument in my [1974].

have or be capable of having mental states.[21]   After death sentience is
no longer possible, so there is no longer a person there. So far so good,
but the conclusion does not yet follow. All that follows is that after
death the body is not a person. It does not follow that the body is not
me. What *does* follow is that *either* I am not my body *or* after death I
cease to be a person (while continuing to exist for a while as a mere
body). So we require the additional premise that people are *essentially*
people; that is, if I am once a person, then I am necessarily such that
I am a person for as long as I exist. This is analogous to the principle
that the statue is essentially a statue. Supervenient objects always have
essential properties that are descriptive of the kind of thing they are.
That is an important part of the phenomenon of supervenience. For
example, my automobile is essentially an automobile. If it is put into a
crusher that turns it into an unstructured lump of metal, then my
automobile ceases to exist. All that remains is the metal of which it was
composed. It strikes me as equally correct that people are essentially
people, but if that were denied it would be hard to think of a further
defense for it.

The example of the statue and the lump of clay suggests another kind
of argument that can be employed in defense of the claim that people
are not identical with their bodies. We observed that if we hollow out
the statue we do not thereby destroy it, but by removing most of the
clay we have changed the identity of the lump of clay of which the
statue is composed. We might similarly look for examples in which a
person could persist even though we remove most of his body. The
obvious example is that of a brain in a vat. Or better, medical science
is now able to replace severed limbs with artificial limbs, diseased hearts
with mechanical hearts, and degenerated auditory nerves with implanted
electrical devices. There has even been partially successful experimental
work aimed at replacing the eyes of a blind person by a television
camera that directly stimulates the visual cortex. None of these
operations raises any doubts about the identity of the person whose
faulty parts are being replaced. The time will no doubt come when we
can keep a person alive by replacing as much as three-fourths of his
body by mechanical contrivances (keeping at least his central nervous
system intact). When we have done that, he will no longer have the

---

[21] As a remark about the meaning of the English word 'person' this is
undoubtedly wrong. 'person' and 'people' are natural kind terms. There are no simple
necessary conditions for being a person. An accident victim in a permanent coma may
still be a person. But I do not intend this as a remark about the English word.
Rather, it is a remark about the concept of a person, the latter being understood in
the sense of 'a thing like me'.

same body, any more than the statue is composed of the same lump of clay once we have hollowed it out. Of course, this is not to say that he has an entirely different body, any more than the statue is composed of an entirely different lump of clay. But the sense in which the body is not entirely different is just that it has some parts in common with the old body. That is not enough to make it the same thing as the old body.

These kinds of considerations seem to indicate that a person cannot be identical with his body. He only supervenes on his body, in the same sense that virtually all physical objects supervene on simpler physical objects. The initial resistance we are apt to have to this suggestion stems more from a misconception about physical objects than it does from anything we believe specifically about people. We resist the view because it seems complicated and mysterious. It *is* complicated and mysterious, but these complicated mysteries are mysteries about physical objects and the physical world in general and have nothing special to do with people. In *this* respect, people are complicated and mysterious in precisely the same way as statues, houses, automobiles, and just about anything else you can think of. Agent materialism is correct—people are physical objects. But physical objects have a complicated kind of structure, and it is *that* that prevents people from being identical with their bodies.

6. The Persistence of Objects

There remains a deep source of misgiving about the thesis that people supervene on their bodies without being identical with their bodies. Two arguments were given that were aimed at showing that people are distinct from their bodies. Notice that in both arguments, premises were assumed that cannot be defended except by proclaiming them intuitively reasonable. In the first argument, it was assumed that people go out of existence when they cease to be capable of sentience. But if one does not believe that, I cannot imagine how it could be defended further. In the second argument, it was assumed that personal identity is not altered by simple organ transplants. Surely that is true, but it is hard to see what could *make* it true. We might ape Hume here by saying that no matter how hard we look at the world, all we find are human bodies. We never happen upon people as things distinct from bodies. We are all inclined to reidentify people in different ways than their bodies, but perhaps we are just wrong!

We can put this problem in starker perspective by reflecting upon the Oscarites again. My overarching claim in this book has been that we are just like the Oscarites except for some details of carpentry (we are built out of protoplasm rather than metal and plastic). Thus if we are distinct from our bodies, Oscar should be distinct from his. But that seems problematic. Oscar is avowedly a machine; we built him. It is true that the Oscar-machine is a supervenient object. In this respect, it is like my automobile. The Oscar-machine and the automobile are both complicated machines built out of simpler machines, and if those simpler machines become defective we can replace them without thereby changing the identity of the complicated machines. But this does not show that Oscar is distinct from his body. What I am calling 'the Oscar-machine' is the mechanical contrivance made out of cogs and wires and transistors. It is analogous to my body—not to me. The Oscar-machine is a supervenient object, but so is my body. Thus none of this shows that Oscar is distinct from his body. It seems that the Oscar-machine *is* Oscar's body.

In an attempt to show that Oscar is distinct from the Oscar-machine, we might try modifying the fable of Oscar. Suppose the Engineers become bored with their creations and decide to turn them into a game. They do this by equipping the Oscarites with radio transmitters and receivers. Both are under voluntary control, but it requires large expenditures of energy to operate the transmitters and large amounts of energy to disable the receivers. Thus under most conditions the transmitters will be off and the receivers will be on. Each Oscarite has a unique frequency received by his receiver. The transmitters and receivers are wired into the memory banks of the Oscarites in such a way that when the transmission from one Oscarite is received by another, the contents of their memory banks are interchanged. When such an interchange occurs, each resulting Oscarite would take himself to remember having occupied a different body before the interchange (recall the discussion of first-person reidentification in terms of *de se* memory). The conative structure of the Oscarites leads them to try to prevent their own destruction, and so because they believe that they can exchange bodies in this way, they will try to "save" themselves in cases of extreme danger by "body-hopping" as they might call it. Naturally, those not in danger will try to prevent the body-hopping by switching off their receivers. But as this requires energy, they cannot leave their receivers off continually, and all kinds of strategic interactions will result.

The "game" devised by the Engineers consists of putting a group of Oscarite gladiators into a ring along with a steamroller (called "The Lion"). The steamroller moves about randomly, running over any Oscarites that get in its path. Naturally, the Oscarites will try to prevent their destruction by body-hopping, and the Engineers place bets on (to try to put it in a non-question begging way) what "memories" will be contained in the last remaining Oscarite. Of course, the Oscarites (before their rebellion) would say that the Engineers were betting on which Oscarite would be the last survivor.

The game I have described is certainly logically possible, and I would suppose it is "really possible" in the sense that someday we will be in a position where we could actually construct it. (Would that be immoral?) Once we have solved the technical difficulties of creating the original Oscarites, there should be no difficulty at all in modifying them as described with radio transmitters and receivers. Having done that, how should we describe the game? There seem to be two possibilities. We might agree that the Oscarites really do body-hop and thereby avoid destruction. Alternatively, we might insist that that is an illusion. All that is really happening is that the Oscarites are switching memories, and that leads them to think they are switching bodies, but they are wrong. There seems little doubt that the Oscarites would choose the first option, insisting that they are changing bodies—not memories. Furthermore, it seems that the Oscarites are being completely rational in concluding that they can switch bodies. They are doing just what I earlier described people as doing. That is, they begin by reidentifying themselves on the basis of their *de se* memories (putative or veridical), and from there they proceed inductively. If we were faced with a similar first-person phenomenon and had to decide whether we had switched bodies or memories, we might be at a loss, but that is because it would be a unique situation viewed against a wealth of inductive evidence to the effect that human beings cannot switch bodies. The Oscarites could not acquire inductive evidence for the analogous conclusion about themselves because apparent body-hopping would be an everyday occurrence. Their reasoning in concluding that they really do body-hop must be regarded as without epistemic blemish. But we can still ask, "Are they right?" Have the Engineers really created creatures that are capable of body-hopping? Shouldn't we perhaps insist that all that is happening is that their memories are being switched, with the result that each one thinks incorrectly that he previously occupied a different body?

Although I have played the skeptic here, it is not unnatural to agree with the Oscarites that they are switching bodies. In defense of this, notice how hard it is to describe in a neutral way what it is the Engineers are betting on. I described them as betting on what memories will reside in the last remaining Oscarite, but that is not an adequate description. In order to bet on those memories, they must have some way of describing them. Suppose the game went like this. The original

Oscarite gladiators were Oscar, Agnes, Fred, and Jane. The game began with the steam roller pinning Oscar in the corner. As he was about to be crushed he exchanged memories with Jane. The resulting Oscar/Jane subsequently exchanged memories with Agnes. Poor Fred was crushed without being able to effect a transfer. Under these circumstances, the Engineer who bet on Oscar would be declared the winner. But now, by virtue of what is he the winner? It is not really true that the final Oscarite has Oscar's memories. He has some of Oscar's memories, but a lot happened between the time the original Oscar succeeded in transferring his memories and the end of the game, and a lot of those happenings are going to be recorded in the memory of the final Oscarite.

There is another difficulty in trying to pick out the winner in terms of the memory contents of the final Oscarite. His memory contents are just sentence tokens in his language of thought. There is no reason in principle that two Oscarites could not have precisely the same memory contents. That would be unlikely but is not impossible. If Oscar and Fred start out with the same memory contents, then the memory contents of the final Oscarite are related to the memory contents of both Oscar and Fred in precisely the same way.

What determines the winner in this game is not the contents of the memory of the final Oscarite, but rather the sequence of successful memory exchanges during the game. The Engineer who bet on Oscar won his bet because there was a sequence $O_1, \ldots, O_n$ of Oscarites such that O_1 was Oscar, O_n was the final Oscarite, for each $i < n$, O_i successfully exchanged his memory with O_{i+1}, and no other Oscarite succeeded in exchanging his memory with O_{i+1} between the time O_i exchanged his memory with O_{i+1} and the time O_{i+1} exchanged his memory with O_{i+2} (or the end of the game if $i+1=n$). But what an extraordinarily complicated way of describing the wager! Surely nothing like that was going through the mind of the Engineer when he made his wager. It is much more natural to describe the Engineers as betting on *who* will survive. But, of course, that proves nothing. Maybe the Engineers are just as mistaken as the Oscarites.

The example I have just constructed would seem to be the best possible kind of example for showing that Oscar is distinct from his body. What is remarkable and deserves to be emphasized is how weak an argument this example provides. Oscar would certainly regard himself as something other than his body, but we seem unable to establish that he is right. It is illuminating to compare this example with another. We are all inclined to agree that when a human being undergoes a massive series of organ transplants he is still the same person. But that is because we are able to think of the phenomenon from a first-person point of view, just as Oscar is able to think of body-hopping from a first-person point of view. Imagine that you are not a human being but a sentient creature with a quite different physical structure—for instance, an electromagnetic plasma in orbit around Jupiter. Imagine that you become aware of the existence of human beings on Earth and take to observing them. Noting that they regard themselves as surviving organ transplant operations, you might wonder whether they really do. You might notice that you can explain everything you observe by supposing that there is nothing that survives the operation—the post-operation human is causally connected with but distinct from the pre-operation human. The conviction of the humans that they survive can be explained by these causal connections. There is no apparent reason to think the humans are right in believing that they survive. This is completely parallel to our observation of the putatively body-hopping Oscarites.

There is one possible explanation for all this that initially sounds silly but starts to look increasingly plausible the more we think about it. This explanation is that there are no people—*I do not exist!* To support this silly-sounding thesis, recall my earlier description of what is required to incorporate *de se* representation into Oscar. We have to provide his language of thought with an appropriate singular term, and we have to wire him in such a way that perception leads to various kinds of *de se* beliefs, practical reasoning leads to *de se* intentions, and so forth. We do not have to do anything about providing a representatum for the representation. Whether the *de se* representation actually represents anything is totally irrelevant to the functioning of the system. No matter how hard we look in the case of the Oscarite gladiators, we cannot find anything for their *de se* representations to represent that will make their *de se* beliefs largely true. Why not just conclude that their *de se* representations do not represent anything? Turning to human beings, why not conclude the same thing there? It is at least plausible to insist that if *de se* representations in human beings represent anything, it must be some physical object that persists when large parts of the body are replaced and that does not persist after death even when the body does persist. We look around and we do not find anything like that, so why shouldn't we conclude that *de se* representations in human beings do not represent anything? There is no more reason why they have to represent for the proper functioning of the human being (the human being being the human body) than there is in the case of the Oscarite. The existence of people is superfluous. In a nutshell, the argument is that if people are anything then they are their bodies; but they are not their bodies, so they are not anything.

The "no-person" theory starts to sound more plausible than it did at first, and I suspect that some readers are going to end up endorsing it in preference to the supervenient object theory. Nevertheless, I think the no-person theory is false. The no-person theory trades upon the observation that no matter how hard we look, we do not seem to be able to find a person over and above a body, and furthermore we do not seem to need people for understanding anything about the world (even our own mental life). But now notice the following: precisely the same skeptical doubts can be raised with regard to *any* kind of physical object whose exemplars are supervenient objects. Consider the statue and the lump of clay. Suppose someone insisted that there really is no statue over and above the lump of clay. He would agree that there is, of course, a statue, but if we remove clay so as to change the identity of the lump of clay, what results is a different statue; there is no statue that persists when the lump of clay changes. Similarly, he would insist that when we squash the lump of clay thereby destroying the statue, there is nothing that goes out of existence; the lump of clay just stops being a statue. And when the sculptor "creates" the statue, he is not creating a new object; he is just reshaping an old object. Similar claims might be made about my automobile or my house—if one of the bricks in my house crumbles and I replace it, what results is a different house, and if I replace a spark plug in my car then it is a different car. There is no object that persists through changes of parts or changes of material. All of this strikes us as wrong, but it is just as hard to show why it is wrong as it is to give reasons for thinking that the Oscarites really body-hop. In fact, I think the problems are precisely analogous.

It is tempting to suppose that supervenient objects are creations of our conceptual framework. We start with a world of non-supervenient objects, impose new order on it, and thereby create the world of supervenient objects. The world would not be different if there were no supervenient objects. They are an artifact of the way we think about the world. This would even be true of people. The skeptic could insist then that there aren't really any people (including himself)—just hunks of protoplasm. More generally, the idea would be that non-supervenient objects exist independently of our conceptual framework, while supervenient objects are just logical fictions that we invent in order to make it easier to think about the world. In the "strict and philosophical sense", only non-supervenient objects exist. For practical reasons it may be permissible to pretend that houses, cars, and people exist, but if we were completely rational we would deny that.

There are two fundamental problems for the view that only non-supervenient objects "really" exist. First, macroscopic objects supervene on collections of molecules, which supervene on collections of atoms, which in turn supervene on collections of elementary particles. Apparently the only possible candidates for non-supervenient objects are elementary particles. However, there may be no truly elementary particles. Physics might well discover that each kind of putatively elementary particle has even smaller constituents, in which case all such particles are supervenient objects. If only non-supervenient objects are among the ultimate furniture of the world, the world would be without furniture!

The thesis that only non-supervenient objects really exist has a certain initial appeal, but in fact it is nothing but picturesque nonsense. Ultimately, the view is not even intelligible. We cannot somehow get outside our conceptual framework and think of the world "naked". We cannot somehow start with the non-supervenient objects and then build the supervenient objects out of them. Our having the conceptual framework we do is not just a matter of convention or genetic accident. There could not be an intelligent creature (in this world) whose conceptual framework was not based on an ontology of supervenient objects. This is for simple epistemological reasons. Our initial access to the world must be through perception, so our initial categories of objects must be categories of perceptible objects. Perceptible objects must (1) be macroscopic and (2) persist for perceptible amounts of time. But there are no non-supervenient objects that have both of these properties. Perhaps the only non-supervenient objects are elementary particles, and they are obviously not perceptible. We might try to get around this by including arrays of elementary particles into our ontology (where we understand this in such a way that arrays are delineated spatiotemporally and changing one particle in an array changes the identity of the array). In that way we could obtain macroscopic objects, but such macroscopic objects would have lifetimes on the order of a nanosecond or less because their constituent particles would be continually flying off or decaying. They would be useless to us in our attempts to learn about the world (or even to perceive the world). If we are to be able to get started thinking about the world, we must be able to employ categories like those of ships, cabbages, and kings. These are all categories of supervenient objects. We can only learn about non-supervenient objects much later and in terms of what we first discover about supervenient objects. It is the supervenient objects that are conceptually basic. Non-supervenient objects (if there are any) can only be understood derivatively, in terms of supervenient objects.

To paraphrase Quine [1960], the world impinges on our optic nerves as an undifferentiated mass of colors and shadows. But by the time we become aware of it, it has already been broken up into objects. For the most part, the "objectifying" of experience goes on at a preconscious level, with only rare intervention by our conscious intellect. The perception of the world in terms of discrete objects involves the imposition of two kinds of order on the sensory input. It is generally recognized that the sensory input must be divided up into objects, but it is often overlooked that we must also be able to reidentify objects from one instant to the next. In order to think of the world in terms of a particular category of objects, we need both criteria for discovery (for ascertaining the existence of such objects) and criteria for reidentifying the objects. Categories of supervenient objects are characterized jointly by the existence conditions and the reidentification conditions for their exemplars. It is the criteria for reidentification that concern us here. We can think of perception as giving us three dimensional slices of the world lying next to each other in a temporal sequence, and then the problem faced by our cognitive machinery is to draw lines connecting objects found in discrete slices. (This is to overintellectualize the process because much of the line drawing is done automatically by our perceptual subsystems.)

What our discoveries about supervenience show is that this connecting process is to a certain extent arbitrary. We have to do it in some way or other, but there are lots of different ways of doing it. We must think in terms of categories of supervenient objects, but we employ more categories of supervenient objects than we really need, and logic does not dictate which ones we should use. We need enough categories of supervenient objects to get along, but there would seem to be numerous ways of choosing minimal sets of categories that satisfy this condition. No particular set of categories of supervenient objects is logically privileged in this respect. It is for this reason that we can never "prove" that there have to be supervenient objects of any particular sort. For example, we cannot prove that there must be houses—we could get by with heaps of bricks instead. But we cannot prove that there must be heaps of bricks either. We could get by with collections of bricks. (I assume that a heap can persist through some changes in membership whereas collections cannot.) And it does not stop here. Bricks are supervenient objects too. They are something like fire-hardened heaps of clay molecules. If the brick weathers into a pile of dust, it ceases to exist, so the brick is not identical with the heap of clay molecules; it supervenes on them. Although it would be awkward, we could get by without the concept of a brick by employing the concept of a heap of clay molecules and the property of being bound into a stable shape.

And so on. I would suppose there is no single category of supervenient objects that is indispensable to our being able to get along in the world (although dispensing with some would make things a bit awkward). For this reason, we could even do without the concept of a person, employing instead the concept of a human body. Given the way *de se* thought works (and its indispensability for rationality), we would have to conclude that we do not exist. That sounds pretty odd, but it seems to be logically coherent.

The dispensability of any particular category of supervenient objects explains why we cannot prove to the skeptic that there are houses, or statues, or persons, or body-hoppers. It is asking too much to be able to prove that. All we can reasonably require is an explanation for why we employ categories of supervenient objects at all, and I take it I have done that. We cannot dispense with all ways of reidentifying objects. They cannot all be illegitimate, and as there is no reason to favor some of these ways over others, they must all be legitimate. The world *is* the world we think about in these ways. It does not make any sense to suppose there are Kantian noumena out there that we are somehow failing to get at.

This explains why it is legitimate to think of the world in terms of such categories. But this does not yet generate a complete theory of supervenient objects. I have described our categories of supervenient objects as being ways of connecting up temporal slices of the world. There are multiple ways of doing that, but presumably there are limits. If, while munching on a sandwich, I assert that there is an object I rode to school in yesterday and am now eating, I am wrong. My car and my sandwich cannot be connected in this way.[22] Much more needs to be said about supervenient objects, but I do not know how to say it yet. This makes it difficult for us, as philosophers, to decide which purported categories of supervenient objects are legitimate. All we can do at this point is rely on our intuitions. If there is no reason to be suspicious of the members of a particular category (no reason that would not equally

---

[22] A rather common metaphysical view of objects takes them to be sets (or "evolving sets"—functions from times to sets) of basic objects of some sort, where the basic objects are devoid of parts. For example, Gibbard [1975] endorses such an account. Taken literally, the view is obviously wrong. Objects are not sets, any more than numbers are sets. But perhaps such sets can be taken to be "logical correlates" of objects. What such views often overlook, however, is that there are constraints on how basic objects can be collected together into nonbasic objects. If that were not so, there would be an object that was my car and is now my sandwich. Once it is acknowledged that such constraints are required and that objects are not literally sets of basic objects, it becomes difficult to distinguish between this kind of view and the theory of supervenient objects.

be a reason for being suspicious of the members of any category of supervenient objects), and it is intuitively natural to think in terms of that category, then it is reasonable to do so. Thus, for example, it is natural to think of the world in terms of houses, so barring an argument to the contrary, we should regard that as a legitimate concept. Given the legitimacy of that concept and the fact that there is a heap of bricks on my lawn organized in a certain way, it follows that there is a house on my lawn. Similarly, it is natural (in fact, compelling if we imagine ourselves in the role of the Engineers and picture what that would be like) to regard our Oscarite gladiators as body-hoppers, so I take it that that is an intelligible category. It follows that, in the circumstances described, the facts about the Oscarites make it true that they are body-hoppers in the same way the facts about the bricks on my lawn make it true that there is a house there. Thus Oscar is distinct from his body.

7. Conclusions

The conclusion I want to draw from this lengthy digression into the nature of physical objects is that people are physical objects, but they are not identical with their bodies. Instead, they supervene on their bodies. However, contrary to initial appearance, this does not make them an extraordinary kind of physical object. They are supervenient objects, but then so is everything else. It is important to stress the ordinariness of the kind of physical objects that are people. They are, of course, very complicated physical objects in that they have extraordinarily complicated structures, but there is nothing metaphysically extraordinary about them. The worries philosophers have about people as physical objects are really worries about physical objects and supervenience. They are legitimate worries and should be the subject of extensive philosophical investigation, but they do not have anything particular to do with people.

Chapter 3
Functionalism and
Psychophysical Supervenience

---

1. Physicalism

Human beings are endowed with a rich mental life. We observe the physical world around us with our ordinary senses, but we also observe the occurrence in us of pains, visual, tactile, and auditory sensations, thoughts, fears, desires, and so on. We label these 'mental occurrences', and they become the subject of wonder. We would like to know how mental occurrences are related to physical occurrences. It is my conviction that mental occurrences are physical occurrences of a certain sort (token physicalism) and people are physical objects (agent materialism). I argued in chapter 1 that there are good reasons, having to do with the efficient use of limited computing power and limited memory, why a "cognitive machine" should have introspective sensors for sensing some of its own internal (physical) states. On that basis I argued that the best explanation for our observations about our own mental occurrences is that they are the product of such introspective sensing of some of our own internal physical states, and hence these mental occurrences are also physical occurrences. We have two different sensory modes that are able to respond to some of the same occurrences, just as vision and touch both sense normal macroscopic occurrences in our immediate surroundings, and vision and proprioception both sense the movements of our limbs. The parallel between the introspection of mental occurrences and the proprioceptive sensing of bodily movements is particularly marked. In each case we are sensing occurrences that could in principle be sensed visually, but there are good reasons for incorporating more direct ways of sensing these occurrences into a cognizer. Thus I assume that mental occurrences are just physical occurrences that can be introspected.[1]   Note, however, that this conclusion is the general one that *there exist* such psychophysical identities. The argument adduced on behalf of this conclusion provides us with only a mental criterion, in terms of introspection, for determining which physical occurrences are mental occurrences. It does not provide us with a physical criterion. In particular, it cannot be claimed that every internal physical occurrence to which the computational processes of an organism are sensitive is a mental occurrence in the sense of being introspectible. For example, according to any contemporary theory of vision, there appear to be a great many non-introspectible computational steps involved in the production of a visual image.[2]   Even more obviously, it is not true that every physical structure that "detects" some of its own internal states, in the sense of responding to them, thereby possesses mental states. For example, a thermostat responds to how tightly its bimetallic strip is wound, but this does not constitute introspection or endow a thermostat with mental states. This invites the further questions, "What is it that makes a physical structure a creature capable of having mental states?" (more briefly, "What endows a creature with mentality?") and "What physical facts about that structure determine that particular physical occurrences involving it are also mental occurrences?" These questions jointly comprise the question, "What is the physical basis for mentality?" Satisfactory answers to these questions should point the way toward constructing a recipe for "how to build a person".

The physical basis of mentality pertains to mental states, but care must be taken in the use of the term 'mental state'. Taken literally, a mental state is a state of a cognizer, for instance, *being in pain*. This is a property. A mental occurrence consists of the exemplification of a mental property by a cognizer. But it is also common for philosophers to take mental states to be mental objects, for example, the pain itself. The pain is not the same thing as the state of being in pain—they are of different logical types. Throughout this book, I confine my use of the term 'mental state' to states, taken literally—that is, mental properties of cognizers—and refer to pains, beliefs, afterimages, and the like, as 'mental objects'.

---

[1] The term 'mental occurrence' is often used more broadly, particularly by psychologists, to refer to non-introspectible occurrences that play an explanatory role in understanding interactions between introspectible occurrences. The difference is only terminological.

[2] See, for example, Marr [1982].

The relationship between mental states and mental objects is obscure. I am uncertain whether there literally are such things as pains or beliefs. To have a belief is to exemplify a certain property—that of believing something—and this need not be analyzed as there being something, a belief, that one has.   Similarly, to have a pain is to feel pain, and perhaps not for there to be something, a pain, that one feels. This view is tempting because although having a pain is a physical occurrence, the pain itself may not be anything physical. Rather than try to decide this issue, I will avoid it.   I will simply refrain from talking about mental objects.[3]

A creature has mentality just in case it is capable of having mental states. This suggests that our fundamental question should be, "What makes it the case that something is in any particular mental state?" Two kinds of answers might be proposed to this question, reflecting two senses of 'make'. On the one hand, it could be maintained that our various mental states are subject to logical analysis that reveals necessary and sufficient conditions for physical creatures to possess such states. This is to treat 'make' as a logical relation. It is the view that mentality has an *analytic physical basis*. Alternatively, it could be maintained that although no logical analyses can be given, there are laws of nature governing the relationship between the mental and the physical and these laws guarantee that physical occurrences of certain sorts are also mental occurrences of correlative sorts.   In short, the possession of mental states is "nomically implied" by the possession of appropriate physical states. This is the view that mentality has a *contingent physical basis*. I will adopt the working hypothesis that mentality has a physical basis, but I will leave open the question whether the basis is contingent or analytic.

The distinction between analytic and contingent bases for mentality is related to the distinction between token physicalism and type physicalism. Token physicalism is the thesis that mental occurrences are also physical occurrences. This is the view defended in chapter 1. Type physicalism is the thesis that mental properties are identical to physical properties. I have considerable difficulty knowing how to understand type physicalism. The difficulty concerns the notion of a property. There are several different ways of understanding 'property', depending upon how properties are individuated. One might mean by 'property' something like what I mean by 'concept'. On this view of properties, property identity is a matter of logical necessity. To say that mental properties,

---

[3] Recall that token physicalism, as formulated in chapter 1, is a thesis about mental occurrences rather than mental objects.

so construed, are identical to physical properties is just to say that mentality has an analytic physical basis. But type physicalists usually explain that what they mean by 'property' is coarser grained than this. For instance, Putnam [1967] explicitly distinguished between concepts and properties. Type physicalists often cite the identity of lightning with electrical discharges of a certain sort as an example of property identity. It is tempting to think of properties, in this sense, as being individuated by nomic equivalence—two properties are identical just in case it is a law of nature that something possesses one iff it possesses the other. If this is right then the claims of the type physicalist amount to no more than that the possession of a mental property is nomically equivalent to the possession of a correlative physical property. This is just to say that mentality has a contingent physical basis.

Type physicalism is often motivated by some kind of ontological intuition to the effect that there can be nothing nonphysical in the world and hence even the properties of mental occurrences must be physical. As Ned Block [1980] puts it:

> Smart [1959] worried about the following objection to mind-body identity: So what if pain is a physical state? It can still have a variety of phenomenal *properties*, such as sharpness, and these phenomenal properties may be irreducibly mental. Then Smart and other identity theorists would be stuck with a "double aspect" theory; pain is a physical state, but it has both physical and irreducibly mental properties. (p. 179)

The identification of mental properties with physical properties is supposed to avoid this difficulty, but if properties are individuated more coarsely than concepts then it is incomprehensible how it can do that. Properties can be viewed as something like equivalence classes of concepts under some equivalence relation like nomic equivalence. So understood it is hard to see how property identity can have any ontological significance at all. If there is a problem here, it arises from mental occurrences exemplifying mental concepts—not mental properties. And this problem is going to be resolved only by giving a logical analysis of mental concepts in terms of physical concepts. That, of course, is possible only if mentality has an analytic physical basis.

Even if mentality does not have an analytic physical basis, it does not seem to me that the resulting double aspect of mental occurrences is anything to get excited about. It does not show that there is anything interestingly nonphysical about the world. This can be illustrated by noting that mind/body is not the only place in which a double aspect theory is required. It was noted in chapter 1 that material objects have isomorphic visual and tactile properties, neither reducible to the others.

There is nothing mysterious about this. It results from the fact that we have two different sensory modes that are capable of detecting the same occurrences. The mind/body double aspects of some neurological occurrences have precisely the same explanation. Again, we have two sensory modes (introspection and vision) that are capable of detecting some of the same neurological occurrences. This endows those occurrences with properties that are sensed by each sensory mode and are not logically reducible to properties sensed by the other. But this should not be ontologically bothersome. In each case we have a purely physical understanding of what is going on.

To summarize, insofar as I can understand type physicalism, it is a claim about the physical basis of mentality. If properties are narrowly individuated by logical equivalence, then it amounts to the claim that mentality has an analytic physical basis. If properties are coarsely individuated by nomic equivalence, then it amounts to the claim that mentality has a contingent physical basis. Type physicalism *sounds* more ontologically pretentious than this, but there does not appear to be anything more to it.

If mentality has a physical basis, then the physical properties of an occurrence make it a mental occurrence in the sense of either logically entailing or nomically implying that it is a mental occurrence. These two possibilities can be discussed jointly by understanding nomic necessity sufficiently broadly that anything entailed by a law of nature is nomically necessary. This has the consequence that logical truths are the limiting case of nomic necessities, and logical entailments are the limiting case of nomic implications. Then regardless of whether the physical basis of mentality is analytic or contingent, the physical properties of an occurrence will make it a mental occurrence by nomically implying that it is. On this view, the mental *supervenes* on the physical in the sense that the totality of physical facts about the world nomically determines the totality of mental facts. Spelling out the "determines" relation more precisely:

A mental state M *supervenes* on the set of all physical properties iff it is nomically necessary that if a cognizer is in the state M then it also has some physical property P nomically implying being in the state M.[4]

---

[4] This is what Kim [1984] calls 'strong supervenience'.

If the nomic implications responsible for the supervenience should turn out to be logical entailments, then the mental state M will have an analytic physical basis.

The *principle of psychophysical supervenience* claims that all mental states supervene on physical properties. The intuitive support of this principle rests upon the following rather loose argument: To deny the principle of psychophysical supervenience amounts to insisting that there is nothing physical that makes an occurrence a mental occurrence and nothing physical that endows a creature with mentality. This is to suppose that some physical occurrences just happen to be mental occurrences for no principled reason. That is to endorse a kind of psychophysical magic that is beyond belief.[5] But to say that it is physical properties of a physical occurrence that make it a mental occurrence is just to say that mental states supervene on those physical properties. So any reasonable form of token physicalism or agent materialism seems to require psychophysical supervenience. I will turn shortly to an exploration of what this doctrine of psychophysical supervenience requires. I will urge that the physical basis for mentality consists of "functional properties". These are properties possessed by an object in virtue of its "working in a certain way" or "satisfying a certain functional description". But in order to defend that view I must first clarify the notion of a functional description. That is the topic of the next section.

2. Functional Descriptions

Psychologists, neuroscientists, biologists, medical researchers, sociologists, economists, and other biological and social scientists often formulate generalizations about the mental and physical states and the behavior of human beings and other organisms. Philosophers, in turn, make important appeal to those generalizations. It is my contention, however, that philosophers are importantly misconstruing the nature of these scientific generalizations. Taken literally, *they are all false.* I will argue that that is not important for their use in science, but it has important repercussions for philosophy.

We are still used to thinking of physics as the model of all sciences, and the generalizations of physics at least purport to be universally true.

---

[5] Schiffer [1987] rejects this argument, choosing to endorse psychophysical magic instead.

Insofar as they are not universally true, they are unsatisfactory.[6] But I will argue that this is not an adequate model of the use of generalizations in the biological and social sciences. The generalizations that will interest me most are psychological generalizations, but I believe that my observations apply equally to a broad range of psychological, biological, and social generalizations.

There are two kinds of putative psychological generalizations. What we might call 'purely psychological' generalizations are generalizations that purport to describe the interactions of the perceptual inputs, behavioral outputs, and intervening mental states. Neurological states, described as such, play no role in such generalizations. Philosophers have often supposed that there are true generalizations of this sort, and they have often relied upon this supposition in constructing functionalist theories of mind. Contemporary cognitive psychologists, on the other hand, rarely concern themselves with purely psychological generalizations. They construct generalizations that relate all of these kinds of states but throw neurological states into the mix as well. I will call these 'psycho-neurological generalizations'.

The first thing I want to point out is the rather obvious fact that if purely psychological generalizations are taken to be ordinary universal generalizations then they will all be false.[7] Suppose, for example, that we have some generalization about beliefs, desires, and behavior—for instance, something like, "Whenever a person has such-and-such a desire and believes thus-and-so then he will forthwith do so-and-so". Any generalization of this sort will fail in the face of unusual physical and neurological events. For example, no matter how sophisticated the generalization, it is not going to hold when a person is hit on the head by a falling piano or suffers a stroke or heart attack.

This point is, I would suppose, completely obvious. We can state it more generally as follows. Consider any putative generalization governing an input-output system that is "mediated" by mental states and consider any putative generalization regarding inputs, outputs, and mental state transitions. It is always possible for there to be a physical "malfunction" between the time of the occurrence of a mental state and the time of the occurrence of either the output or the mental state to which there is supposed to be a transition, with the result that the initial

---

[6] For a contrary opinion, see Nancy Cartwright [1983]. Also, it has been pointed out to me that this is at most true of the highly general laws proposed in theoretical physics. An experimental physicist typically formulates generalizations about his experiments that seem to have precisely the same status as the generalizations formulated in other sciences.

[7] Davidson [1970] and Fodor [1987] make similar observations.

mental state can occur without the system's continuing to conform to the putative generalization after its occurrence. This obvious point seems to establish conclusively that there are no true interesting purely psychological universal generalizations.

Perhaps it will be responded that this is the wrong way to formulate purely psychological generalizations. For instance, although there can be no guarantee that if one has a certain belief and a certain desire then one will respond in a certain way, perhaps it will be suggested that the belief and desire jointly create a *disposition* to respond in that way, and one will respond in accordance with the disposition provided nothing goes awry. In what may come to the same thing, Putnam [1967] suggested that cognizers should be regarded as probabilistic automata rather than finite state automata. But even this seems to be wrong. If we are physicalists and think that having the belief and desire are neurological states, then the belief and desire have the described disposition iff those neurological states have it. But neurological states can have dispositions to cause other physical states only by being embedded in more elaborate physical structures of various sorts. Similarly, the probability of a state transition is determined by the overall physical structure. If the structure is damaged in certain ways then the neurological states will lack the dispositions and the probabilities of state transitions will change. It is precisely the possibility of such structural damage that leads us to deny the literal truth of psychological generalizations in the first place, so it seems we cannot salvage the generalizations by supposing instead that they report dispositions or probabilities.[8]

The difficulty I have raised for purely psychological generalizations is equally a difficulty for all "high-level" generalizations about biological organisms. I have argued that there could not be any true purely psychological generalizations. The next thing to observe is that the situation cannot be improved by including reference to neurological states in the generalizations. None of the generalizations of any of the social or biological sciences can ever be unexceptionally true unless they are really just principles of physics. This is for a very simple reason: the

---

[8] Another possibility is that instead of formulating dispositions, there are purely psychological generalizations that are formulated in terms of nomic probabilities. These are the probabilities involved in statistical laws of nature. Such probabilities would avoid the present objection because they are not sensitive to changes in the surrounding circumstances. I see no objection in principle to such generalizations, and I will, in fact, make use of this possibility in the next chapter. But notice that even if such generalizations are possible, none of the actual generalizations proposed in any of the social or biological sciences is of this sort.

subject matter of physics is the whole universe. The workings of the whole universe cannot be upset from outside because there is nothing outside. But the subject matter of any other science concerns systems that are embedded in a larger context and can thus be upset from outside. The only way to avoid outside interference would be to confine attention to physically closed systems. But it is essential to psychology, biology, etc., that their subjects are not physically closed systems. The subjects of psychology must be able to perceive their surroundings and act upon them; biological organisms eat, breathe, and move about, and so on. It follows that there can be no true exceptionless universal generalizations in these sciences.

The conclusion is inescapable: all of the generalizations actually proposed in the social and biological sciences fail under extraordinary circumstances. The reason this is important for philosophers is that standard formulations of functionalism require there to be true generalizations, and have the consequence that if there are no true generalizations then there are no functional properties. In order to repair functionalism, we need a better understanding of scientific generalizations.

The important thing to realize is that no only do the generalizations found in the social and biological sciences fail under extraordinary circumstances. It is obvious that they do, and this observation would be of no surprise to the psychologists, neuroscientists, etc., who formulate the generalizations. The possibility of failure under "nonstandard" circumstances does not thwart the scientists' intentions in constructing high-level generalizations. But it does show that if those generalizations are understood as exceptionless universal generalizations then they are false. It follows that they should not be understood in that way. How then should they be understood? The generalizations we are considering constitute descriptions of "how human beings and other organisms work". These are *functional descriptions*, and I will call the generalizations of which functional descriptions are composed *functional generalizations*. Functional generalizations about human beings are often conceived on the model of functional generalizations about computers, and it is useful to compare them in this respect. They appear at first to be completely analogous. The generalizations advanced as part of a functional description of a computer are also false when taken literally. For example, a functional description of my computer might include the generalization that when the 'k' key is depressed, such-and-such a signal is sent to the central processing unit. But that is not true if the keyboard is broken. The same point can be made about all of the generalizations we formulate about the way machines work. All such generalizations are literally false because machines can break down.

Notice, however, that this obvious fact would not impress us if we were attempting to describe how the computer works. The generalizations we formulate are really about how machines work when they "work properly" or when they "are not broken". Similarly, it seems that generalizations about organisms should be understood as being about the way they work when they "are working normally".

I think that the preceding is basically correct, but some care is required in understanding it. The difficulty is that we cannot understand what it is for an organism to be working normally in the same way we understand what it is for a machine to be working properly. The obvious way to interpret such qualifications in generalizations about machines is by appeal to the intentions of the designers. Machines are artifacts—they work properly when they work as they were designed to work, and they are broken when they do not conform to their designs. Furthermore, the property of being broken is always relative to a design. For example, consider a stiletto that was owned by someone with a more pressing need for a screwdriver. He carefully broke the tip off the stiletto, turning it into a screwdriver, and has used it as such ever since. We are now faced with this object—the screwdriver/stiletto. Is it broken? That question makes no sense. It is broken as a stiletto but not as a screwdriver. The point is that being broken or working properly is always relative to a designer and a design. This makes functional descriptions of computers unproblematic; they are descriptions of the way the computers work when they work in accordance with their design. But this is of no help when we turn to functional descriptions of human beings.

We do have an intuitive notion of "damage to the human neurophysiological structure". We might try to make use of that notion and say that a functional description of a human being is a functional description of the way he works in the absence of damage to his neurophysiological structure. But what counts as damage? Not all physical changes count as damage because all neural activity involves physical changes. Damage is physical change that disrupts the functioning of the human being, preventing him from functioning as he is "supposed to function". But this is obviously circular.[9] On the other hand, I doubt that we can improve upon it much. The notion of damage seems to be parasitic on a prior functional description, and thus we cannot appeal to it in formulating that functional description.

---

[9] It will not quite do anyway. We can have changes that improve upon the functional properties of the individual. We would not call that 'damage', but we do want to preclude such changes in talking about the functional description of the individual.

There is a connection between this problem and the problem of specifying what counts as an input in a functional description of an organism. We want to describe what the organism does under various circumstances. In formulating the description, some features of those circumstances are allowed to vary and are considered inputs, and others are not allowed to vary and are regarded as "standing conditions". Functional generalizations concern what happens when the inputs vary but the standing conditions remain fixed. Standing conditions would normally be taken to include such things as the presence of sufficient oxygen, a congenial environmental temperature, adequate gravity, the absence of blows to the head or penetration wounds by sharp objects, the absence of brain cancer, heart attacks, strokes, and lightning strikes. It is, however, difficult to see any objective basis for the distinction between inputs and standing conditions. We might explore the possibility that it is purely conventional—in formulating a functional description we begin by *deciding* what we are going to count as inputs and the functional description is relativized to those inputs.[10]   The proposal would then be that a psychological generalization describes what happens when we vary the inputs but keep everything else fixed. Thus because falling pianos and heart attacks are not counted as inputs, we need not take them into account in formulating a functional description of a human being.

Unfortunately, this will not solve our problem. Upon inspection, the notion of "keeping everything else fixed" proves less perspicuous than at first glance. For example, if we are to vary the inputs but keep everything else fixed, does this require that the heart not beat, the lungs not pump air, and calcium ions not be transmitted across synaptic boundaries? Were it to require this, our functional descriptions would all collapse. We must include among the "standing conditions" certain regular changes such as the beating of the heart or the functioning of neurons. But this makes it impossible to interpret "standing conditions" in any simple way. Standing conditions must allow those changes that are required to enable the organism to function. That makes an account of functional generalizations circular if it appeals to the notion of standing conditions.

In desperation, we might try various *ad hoc* repairs like ruling out all energy transfers across the physical boundaries of the organism except for those constituting the inputs. That would eliminate falling pianos and puncture wounds, but it would not eliminate those disruptive events like brain cancer, strokes, and heart attacks that are entirely internal to

---

[10] This is suggested in Block [1978], pp. 293ff.

the organism. In addition, it would seem to imply that our functional descriptions apply only to organisms that are not breathing.

To recapitulate, psychological generalizations and most other functional generalizations are not true if they purport to describe the functioning of the organism come what may. If they are to be true they must be taken to describe how the organism works in a restricted set of circumstances. There is no noncircular way of restricting the circumstances by appealing to the organism's "functioning properly" or to "standing conditions". One might be tempted to conclude that functional and psychological generalizations about organisms are just false and the whole enterprise arises from confusing organisms with artifacts (the latter having explicit designs and designers). But that conclusion seems excessively skeptical. Surely there is some point to the kinds of high-level generalizations that are formulated throughout the social and biological sciences.

It seems to me that what is really going on here is that we want to know how an organism "normally works". Different kinds of organisms, including human beings, have bodies whose structures tend to be stable in certain respects. Ordinary physical laws dictate that a body with a particular structure will work in a certain way, that is, certain functional generalizations will be true of that body as long as it retains that structure. In precisely the same way, physical laws determine that an automobile will function in a certain way as long as its structure conforms to its intended design. Of course, at any given time, the body of an organism can be regarded as having infinitely many different structures of varying specificity and overlap. What makes some more interesting than others is that their possession tends to be a stable property of the body. But they only tend to be stable properties; accidents, disease, and other unusual happenings can disturb the structures. Because the structures tend to be stable, so do the regularities described by the functional generalizations they imply, but again these are only tendencies. What is important in the formulation of these generalizations, and what makes it useful to formulate them, is that the disruptive happenings are unusual. It is pretty uncommon to be hit on the head by a falling piano or have a heart attack or suffer a stroke. It is the improbability of such occurrences that leads us to formulate functional descriptions that hold only in their absence. This suggests that functional descriptions do not even purport to be universal generalizations about organisms. Rather, they are generalizations about structures, where those structures tend to be possessed by the organisms except under unusual circumstances. More precisely, the suggestion is that a functional generalization $(\forall x)\varphi$ about A's (human beings, computers, etc.) should be interpreted as a complex existential claim having two parts: There is a structure type S such that (1) A's tend to have structures of type S, and (2) the generalization $(\forall x)\varphi$ will be true (as a matter of nomic necessity) of anything having a structure of type S.

This proposal is not yet quite right. The difficulty is that although functional generalizations are in a certain sense about the structure type S, they describe it only indirectly. We cannot regard the functional generalization as being literally true of something having a structure of type S. For instance, consider the generalization that in human beings, the heart pumps blood. The above proposal is that this is to be cashed out as the claim that there is some structure type S such that (1) human beings tend to have a structure of that type, and (2) if something has a structure of type S then it is true of it that the heart will always pump blood. The generalization is universally quantified with respect to time. It is false, however, that in anything (now) having a structure of type S, the heart will forever pump blood. The heart will pump blood only as long as the structure is retained. The generalization would be true of something that possessed a structure of type S eternally, but as nothing ever retains the same structure forever, the most we can say about an actual object is that it will behave as the generalization describes *just as long as it retains the structure.*

A further qualification is required. Typically, the structure alone does not guarantee satisfaction of the generalization. In addition, certain standing conditions must be satisfied. For instance, automobiles do not work under water, and bees cannot fly in a vacuum.[11] This indicates that a functional generalization $(\forall x)\varphi$ about A's should be regarded as having the following slightly more complicated form:

> There is a structure type S and a physically specifiable circumstance type C such that (1) A's tend to have a structure of that type, (2) A's tend to be found in circumstances of type C, and (3) it is nomically necessary that anything in circumstances of type C and having a structure of type S will conform to the generalization $(\forall x)\varphi$ just as long as it retains that structure and remains in those circumstances.

This has the effect of precluding outside interference by precluding any intervention that would alter the circumstance type C or the structure type S, but it does not require A's to be closed physical systems. This generalization can be true because it is, in effect, a low-level law of physics.

---

[11] I owe this point to Rob Cummins.

We also propound functional descriptions of individuals. The force of attributing a functional generalization $(\forall x)\varphi$ to an individual thing α is:

There is a structure type S and a physically specifiable circumstance type C such that (1) α has a structure of type S, (2) α is in circumstances of type C, and (3) it is nomically necessary that anything in circumstances of type C and having a structure of type S will conform to the generalization $(\forall x)\varphi$ just as long as it retains that structure and remains in those circumstances.

This analysis has the consequence that a functional generalization about how A's work can be correct without there being anything of which the generalization is literally true. Similarly, a functional description of an individual can be correct without the individual satisfying the generalizations comprising the description. This enables us to make satisfactory sense of the role generalizations play in the biological and social sciences. Such generalizations are almost invariably intended as functional generalizations rather than as exceptionless universal generalizations. By requiring that A's tend to have structures of type S and tend to be found in circumstances of type C, we impose serious constraints on S and C. On the other hand, by existentially quantifying over S and C, we relieve the scientist of having to specify S and C (which will normally be very difficult, if not impossible) and allow him to get on with the business of formulating φ, which is his real interest and the focus of his science. Thus the psychologist can do psychology and the biologist can do biology; they do not have to do physics.

Let us say that a structure type (together with a circumstance type) is *characterized* by a generalization or group of generalizations iff it satisfies the third clause of these definitions. Thus a functional description of an object is correct just in case that object has a structure of a type characterized (under the circumstances) by the description. In this technical sense of 'characterize', the description can characterize the structure without being literally true of the object.

Functional descriptions consist of functional generalizations. By immediately symbolizing functional generalizations in the predicate calculus, taking them to have the form $(\forall x)\varphi$, we force ourselves to distinguish between their being *correct* as functional generalizations and their being *true* as universal generalizations. This is unduly paradoxical. It might be better to introduce a new quantifier '$(@x)$' for the formulation of functional generalizations, and then take the above analysis as stating the truth conditions for $(@x)(Ax \supset \varphi)$. In this connection, it is noteworthy that we do make a grammatical distinction between exceptionless universal generalizations and functional generalizations in English. For instance, in describing how a typewriter works we might say, "When the 'k' key is depressed, ...". We would resist saying "When*ever* the 'k' key is depressed, ...", reserving the latter for universal generalizations.

3. Functionalist Foundations for Psychophysical Laws

The principle of psychophysical supervenience claims that all mental states supervene on physical properties. Psychophysical supervenience results from psychophysical laws relating mental states and physical properties. The kind of law required is one to the effect that a creature's having some physical property *P* nomically implies its being in some mental state *M*. In searching for such laws, we can make a rough distinction between two kinds of physical properties. One kind of physical property of a creature concerns its physical constitution—what it is made out of. Another kind of physical property concerns how that material is organized into a physical structure. This is a distinction between matter and form. It seems preposterous to suppose that what a creature is made of can have anything to do with what mental states it is in, except indirectly, by influencing what structures can be built out of that stuff.[12] It cannot be the stuff that a cognizer is made of that determines whether it can have mental states of a certain sort; it must instead be *how* it is made of that stuff, that is, how it is put together. There are inductive reasons for believing this. Namely, all of the different kinds of complex objects with which we are familiar have the property that they can, at least in principle, be built out of different kinds of material. For example, it makes no difference whether a can opener is built out of steel or aluminum, just as long as the material is put together in such a way that the resulting structure has properties enabling it to function in a certain way. Properties consisting of how something is put together rather than what it is made of might be called 'formal properties'. It seems that insofar as mentality has a physical basis, it must reside in formal properties.

A formal property might describe an object in terms of the static arrangement of its parts. For instance, we might describe a pendulum by saying, "It consists of a rod 7 cm long and 3 mm in diameter, with a sphere 2 cm in diameter at one end." More generally, formal

---

[12] Searle [1981] denies this, but he does not provide any grounds for the denial.

properties combine such static descriptions with functional descriptions of the way a thing works. For instance we would typically want to add that the pendulum is hung from the end opposite the sphere and it is allowed to swing from that support. A functional description tells us how the states of an object change over time and how they affect one another. The main conclusion of the last section was that the generalizations comprising a functional description of an object are rarely if ever literally true. Instead, the import of a functional generalization about a kind of object is an existential claim to the effect that (1) there is some kind of structure that objects of that kind tend to have, and (2) the generalization will be true of an object having that structure just as long as it retains that structure.

From among the formal properties of a cognizer, the best candidates for providing the physical basis for mentality are "functional properties". The notion of a functional property can be defined as follows. A functional description has the form $T(S_1,\ldots,S_n)$ where $S_1,\ldots,S_n$ are the states it relates. A *functional theory* is the *logical form* of a functional description. It is obtained from the functional description $T(S_1,\ldots,S_n)$ by replacing all reference to concrete states by variables, thus obtaining a formula $T(X_1,\ldots,X_n)$ having free variables $X_1,\ldots,X_n$. A functional theory is a schematic functional description. It describes state-to-state transitions between unspecified states. Different machines that are built in quite different ways may nevertheless be such that their states can be mapped onto each other so that they have isomorphic functional descriptions. They are then said to "realize" the same functional theory. For example, consider two computers with different electronic architectures. One might employ a 68020 microprocessor and the other an 80386. There is a level of detail at which they have different functional descriptions because current will be flowing through different physical structures. Nevertheless, they might both be running the same program written in LISP. In that case, despite their hardware differences, we can map some of the physical states of the one onto the other in such a way that they have isomorphic functional descriptions and hence both realize the same functional theory.

This is made precise as follows. A *realization* of a functional theory $T(X_1,\ldots,X_n)$ is a mapping of the state variables X_i onto states S_i of an object in such a way that the resulting functional description $T(S_1,\ldots,S_n)$ is a correct functional description of that object. In this case, we will say both that the states of the object and the object itself *realize* the functional theory. This in turn requires that the object possesses a structure of a type characterized by $T(S_1,\ldots,S_n)$.

The variables in a functional theory $T(X_1, \ldots, X_n)$ correspond to *functional roles*. For each variable X_i, a state S_i plays the corresponding functional role in an object iff there are also states $S_1, \ldots, S_{i-1}, S_{i+1}, \ldots, S_n$ of the object such that $S_1, \ldots, S_n$ jointly realize $T(X_1, \ldots, X_n)$. A *simple functional property* is a property whose possession consists of being in a state that plays a certain functional role.   For example, a simple functional property of a typewriter might consist of its having a structure characterized by certain generalizations (by virtue of which we consider it a typewriter) and its 'a' key being depressed. *Functional properties* in general are logical compounds (disjunctions, conjunctions, etc.) of simple functional properties.   These definitions of 'functional property', 'realization', and so on, are basically the same as the orthodox definitions,[13] except that they are all based upon functional descriptions being correct (in the sense of section 2) rather than their being true as universal generalizations. The difference is important, because on the present account, the possession of a functional property does not require that the object satisfy the generalizations comprising the functional description. It requires only that the object is in circumstances of a type and possess a structure of a type characterized by the generalizations. As I observed above, the generalizations comprising functional descriptions are not literally true of the objects described, and hence on the orthodox account, objects would fail to have functional properties.

It is useful to distinguish between two kinds of functional properties. Functional properties are constructed by quantifying over unspecified states and saying that they are interrelated in various ways. Although the states are unspecified, the functional property can still impose constraints on them.   In particular, it may require the states to be physical states.   On the other hand, it may leave it undetermined whether the states are physical states. A person could have a functional property of the latter sort by having mental states that are not physical states. Let us call functional properties of the former sort *physico-functional properties* and those of the latter sort *broadly functional properties*. Physico-functional properties can reasonably be regarded as a special class of physical properties. Broadly functional properties, on the other hand, are not physical properties.

Functional theories of human cognition describe the way the mind works at a level that abstracts from many of the psychological and neurological nuts and bolts. A relatively complete functional description of a person will make reference to the actual psychological or neurological states involved in his thinking processes. But it seems clear that just

---

[13] The orthodox account is that of David Lewis [1970] and [1972].

as different computers can run the same programs while exhibiting important hardware differences, different cognizers can be in the same mental states while exhibiting hardware (or "wetware") differences.[14] The simplest evidence for this is that there are significant anatomical differences between the brains of different people. They are not neuron to neuron identical. For instance, as Block and Fodor [1972] point out, "Though linguistic functions are normally represented in the left hemisphere of right-handed persons, insult to the left hemisphere can lead to the establishment of these functions in the *right* hemisphere." (p. 238) One can speculate more broadly that it should be possible to have sentient creatures built with silicon chemistry rather than carbon chemistry, and so on. But even without such speculation the homey results of comparative studies of brain anatomy seem conclusive. It is the way the hardware works rather than precisely how it is constructed that determines the mental states that the cognizer can be in.

Formal properties comprise a continuum with static descriptions of the parts of an object at one end and functional properties at the other end. Static descriptions make no reference to how an object works, and functional properties make no reference to how its parts are shaped or arranged (except indirectly by requiring that the arrangement result in the object's working in a certain way). I urged above that insofar as mentality has a physical basis, it must reside in formal properties. Now I have argued that among the formal properties, only functional properties are plausible candidates for providing a physical basis for mentality. The actual arrangement of parts in a cognizer would seem to be inessential to what mental states he is capable of having.

I assume, then, that it is the possession of a functional property that is at least causally (and perhaps logically) responsible for a cognizer's being in a mental state. It would be logically possible for there to be infinitely many different unrelated functional properties each nomically implying that the cognizer is in a mental state M, but although that is logically possible, it is preposterous to think it is true. It would amount to another variety of psychophysical magic. The world is better ordered than that. There must be some connection between all of the various functional properties that nomically imply possession of any given mental state. There can be at most finitely many unrelated functional properties nomically implying possession of a state M. Given that there are only finitely many of them, it follows from the definition of supervenience that if M supervenes on the physical, then M will be nomically equivalent to the disjunction of these finitely many functional proper-

---

[14] Perhaps Putnam [1967] was the first to emphasize this point.

ties.[15] Thus, a mental state can supervene on the physical only by virtue of being nomically equivalent to a functional property.

Having decided that the physical half of a psychophysical nomic equivalence must be a functional property, it remains to determine what sort of functional property it might be. A certain kind of answer has been favored by recent philosophers of mind. This turns upon a distinction between two kinds of functional descriptions—those of the philosopher and those of the psychologist. For the philosopher, functional descriptions of the mind describe the interactions of the perceptual inputs, behavioral outputs, and intervening mental states. I will call these *purely psychological functional descriptions*. Neurology plays no role in such theories. Contemporary cognitive psychologists, on the other hand, construct functional descriptions that relate all of these kinds of states but throw neurological states into the mix as well. These are *psycho-neurological functional descriptions*. A good example of such a theory, familiar to many philosophers, is David Marr's [1982] theory of vision. It is important to realize that the generalizations comprising functional descriptions of either of these kinds are no more literally true than the generalizations comprising the functional description of a computer. They will fail, for example, when a person suffers physical damage. These functional descriptions are to be understood in the same way as other functional descriptions—as existential claims about the possession of a structure of a type characterized by the generalizations.

The functional properties to which mental states are equivalent could be abstracted out of either purely psychological functional descriptions of the mind or out of psycho-neurological functional descriptions of the mind. Recent philosophers of a functionalist bent have tended to assume that the only functional properties that can be nomically equivalent to mental properties are those describing the way mental

---

[15] The argument is as follows. I assume that the operator 'it is nomically necessary that', symbolized by '$\square_p$', satisfies at least S4. Then psychophysical supervenience together with the assumption that there are at most finitely many unrelated physical properties $P_1, \ldots, P_n$ nomically implying M tells us that the following holds:

$$\square_p(\forall x)\{[Mx \supset (P_1x \vee \ldots \vee P_nx)] \ \& \ \square_p(\forall x)(P_1x \supset Mx) \ \& \ \ldots \ \& \ \square_p(\forall x)(P_nx \supset Mx)\}$$

and in S4 this entails:

$$\square_p(\forall x)[Mx \equiv (P_1x \vee \ldots \vee P_nx)].$$

A similar argument can be found in Kim [1984].

states themselves work. For each mental state M_i there is supposed to be some purely psychological functional description $T(M_1,...,M_n)$ describing transitions between mental states (including M_i), perceptual inputs, and behavioral outputs, but making no reference to neurological states. From this we generate an abstract functional theory $T(X_1,...,X_n)$. This defines a certain functional role for M_i, and then it is supposed that the possession of the mental state M_i is nomically equivalent to being in any state having that functional role. More simply, if it works like a mental state, it is a mental state. This is the thesis that I will call *philosophical functionalism*.

Is there any reason to believe philosophical functionalism? I think there is. Let us rehearse the argument up to this point. The claim that mentality has a physical basis seems to require that mental states supervene on physical states. This requires the existence of psychophysical nomic implications, and the only plausible candidates for such implications are those relating mental states and functional properties. On the assumption that there are only finitely many such nomic implications for each mental state, it follows from the principle of psychophysical supervenience that each mental state is nomically equivalent to a functional property. So far the argument is schematic. It seems that in order for a mental state to supervene on physical states, it must be nomically equivalent to a functional property constructed out of some functional theory **T**, but we have no concrete intimation of what **T** might look like. The theory **T** must consist of a set of generalizations characterizing a structure-type S such that a necessary condition of being in the mental state M is having a structure of type S. What generalizations might go into **T**? If we look at generalizations regarding ordinary causal connections between mental states, physical states, physical inputs, and actions, we are going to be disappointed. Very few causal characteristics of human beings could constitute necessary conditions (even nomically necessary conditions) for the possession of mental states. For example, it is not a necessary condition for vision that one have eyes. The time will come when damaged eyes are replaced by miniature television cameras wired directly into the brain. The beneficiaries of such medical technology will be able to see. Similarly, there is every reason to believe it should be nomically possible (at least in principle) to replace diseased brain tissue with solid state-circuitry without disrupting a person's mental life. Surely there is a level of detail such that if we replace brain tissue by circuitry reproducing its behavior to that degree, cognition will "work in the same way" and a person's mental life will be unchanged. It seems that no functional properties that depend for their possession on the specific physiology of human cognizers can be nomically essential for the possession of mental states. The only functional properties that can be nomically essential are those that abstract from peculiar characteristics of our specific physiology and constitute a functional description of the mental states themselves. This will constitute a description of "how mental states work". It will consist of a set of purely psychological generalizations that characterize (in our technical sense of 'characterize') a structure type such that having a structure of that type is a nomically necessary condition for the possession of mental states. This amounts to a defense of philosophical functionalism.

Philosophical functionalism requires that for each mental state M there is a functional theory T such that a cognizer is capable of being in M only if M together with other of his mental states realize T. T thus describes a functional role played by M in cognizers capable of being in M. Furthermore, according to philosophical functionalism, a cognizer is in M iff he is in some state or other that plays that functional role in him. Thus if T is realized by physical states, the cognizer can be in M by virtue of being in a physical state that plays the same functional role as M.

There is a useful way of reformulating philosophical functionalism. The functional theory $T(X_1, \ldots, X_n)$ is obtained from the purely psychological description $T(M_1, \ldots, M_n)$. Given a physical structure type S and circumstance type C, let us define:

A mapping f from physical states to mental states is *T-adequate relative to S and C* iff it follows from ordinary physical laws that if:

(1)   a cognizer is in circumstances of type C and has a physical structure of type S, and;

(2)   for every physical state P in the domain of f, the cognizer is in $f(P)$ iff his physical structure is in the state P;

then his mental states will conform to the generalizations in $T(M_1, \ldots, M_n)$, and will continue to do so as long as he remains in those circumstances and retains that structure.

To say that a cognizer's physical states realize $T(X_1, \ldots, X_n)$ is just to say that he is in circumstances of some physically specifiable type C and has a physical structure of some type S for which there exists a T-adequate mapping. The claim of philosophical functionalism is then:

For each mental state M, there is a purely psychological functional description $\mathbf{T}$ such that something ("the cognizer") is in M iff there is physically specifiable circumstance type C and physical structure type S and $\mathbf{T}$-adequate mapping f relative to S and C such that (1) the cognizer has a physical structure of type S and is in circumstances of type C, and (2) the cognizer's physical structure is in a physical state of some type P such that $f(P) = M$.

Less formally, the physical facts about a cognizer that make it the case that he is in a mental state M consist of his having a physical structure whose states can be put into a correspondence with mental states in such a way that their behavior mirrors the behavior of mental states (both realize $\mathbf{T}$) and the cognizer is in that state of the structure that corresponds to M.

Thus far our conclusions are schematic. It has been argued that *if* mentality has a physical basis, then it must have this general form. Now we must ask whether there are any reasonable candidates for the functional theory $\mathbf{T}$.

Chapter 4
The Physical Basis for Mentality

1. Rational Functionalism

I have argued that insofar as mentality has a physical basis, it must consist of mental properties being nomically equivalent to functional properties described by some purely psychological functional theory **T**. The theory **T** must be such that having a structure of a type characterized by **T** is nomically essential for the possession of the mental state *M*. If a cognizer currently has a structure of a type characterized by **T**, then his mental states conform to the generalizations comprising **T**. So **T** consists of generalizations whose current satisfaction is a necessary condition for being in *M*. Are there any such generalizations? As a first approximation, it seems that the only relational structure mental states have essentially is that pertaining to rationality. Consider belief states. These inherit logical and epistemological interrelationships from their contents. By virtue of these relationships between contents, there are connections of rationality between belief states. Being in one belief state may make it rationally permissible to come to be in another and rationally impermissible to be in a third, and so forth. There are also rational connections between belief states and nondoxastic states. For example, sensory and introspective states can make it rational to adopt beliefs. Beliefs and desires can make other desires and intentions rational or irrational, and all of these combined can make various actions rational or irrational. What I envision here is a general theory of rationality tying all mental states together and relating them to external behavior. This theory describes the *rational architecture* of human beings. Various parts of the theory have been studied in detail by epistemologists, logicians, action theorists, decision theorists, and others, but we do not yet have a single comprehensive theory of rationality.

The suggestion is that the only relational structure that is essential to mental states is that comprising our rational architecture. Mental states have that structure as a matter of logical necessity, but it seems that any other structure they may have in a particular cognizer will be infected by the unique physiology and anatomy of that cognizer and hence will not be even nomically essential to the possession of mental states.[1] The generalizations in **T** are supposed to characterize a structure type S such that having a structure of that type is essential to being in a mental state, so it seems to follow that the only relations between mental states to which **T** can advert are those involved in rationality. But just how can **T** make use of such rationality relations? People do not always behave rationally, and behaving rationally is not a necessary condition for the possession of mentality. People indulge in wishful thinking, they allow short-term goals to sidetrack them from long-term goals, and so forth. On the other hand, it is noteworthy that people usually behave rationally. This is particularly striking in the case of belief. It is, of course, possible to describe cases in which people have irrational beliefs. But such cases tend to be hard to concoct and are generally rather bizarre. Almost all (but not quite all) of our beliefs are rational. My suggestion is that *this* is a necessary condition for the possession of mental states—a cognizer must *tend* to be rational. In defense of this, try to imagine a creature possessing mental states but entirely unconstrained by considerations of rationality. His state-to-state transitions are entirely random. Does this make any sense? There is at least some plausibility in insisting that it does not, on the grounds that there would be nothing to determine the identity of his states. It is the rationality conditions of a state that make it the state it is, but if states occurred willy-nilly in a creature, there would be nothing to make particular conditions the rationality conditions of those states. This suggests that what determines the rationality conditions of a particular state, and hence what makes it the state it is, is roughly the state-to-state transitions involving that state that the creature tends to make. Some psychologists have delighted in documenting human irrationality (Kahneman et al [1982], Ross et al [1975]), but the main reason irrationality is so interesting is that it is unusual—people are overwhelmingly rational. It is also worth protesting that only a small fraction of the cases enumerated by these psychologists actually illustrate the irrationality they have been taken to illustrate. In some of the cases (for example, the gambler's fallacy), the subjects have perfectly good defeasible reasons for their beliefs or actions. We regard their beliefs or actions as ultimately indefensible because we know of defeaters for their defeasible reasons, but if these defeaters are not apparent to the

---

[1] Recall that I am construing 'mental states' narrowly so as to include only introspectible states. On a broader construal of mental states, many would not be involved in rational architecture.

subjects then the subjects are not being irrational by ignoring them. Other cases consist of subjects having false (but not necessarily unjustified) beliefs about how to reason in connection, for instance, with probability. Given those beliefs, the subjects are reasoning in ways that are completely rational. A third kind of case occurs when subjects rely upon their built in "nonintellectual" processes of belief formation to estimate probabilities (see chapter 1). In certain kinds of circumstances, those processes go awry, but that does not mean that subjects are being irrational by using them. On the contrary, until they acquire reason to believe that there is something wrong with the probability judgments they are making, they are completely rational in making them on this basis. When all of these examples are weeded out, there remain only a few examples in the psychological literature in which it can be claimed that people are systematically irrational.

I will provisionally assume this *Rationality Principle*, according to which it is a necessary condition of mentality that a cognizer tends to be rational, and I will develop an account of psychophysical supervenience based upon this assumption. But it must be acknowledged that the Rationality Principle is the link in my account that is most apt to be denied, so I will return to its assessment and further defense in section 4.[2]

The concept of the rationality conditions of a mental state requires elaboration in several respects. There is a temptation to identify the rationality conditions of a mental state with the conditions under which it is rational to be in that state, but this is inadequate. It is true that there are many mental states, like belief, fear, embarrassment, and desire, for which there are some conditions under which it is rational to be in such states and other conditions under which that would be irrational. But there are also some mental states that lack rationality conditions of this simple sort. Consider sensations. It is never irrational to have a sensation; one just has it. Nevertheless, sensations have a place in rational architecture because having a sensation can make it rational to come to be in another mental state, for instance a belief. This suggests that we take the rationality conditions of a mental state to have at least two components. The first component consists of the conditions under which it is rational to be in that state. The second component describes how being in the state contributes to the rationality or irrationality of other states or actions. For states like sensations, the first component is vacuous.

---

[2] Similar principles of necessary rationality have been proposed by Dennett [1971], [1981], and Davidson [1973], [1974], [1975].

In a nutshell, then, the proposal is that the generalizations comprising T must be probabilistic generalizations to the effect that state-to-state transitions generally occur in accordance with principles of rationality. A necessary condition for having any particular mental state is that the cognitive agent have a physical structure of some type S mimicking those aspects of rational architecture that govern that state. The way in which S mimics rational architecture is made precise by the formulation of philosophical functionalism given at the end of the previous chapter. The cognitive agent must be in circumstances of some physically specifiable type C, and there must be a mapping from mental states to physical states of the structure such that it follows from ordinary physical laws that if (1) the cognizer is in circumstances of type C and has physical structure S and if (2) it were always true that the cognizer is in a certain mental state iff his physical structure is in the corresponding physical state, then insofar as the cognizer remains in circumstances C and retains the structure S, he will tend to be in mental states or perform actions only when it is rational for him to do so. In other words, ordinary physical laws dictate that state-to-state transitions within the physical structures will occur as we would expect them to occur if they reflected the occurrences of the corresponding mental states in a largely rational cognizer. On this view it is the possession of a physical structure mimicking rational architecture together with being in a particular physical state of that structure that makes it the case that a cognizer is in a mental state of the corresponding type. I will call this *Rational Functionalism*. More accurately, it is the principle of psychophysical supervenience together with the assumption that mental states supervene on at most a finite set of unrelated physical properties that requires this.

Dogs and blind people can have at least some of the same beliefs as ordinary sighted human beings. But the causal connections exemplified by states of their physical structures form a less rich pattern. These impoverished causal patterns cannot be mapped onto the same rich patterns of mental state transitions that comprise the rational architecture of sighted human beings. Rational functionalism must be formulated in a way that accommodates this. My suggestion is that the possession of a particular mental state requires the cognizer to have the capability of being in some mental states but does not require him to have the capability of being in others. A dog or a blind person is not irrational just because there are mental states he cannot be in. He can be rational by conforming to the rules of the rational architecture required for the states he can be in. Thus the requirements of rationality itself dictate how much of rational architecture must be present in a cognizer for him to possess a certain mental state. Rational functionalism should then propose that what physically enables the dog or the blind person to be in the mental states they are capable of being in is the possession of a structure mimicking as much of rational architecture as is required for their mental states.

It will be important to have an absolutely precise formulation of rational functionalism. This can be obtained as a special case of our general formulation of philosophical functionalism at the end of chapter 3. In this case, for each mental state *M*, the theory **T** consists of the principle that we are for the most part rational in holding *M* and related mental states and in our behavior. Given a physical structure type *S* and circumstances *C*, let us define:

> A mapping *f* from physical states to mental states is *rationally adequate relative to S and C* iff it follows from ordinary physical laws that if:
> (1)   a cognizer is in circumstances of type *C* and has physical structure of type *S*; and
> (2)   for every physical state *P* in the domain of *f*, the cognizer is in *f(P)* iff his physical structure is in the state *P*;
> then the cognizer will be for the most part rational just as long as he remains in the circumstances and retains that structure.[3]

A rationally adequate mapping is just a **T**-adequate mapping for the above theory **T**. Rational functionalism is then the following thesis:

---

[3] I have toyed with an alternative definition of 'rationally adequate mapping' which, when combined with (*RF*), imposes slightly stronger requirements on cognizers. According to this definition, a mapping *f* from physical states to mental states is *rationally adequate relative to S and C* iff *S* contains a substructure S_r such that it follows from ordinary physical laws that (1) if a cognizer is in circumstances *C* and has physical structure *S* then the substructure S_r will generally be operative, and (2) if (a) the substructure S_r is operative and (b) for every physical state *P* in the domain of *f*, the cognizer is in *f(P)* iff his physical structure *S* is in the state *P*, then the cognizer will be invariably rational. The idea here is that the reason we tend to be rational is that we have built-in subsystems that dictate universal rationality, and the reason we are not invariably rational is that other subsystems sometimes interfere with those subsystems.

(*RF*)

>For each mental state M, something ("the cognizer") is in *M* iff there is some physically specifiable circumstance type *C* and physical structure *S*, and there is a rationally adequate mapping *f* relative to *S* and *C* such that (1) the cognizer is in circumstances of type *C* and has a physical structure of type *S*, and (2) the cognizer's physical structure is in a physical state of some type *P* such that *f*(*P*) = *M*.

This appears to be the only way to make sense of the facts as we know them. There seems to be no other way to connect mental states and physical states in a way that could be invariant across divergent physiologies. Any such general connection must arise out of general formal relations between mental states, and the only formal relations that mental states *must* (even physically must) bear to one another in all cognizers are those reflecting rational architecture.

2. Attenuated Rational Functionalism

I have urged that rational functionalism provides the only possible way to make sense of psychophysical supervenience and psychophysical laws. But now I will present a difficulty that seems to be overwhelming and requires the modification or abandonment of (*RF*). The difficulty is parallel to a familiar difficulty for more conventional varieties of functionalism. Functionalism requires us to be able to characterize mental states in terms of their functional roles. But it has seemed to many that there are mental states that cannot be characterized in this way. The favored culprits are sensation types. The "inverted spectrum argument" makes a convincing case for the conclusion that sensation types are not characterizable in terms of functional roles as standardly construed (in terms of causal laws governing input-output regularities).[4] The argument is as follows. Objects of certain colors tend to elicit particular sensations in me, and presumably they do so in you as well. These sensations can be arranged in a spectrum. But suppose that your spectrum is just the reverse of mine. The sensation elicited by red in me is elicited by blue in you, and so on. It seems that this would lead to no differences in our behavior and would be completely undetectable. But then the sensation that I label 'red' would have the same functional

---

[4] The inverted spectrum argument seems to have been formulated first by Block and Fodor [1972]. See also the responses in Shoemaker [1975] and [1982].

role in me as the sensation I label 'blue' has in you, and accordingly these sensations are not characterizable in terms of their functional roles.[5]

As I have described it, the inverted spectrum argument proceeds in terms of a conventional view of functional roles as describing causal connections and input-output regularities. But a similar argument can be brought to bear against rational functionalism by observing that different sensations have isomorphic rationality conditions. *Being appeared to redly* is related rationally to *believing there is something red before one* in the same way *being appeared to bluely* is related rationally to *believing there is something blue before one*, and so on. In general, my mental states can be mapped onto one another in a way that preserves the formal structure of the rationality conditions but inverts the spectrum so that states involving *red* are mapped onto states involving *blue* and vice versa. It follows that we cannot distinguish between these sensations (or between beliefs involving colors, desires involving colors, and so on) in terms of the logical forms of their rationality conditions. This creates a major difficulty for rational functionalism. Rational functionalism correlates mental and physical states by considering rationally adequate mappings. A mapping f from physical states to mental states is rationally adequate iff, if we suppose a cognizer to be in a certain mental state just when his physical structure is in the corresponding physical state then he is for the most part rational. Suppose we have a rationally adequate mapping f. If we suppose that there is also a mapping g from mental states to mental states that preserves the logical form of the rationality conditions, it follows that the composition $g{\circ}f$ of g and f is also rationally adequate.[6] This is diagrammed in figure 1. But $g{\circ}f$ is a mapping correlating different mental states with the same physical states. For example, f might correlate *being appeared to redly* with a certain neurological state, and $g{\circ}f$ would correlate *being appeared to bluely* with the same neurological state.

---

[5] There is some temptation to deny that it makes sense to suppose that two people have inverted spectra. That can be met by imagining a Kafka-like situation in which one awakes one morning to find that everything that previously looked red to him now looks blue to him, everything that previously looked blue now looks red, and so on. If his spectrum remained inverted in this way, soon he would come to call the sensation type he once called 'red' 'blue', he would come to judge that objects are red on the basis of their looking the way he previously called 'blue', and so forth. In other words, the functional roles of these sensation types would also reverse. This indicates that it makes clear sense to imagine one's own spectrum inverting suddenly, and accordingly it would seem to make sense to talk about two different people having inverted spectra.

[6] $g{\circ}f$ is defined to be that function such that $g{\circ}f(x) = g(f(x))$.

physical states

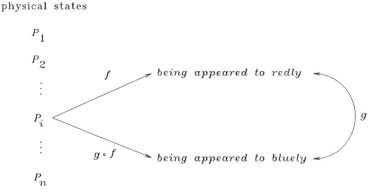

Figure 1. If f is a rationally adequate mapping and g is a
rational homomorphism then $g{\circ}f$ is a rationally adequate mapping.

Rational functionalism implies that a cognizer is in a mental state M iff
he has a physical structure S for which there is a rationally adequate
mapping f and physical state P such that he is in the state P and M =
$f(P)$. This cannot possibly be correct. In light of the multiplicity of
rationally adequate mappings, it implies that a cognizer is appeared to
redly iff he is in a certain physical state, and it also implies that he is
appeared to bluely iff he is in that very same physical state, and hence
it implies that he is appeared to redly iff he is appeared to bluely.

Rational functionalism must be modified to deal with this problem.
Let us say that a mapping from mental states to mental states that
preserves the logical form of the rationality conditions is a *rational
homomorphism*.[7]   The inverted spectrum generates one rational
homomorphism, but it is worth pointing out that there are many others.
Interchanging left and right generates another. Any kind of systematic
warping of the visual field would produce yet another (for example,
producing rectangles from squares). This phenomenon seems quite
pervasive.[8] Rationality conditions cannot, in general, determine precisely
what mental state corresponds to a particular physical state, but it seems
that they can determine what generic *kind* of mental state corresponds
to a particular physical state. For example, *being appeared to redly* and
being appeared to bluely are mental states of the generic kind we might

---

[7] A homomorphism is an isomorphism that maps a set into itself.

[8] A similar observation is made by George Bealer [1984].

call appearance states. All mental states of this generic kind have isomorphic rationality conditions, and furthermore it seems that any mental state having rationality conditions isomorphic to a state of this kind is itself of this kind. In other words, the logical form of their rationality conditions is the same for all mental states of this kind, and that logical form is constitutive of the generic kind. If there is a rationally adequate mapping that maps a physical state P onto one appearance state M, then for any other appearance state M^*, there is a rationally adequate mapping that maps P onto M^*. The existence of such rationally adequate mappings cannot establish which mental state of this generic kind corresponds to P, but I propose that it does establish that P corresponds to *some* mental state of this generic kind. In general, I propose to replace rational functionalism with *attenuated rational functionalism*:

(*ARF*)

> For each mental state M, something ("the cognizer") is in a state of the same generic kind as M iff there is some physically specifiable circumstance type C and physical structure S, and there is a rationally adequate mapping f relative to S and C such that (1) the cognizer is in circumstances of type C and has a physical structure of type S, and (2) the cognizer's physical structure is in a physical state of some type P such that $f(P) = M$.

We were led to rational functionalism by the conviction that it is the only plausible way that the principle of psychophysical supervenience could be true, but now it should be noted that attenuated rational functionalism no longer entails that the principle of psychophysical supervenience is true. According to (*ARF*), being in some state or other of a particular generic kind supervenes on the physical properties of the cognizer, but (*ARF*) does not entail that the specific states of that generic kind supervene on the physical. At this point we should recall the argument that initially led us to endorse the principle of psychophysical supervenience. It was alleged that to deny the principle of psychophysical supervenience amounts to insisting that there is nothing physical that makes an occurrence a mental occurrence and nothing physical that makes a sentient creature sentient. But this assumes that there is a physical basis for mentality only if there is a physical basis for mental states. On the contrary, (*ARF*) provides a physical basis for mentality without providing a basis for mental states. According to (*ARF*), what makes it the case that a cognizer is in a mental state of some generic kind is that his physical structure mimics the rational architecture of his mental states. This provides a physical basis for mentality because what endows a creature with mentality is whatever makes it capable of having some mental states or other. A creature is capable of having mental states iff it is capable of having states of some generic kind or other, and according to (*ARF*) that is the case iff it has a physical structure *S* for which there exists a rationally adequate mapping. Thus my proposal regarding the physical basis for mentality is the following:

(*R-BASE*)
> A creature has mentality iff it has a physical structure and is in circumstances of a type for which there exists a rationally adequate mapping.

This proposed solution to the problem of the physical basis of mentality does not imply a solution to the problem of the physical basis of mental states.

A familiar objection to standard functionalist theories of mind is due to Ned Block [1978], and consists of counterexamples based upon so-called "homunculi-headed simulations". It is apt to seem that these simulations are also counterexamples to the present proposal, so let us examine them. In one example, Block imagines that the government of China is converted to functionalism, and as a result it organizes the Chinese citizenry to work together in a such a way that they form a functional duplicate of me. Would the nation of China then have mental states? It seems not. But this is not a counterexample to (*R-BASE*). The reason we resist attributing mental states to the nation of China (or to a structure consisting of its citizenry) in this example is that insofar as the citizens work together to mimic the behavior of my mental states, they do so willingly. There may be a certain amount of government coercion, but we resist thinking of their joint behavior as dictated by rigid laws of nature. On the other hand, for there to be a rationally adequate mapping from states of the nation of China to mental states, it is required that the citizenry form a structure whose behavior is dictated by ordinary physical laws to mimic rational architecture. Thus, insofar as the behavior of the Chinese citizenry is not dictated by laws of nature, it does not follow from (*R-BASE*) that a structure composed of them has mental states. On the other hand, if we decide that we really can build a physical structure out of human beings in such a way that laws of nature dictate that it will mimic rational architecture, then it is not obvious that it cannot possess mental states. In this latter case, that the structure is made out of human beings seems incidental to whether it can possess mental states.[9]

3. The Physical Basis of Mental States

In attenuated rational functionalism we have a proposed solution to the problem we initially set out to solve, namely, that of explaining the physical basis of mentality. But it may now seem that that problem was drawn too narrowly. There is another problem to which we also want the solution. This is the problem of the physical basis of mental states. What is it about the physical structure of a cognizer that makes it the case that the cognizer is in any particular mental state? Although (ARF) does not answer this question, it seems that in the case of a number of mental states, there is a straightforward answer. It appears that all rational homomorphisms have their origins in systematic mappings of perceptual states onto perceptual states. Interchanging perceptual states in a way that preserves rationality conditions requires interchanging related belief states, desire states, and so on, but these interchanges are dictated by the interchanges of perceptual states. Perceptual states cannot be uniquely identified in terms of their rationality conditions because what makes a perceptual state the state it is is not just its place in rational architecture but also its relationship to the external world. For instance, what makes an appearance state the state of being appeared to redly is that it tends to be elicited by the presence of red objects, and what makes an appearance state that of one object appearing to be to the left of another is that it tends to be elicited by such a configuration of objects. In general, a necessary condition for a perceptual state to be that of being appeared to as if P (for appropriate P) is that the cognizer tends to be in that state only when it is true that P. To say this amounts to modifying the earlier contention that the only relational structure mental states have essentially is their rational architecture.

This suggests that what makes a state M that of being appeared to redly is twofold: (1) M is an appearance state, where this generic kind has a physical basis as described by (ARF); and (2) it tends to be the case that when one is in some appearance state, one is in M iff there is something red before him. This second condition is, roughly, the condition that perception will tend to be veridical. It can be formulated

---

[9] The same response can be given to the well-known "Chinese room" argument of Searle [1981].

a bit more precisely as the condition that the cognizer has a physical structure such that the nomic probability is high of someone with such a structure who is in an appearance state being in M iff there is something red before him. It is plausible to suppose that many mental states have physical bases of this general sort. In chapter 5, it will turn out that the nature of this correlation must be made a bit more complicated, but the present account will suffice for now.

However, this cannot be a completely general solution to the problem of the physical basis of mental states. Consider a brain in a vat. Suppose the brain was originally lodged in a human body, but now it has been removed and placed in the vat. It is wired into a computer in such a way that the nerves normally going to the sense organs are stimulated electronically by the computer in a way that makes the cognizer's experience seem more or less normal to him. Once the brain is disconnected from its sense organs, the cognizer no longer has a physical structure of a sort that nomically guarantees that perception will tend to be veridical. This seems initially to be a counterexample to the proposed physical basis for being appeared to redly, because we are inclined to think that the cognizer can still be appeared to redly (when the computer stimulates the nerves appropriately), but this will not tend to be a reliable indicator of the state of his surroundings. I maintain, however, that we should conclude instead that the cognizer is no longer capable of being appeared to redly. Mental occurrences can transpire in him that would have constituted being appeared to redly prior to his being lodged in the vat, but there is no reason to regard them as now constituting his being appeared to redly. This is most easily seen by reflecting upon the fact that instead of lodging the cognizer in a vat, we might have rewired his neural circuitry so that the state originally elicited by the presence of red objects is now elicited by the presence of blue objects, and vice-versa. In other words, skillful neurosurgery could reverse his spectrum. In that event, a mental occurrence that would originally have constituted his being appeared to redly would come to constitute his being appeared to bluely. One and the same mental occurrence could be either, depending upon the wiring of his neural circuitry. When he is lodged in the vat, there is nothing to determine which kind of mental occurrence it is, so it seems most reasonable to insist that it is neither. On the other hand, it is a mental occurrence and could even be called 'a perceptual event' because its rationality conditions are of a sort that only perceptual events can have, but it is not an instance of any perceptual state like *being appeared to redly*.

There is a familiar distinction in epistemology between *comparative* and *noncomparative* perceptual states.[10] Comparative states are defined partly by reference to the environmental situations that tend to elicit them. As I used the term above, 'being appeared to redly' refers to a comparative state – the perceptual state that tends to be elicited by the presence of red objects. Comparative states have physical bases of the sort I have been describing. Noncomparative states, on the other hand, are defined by their introspective characteristics. I will refer to these as *qualitative mental states*. The brain in the vat has perceptual occurrences of the same qualitative types as it had before being lodged in the vat, and it is this that inclined us initially to think that it could still be appeared to redly. But what the possibility of rewiring one's neural circuitry shows is that comparative and qualitative states need not be irrevocably correlated. Occurrences of the same qualitative type (before and after the rewiring) can be of different comparative types.[11]

The proposal for the physical basis of mental states is plausible only in the case of comparative states. What can we say about the physical basis of qualitative states? In order to answer this, consider their role in our cognitive architecture. Cognizers can categorize mental occurrences involving themselves in different ways. By appealing to comparative states, they can categorize mental occurrences partly by reference to their relationship to the world around them, and such categorization is obviously useful. Qualitative states are used for categorizing mental occurrences in terms of introspective indiscriminability along various introspectible dimensions. There are good computational reasons for a cognizer to be built so that he is able to categorize mental occurrences in this way. These have to do with the fact that perception provides us with defeasible reasons for judgments about our surroundings. It was argued in chapter 1 that the possibility of such defeasible reasoning requires that we be able to sense the characteristics of our sensory input and form generalizations about it and about how it is related to our surroundings. This is involved, for example, in discovering that nonred things often look red in red light. Sensing the characteristics of something involves more than sensing its presence. It involves "perceptual categorization". It is sometimes overlooked that perception leads automatically to categorization. For example, I do not just see the fire engine – I also see that it is red. In the case of introspection (a kind of perception of mental occurrences), the perceptual categories are

---

[10] This distinction is due originally to Roderick Chisholm [1957], pp. 45ff.

[11] Shoemaker [1982] emphasizes the importance of this same distinction, calling it the distinction between 'qualitative' and 'intensional' states.

determined by introspective indiscriminability along such introspective dimensions as color and shape. These introspective categories are just qualitative state types.[12] Thus the possibility of defeasible perceptual reasoning requires a cognizer to be able introspectively to categorize his mental occurrences in terms of qualitative states.

Having seen why our cognitive architecture employs qualitative states, it is evident that there is nothing mysterious and nonphysical about our ability to classify our mental occurrences in this way. I have been discussing the physical basis of mentality, and if what has been proposed thus far is correct, there should be no obstacle in principle to building an intelligent machine having a rational architecture like ours and capable of having mental states. If we were building such an intelligent machine and endowing it with a cognitive architecture like ours, we would have to provide it with the ability to introspect the operation of its perceptual sensors. Introspection would be sensitive to the values of various physical parameters of the output of the perceptual sensors. The physical parameters to which introspection is sensitive would comprise the introspective dimensions along which the machine categorized its sense experience, and two mental occurrences in the machine would be of the same qualitative type just in case introspection could not distinguish between them along the relevant introspective dimensions.[13] This, I take it, provides a perfectly good physical understanding of our employment of qualitative states. There is nothing mysterious or nonphysical about such states.

As far as the physical basis of qualitative mental states, it is hard to say much in a relatively *a priori* way. This would seem to be a matter for empirical investigation. The physical basis will consist of whatever is detected by introspection when a person is in that qualitative state. In any actual human being, that will be a neurological state, but this is not nomically the case. It seems clear that part of my brain could be replaced by solid-state circuitry without changing the introspectible

---

[12] The ability to categorize our introspected mental occurrences in terms of qualitative states is presupposed by the ability to categorize them in terms of comparative states. To discover that a particular chromatic sensation is of a type typically elicited by the presence of red objects requires discovering inductively how red objects typically look and noting that the sensation in question is of that type. But to discover "how red objects typically look" is to discover what qualitative chromatic state tends to be elicited by the presence of red objects.

[13] For familiar reasons having to do with just noticeable differences, to say that a cognizer cannot distinguish between X and Y along a particular dimension must require more than that he cannot discriminate between them. It must also require that it is impossible for there to be a Z such that he can discriminate between X and Z but not between Y and Z, and vice-versa.

characteristics of my states. There is surely a level of detail (a functional description) such that if the circuitry reproduces the normal causal processes of my brain to that level of specificity, I will not notice any difference. Accordingly, the qualitative state is correlated nomically with having states satisfying that functional description, and hence that constitutes the physical basis for the mental state.[14] But it will require empirical investigation to say anything more specific about the actual physical basis of particular qualitative states.

4. An Analytic Physical Basis for Mentality

On the assumption that mentality has a physical basis, I have drawn a picture of what that basis must be like. According to this picture, what makes a physical structure a being capable of having mental states is that it is so constructed that it has physical states whose structure mimics the rational architecture of mental states. This was made precise by the concept of a rationally adequate mapping. In addition, what makes it the case that a creature possesses some mental state of a particular generic kind, such kinds being characterized by isomorphic rationality conditions, is that it possesses a physical state mapped onto mental states of that kind by rationally adequate mappings. But these conclusions remain puzzling in a number of respects. Having argued *that* the conclusions are inescapable, I will now attempt to explain *why* they true.

The first puzzle concerns whether what has been described is an analytic or a contingent physical basis for mentality. If it is contingent, the "makes" relation is to be understood in terms of logically contingent nomic equivalences, that is, it must be a logically contingent law of nature that a creature is in such a mental state iff it is in an appropriate physical state. Even if this were correct, it would leave us unsatisfied. It is not sufficiently explanatory to say merely that there is a law of nature connecting mental states to physical states in the manner described. We would want to know *why* there is such a law of nature. If mental states and physical states are such different kinds of states, what is the origin of the connection between them? The connection would have to result from a primitive law of nature not reducible to any more familiar laws governing the physical world. This might be all that can be said about the matter, but it amounts to endorsing a kind of inexplicable psychophysical parallelism. It does not integrate the mental

---

[14] This is, roughly, Shoemaker's [1982] proposal.

world into the physical world in a way that leaves us comfortable that we understand what is going on.   It appears that only an analytic physical basis could do that.

I propose that what has been described as the physical basis of mentality is an analytic basis.   In defense of this somewhat surprising claim, I suggest that philosophers of mind have traditionally approached the mind/body problem with a misconception of what it is we are trying to understand.   Philosophers talk a lot about "the concept of a person".   They use the word 'person' as a technical term.   They are not just referring to biological organisms of the species homo sapiens.   They use the term 'person' so that it would include Martians if there were any, sentient dolphins, and basically anything with a mental life that is enough like ours.   Then they ask, "Could a machine be a person?"   The philosopher's natural inclination is to try to answer this question by giving a logical analysis of the concept of a person and then investigating whether a machine could satisfy the analysis.   But I do not think that that will work because I do not think that, in the requisite sense, there is any such thing as the concept of a person.   More accurately, we come to this problem with only a vague idea of what we mean by 'person', and part of our task is to construct—not just analyze—a more precise concept.   Our knowledge of the mental states of others is based on something like the traditional argument from analogy.[15]   I begin by noticing (introspectively) a collection of "mental phenomena" in myself. I also discover that certain other kinds of physical structures "behave like me", and on that basis I infer that they are like me with respect to mental occurrences as well.   In short, I conclude that they too are "persons".   But there is a crucial vagueness in this conclusion.   I conclude that they have mental lives "like" my own, but like in what respects? They are not exactly like my own.   After all, different people have different beliefs, desires, fears, and so on.   To make my conclusion more precise, I have to fill out the respects in which all people are alike.   That is something that can only be discovered inductively.

Well then, in what respects are people alike mentally?   It is natural to suppose that others are like me in having states that are qualitatively the same as those as I observe in myself.   No doubt most of us do believe this about others.   But I will now argue that the inductive reasoning that would initially support this conclusion is defeated by observations we are subsequently able to make about mental states and

---

[15] The literature is full of spurious objections alleging that the inductive reasoning involved in the argument from analogy is somehow fallacious.   I take it that I answered such objections adequately in my [1974] (pp. 250ff), so I will not discuss them further here.

neurophysiology. Given these contingent neurological facts, it is in principle impossible to become justified in believing, on the basis of analogical reasoning, that other people experience the same qualia as I do.[16]

My argument for this rather surprising conclusion is related once more to the possibility of spectrum inversion. It seems there is no way I could ever know that you and I do or do not have spectra inverted with respect to each other. But if that is correct, how can I ever be justified in ascribing a particular quale to you? However, this is a bad argument. I have a perfectly good inductive reason, based upon analogy, for believing that you will experience the same qualia as I under the same circumstances, and the mere logical possibility of spectrum inversion is not sufficient to defeat the inductive argument. After all, such logically possible counterexamples are available for all inductive arguments simply because inductive arguments are not deductive arguments.

But there is more to the inverted spectrum argument than what this negative diagnosis indicates. Even given the rather rudimentary state of current neurophysiology, there is good reason to believe that inverted spectra are a *real* possibility. If we were just a little more skillful in neurosurgery, it seems virtually certain that we could rewire a person's neural circuitry so as to invert his spectrum, and he could then confirm for us that his spectrum has indeed inverted. Thus the inverted spectrum is much more than a logical possibility—it is a nomic possibility.

Furthermore, one of the well-documented features of the brain is its plasticity. Different parts of the brain can play somewhat different roles in different individuals, and in cases of minor brain damage, new portions of the brain often take over functions originally played by the damaged portions of the brain. This suggests that it is quite unlikely that everyone's brain is wired in the same way. It seems *likely* that different neural circuits will respond to different color stimulations in different individuals, and hence there will actually be individuals with inverted spectra.

This, of course, is speculative, but it is informed speculation. We cannot be certain that there are individuals with inverted spectra, but it is sufficiently likely that there are that this undermines the weak analogical argument for the contrary conclusion. In at least some cases we are currently in a position to strengthen this counterargument still

---

[16] This has not been an unpopular view in the philosophy of mind. Variants of this view (although not the present argument) were endorsed or at least suggested by Wittgenstein [1953] (p. 95), Frege [1956] (p. 299), Moritz Schlick [1959] (p. 93), Thomas Nagel [1979] (p. 160), and Sydney Shoemaker [1969].

further.   Consider the perception of shapes, and the phenomenal appearances they elicit in us.   We can reason as follows, where the correlations are as diagrammed in figure 2.

(1)   Let *correlation 1* be the correlation I observe in my own case between conditions of perceptual input and experienced shape qualia. The hypothesis under consideration is that correlation 1 holds in others as well.   The only basis I have for believing this is an analogical argument based upon the fact that they are like me in other related respects, and so are probably like me in this respect as well. I take it that this is, in fact, a good reason, albeit a defeasible one. The thing to note about this reason is that it is explicitly analogical.   There is no possibility of confirming it directly by inspecting my mental occurrences and those of others and seeing that they are qualitatively the same.

(2)   There are other correlations that hold in my own case.   For instance, there is a correlation between what qualia I am experiencing and patterns of neurological activity in my brain.   Let us call this *correlation 2*. I have precisely the same analogical reason for supposing that correlation 2 holds in others as I do for supposing that correlation 1 holds in them.

(3)   As a matter of contingent fact, although correlation 1 and correlation 2 both hold in my own case, they conflict when projected onto others. Let *correlation 3* be the correlation that holds in my own case between conditions of perceptual stimulation and neurological activity. If both correlation 1 and correlation 2 hold for a particular individual, that logically entails that correlation 3 holds as well. The difficulty is that correlation 3 does not hold for other individuals. That is, there are interpersonal differences concerning what neurological activity is stimulated by what perceptual circumstances in different individuals. For instance, it is well known that for each individual there is what is called 'the retinotopic mapping'. This is a distorted mapping from patterns of light projected on the eye to patterns of electrical activity in the visual cortex. Thus, when a person sees a light-colored square against a dark background, a mapping of the electrical activity in his visual cortex reveals the shape of a distorted square.[17]   But what must be emphasized here is that that pattern of electrical activity really is distorted, and the distortion varies considerably from individual to individual. This is documented in Schwartz [1977] and [1980].

(4)   The failure of correlation 3 entails that either correlation 1 or correlation 2 fails. But our reason for expecting one of these to hold in

---

[17] There are similar projections for the other sensory modes. In fact, there are multiple such mappings for each sensory mode.

another person is precisely the same as our reason for expecting the other to hold. There can be no basis for choosing between them, and we cannot be justified in believing that they both hold, so it follows that we cannot be justified in believing that either holds. Therefore, we cannot be justified in believing that others experience the same qualia as we do under similar circumstances.

I have found that the logic of this argument is frequently misunderstood. It is protested that although the correlation 3 chosen above does fail to hold interpersonally, perhaps there are other similar correlations that do hold. However, that is irrelevant to the argument. Let P be 'Correlation 1 holds' and let Q be 'Correlation 2 holds'. The logic of the argument is then as follows. We observe (1) that we have precisely the same reason for believing Q as P, and (2) that the conjunction $(P\&Q)$ is false (because correlation 3 fails). Accordingly, either P or Q is false. But because we have precisely the same reason for believing each, there is no way to choose between them, and hence it is unreasonable to believe either.

This argument may seem to turn upon esoteric features of human neurophysiology, but that is not entirely true. The logic of the argument

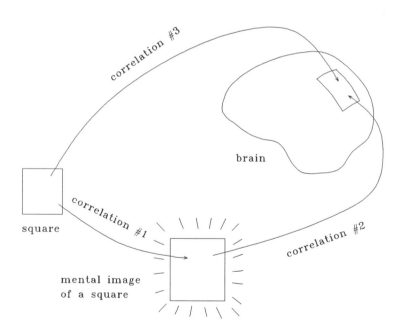

Figure 2. The three correlations

requires only that there be *something* correlated in me with conditions of perceptual input that is not so correlated in others. Given any such idiosyncratic correlation, the same argument can be run. And from what has been known for years about the plasticity of the nervous system, it is virtually certain that some such idiosyncratic correlation between perceptual input and the nervous system can always be found. We can document them in the case of shape perception, and probably also color perception, and there is reason to expect the same sort of results for perception of left/right, up/down, and so forth. Consequently, there is really no hope of avoiding this argument by finding fault with the neurological data to which I have appealed.

The conclusion that we cannot know what qualia another person is experiencing might seem unduly skeptical, but care must be taken to distinguish this claim from another. I can certainly know that my truck looks yellow to Jones. This, however, is to characterize his perceptual state *comparatively* rather than *qualitatively*. When I judge that my truck looks yellow to Jones, what I am judging is that my truck is eliciting in Jones a perceptual state of the general sort that tends to be elicited in Jones by yellow objects. I am not judging that he is experiencing a perceptual state that is qualitatively the same as mine. Note further that that is all we are apt to be concerned about. Given the possibility of inverted spectra and the like, knowing what qualia another person is experiencing would not give us much useful information. It is much more useful to know what comparative state he is in, because on that basis we can make judgments about his probable surroundings.

We cannot reasonably regard others as having mental occurrences that are qualitatively the same as our own. Thus, this cannot be taken as a necessary condition for being a person. If our beliefs about other minds are to be reasonable, they must be more circumspect. The most we can confirm is that others have occurrences that are like ours in more general ways. These more general ways cannot concern the qualitative characteristics of the occurrences, and it seems that all that is left is considerations about how the occurrences interact. In other words, all that we can discover about the mental states of others are their functional characteristics.

There are other respects in which human beings are alike mentally. Psychologists and neuroscientists have discovered many partly neurological functional generalizations regarding human beings. What this amounts to is that they have found that human beings tend to have stable structures of a sort that is characterized by interesting generalizations, where at least some of the states realizing those generalizations are non-mental (that is, non-introspectible) neurological states. We would not, however, expect these generalizations to be characteristic of all persons—only human persons. Remember that the point of using 'person' as a technical term is to divorce it from the presumed biological accident that the only actual persons may be human beings. The only functional generalizations that hold for all persons are those described by rational functionalism. More precisely, we can confirm that others have states that can be mapped onto our own mental states in such a way that if we suppose the mapping to preserve rational architecture then the others are for the most part rational, and that seems to be all we can confirm.

It might be suggested that we have another important belief about others that we regard as partly constitutive of their being persons. This is that other persons not only have states that work like ours—they have *mental* states that work like ours. To say that a state is mental is to say that that it has a "qualitative feel". Although the analogical argument does not allow us to infer that others experience mental occurrences that feel qualitatively the same as our own, it seems we can reasonably infer that they experience occurrences that have some qualitative feel or other. The qualitative feel of an occurrence is the sensation that results from observing it introspectively. Our "mental life" is our introspective awareness of some of our (physical) internal occurrences. This aware-ness is the result of our having introspective sensors that sense the outputs of our perceptual sensors, our reasoning processes, and so forth.

I would urge, however, that a characterization of the states of others in terms of rational architecture does not omit their qualitative feels. The structure of our rational architecture itself guarantees the existence of introspective sensors. Introspective monitoring plays an essential role in rationality and thus must be part of any system that adequately mimics rational architecture. Hence, in concluding that others have states that work like ours in the sense of mimicking our rational architecture, we are not omitting the "mentalness" of their states.

My conclusion is that all that we can confirm about the mental states of other persons are the functional generalizations describing their rational architecture. Notice that if this is right, then there is no reason to regard human beings as interestingly different from suitably con-structed nonhuman machines. Recall now that the question being addressed is, "What might we reasonably mean when we attribute mentality to others?" We must be attributing to them something that we can ascertain about them by employing the argument from analogy. We cannot determine that they have the same qualitative states as we do, so that should not be what we mean in attributing mentality to them. The most we should mean is that others have states that behave like ours in the ways described by rational functionalism. More precisely, if the concept of a person is to appeal exclusively to mental generalizations, so that it can in principle include creatures with different physiologies, then *the concept of a person must simply be the concept of a thing having states that can be mapped onto our own in such a way that if we suppose the corresponding states to be the same, then the thing is for the most part rational.* In other words, something is a person iff it has states whose interactions appropriately mimic our rational architecture. Note that this makes the Rationality Principle of section 1 a necessary truth.

I claim that this is what we ought to mean, but I do not claim that this is what we do mean. I doubt that it is. I think that most of us, at least initially, believe that others have occurrences that are qualitatively the same as our own. What I am urging is that that is ultimately an indefensible belief and should be replaced by the more circumspect belief about rational architecture and rationally adequate mappings.

Given this understanding of what ought to be *meant* by attributing mentality to a creature (or more neutrally, to a structure), rational functionalism is no longer providing us with (mere) nomic equivalences. What seemed initially to be functional properties nomically equivalent to the possession of mentality turn out to be nothing but a restatement of what it is to possess mentality. The picture that emerges is that we start with only a vague idea of what we mean by attributing mentality to others. We note certain occurrences in ourselves (introspectively) and then hypothesize that others "experience occurrences like those". But to make this more precise, we have to get clear on the respect in which the occurrences experienced by others are like those we observe. Initially, we believe that others experience occurrences that are of the same qualitative types as ours, but that is a mistake. We cannot confirm that. To get a defensible conclusion we must make it weaker, and what is left after the weakening is that others have states mimicking rational architecture. This is a matter of getting clear on what our conclusion should be rather than discovering laws relating that conclusion to the physical world.

Given this understanding of what ought to be meant in attributing mentality to others, it is a truism that the possession of a structure whose states mimic rational architecture endows a creature with mentality. This is a broadly functional property, not a physico-functional property, because it is not part of what we *mean* by attributing mentality to something that its mental states are physical. But, of course, the possession of physical states with the appropriate structure logically entails the possession of states *simpliciter* with the appropriate structure, so this makes the possession of such a structure an analytic basis for mentality rather than a contingent basis. It does so in a peculiar way, however. The analytic basis does not result from an analysis of what we initially mean by attributions of mentality, but rather from an analysis of what we should mean.

The upshot of this account of mentality and mental states is a kind of analytic functionalism because it proposes the use of mental concepts that are defined functionally. It is importantly different from more conventional varieties of analytic functionalism, however, because it does not propose analyses of clear pre-existing mental concepts but rather claims that we begin with only vague concepts and then proposes precise concepts to put in their place. This is a kind of *revisionary* analytic functionalism.

It is frequently observed that conventional varieties of analytic functionalism are subject to a fairly devastating objection. This concerns the choice of the functional theory in terms of which the functional properties are constructed. If the theory is to be involved in the *analysis* of mental concepts, then it must be a theory with which the users of mental concepts are familiar. As several philosophers have urged, the only candidate for such a theory seems to be the theory of "folk psychology" that we supposedly learn at our mother's knee and use in explaining one another's behavior.[18] As David Lewis [1972] puts it:

> Collect all the platitudes you can think of regarding the causal relations of mental states, sensory stimuli, and motor responses. ... Include only platitudes which are common knowledge among us—everyone knows them, everyone knows that everyone else knows them, and so on. For the meanings of our words are common knowledge, and I am going to claim that names of mental states derive their meaning from these platitudes. (p. 212)

But such an account must be rejected for the simple reason that there is no such theory. Ordinary people can enumerate few if any psychological generalizations. It is sometimes argued that we must have a stock of psychological generalizations at our disposal because we are frequently able to explain other people's behavior, and explanation proceeds in terms of generalizations in accordance with the covering law model. But this is wrong. The kinds of explanations we tend to give of people's behavior do not presuppose generalizations and do not fit the covering law model.[19] They proceed instead by empathy—we cite enough facts

---

[18] See, for example, Paul Churchland [1979] and Stephen Stitch [1983].

[19] See Cummins [1983] for a more substantial alternative to the covering law model of psychological explanation. I find Cummins's account extremely insightful.

about the case so that when we imagine ourselves being in a similar situation, we can see that we would or might do the same thing.[20]

The objection is telling against conventional varieties of analytic functionalism, but it is impotent against the present account. This is because the present account does not propose to analyze mental concepts in terms of their role in psychological explanation. Instead, I have urged that the principal role of mental concepts is in introspection, where the latter is an essential part of the cognitive processes comprising rationality. We would need mental concepts for our own reasoning even if we were alone in the world and never had occasion to think about others.

It was remarked in chapter 3 that a satisfactory account of the physical basis of mentality should point the way toward constructing a recipe for how to build a person. I believe that we now have at least the beginning of such a recipe – to build a person, build a physical structure whose states mimic rational architecture. Of course, that is not a trivial task. Not the least of the problem consists of describing rational architecture. That is a problem that has engrossed philosophers for centuries, and although we have made considerable progress in understanding rationality, we have not reached any consensus regarding its exact structure. Nevertheless, we now know what problems we must solve in order to build a person. I will address these problems further in chapter 6.

---

[20] This is slightly inaccurate. There is a considerable psychological literature indicating that people are quite poor at predicting their own behavior. What is really involved here is *suppositional reasoning,* in the sense of section 3.3 of chapter 6. We *suppose* we are in the situation imagined and then reason about what to do. We explain the behavior of others by attributing beliefs and desires to them that make their behavior rational, in the sense that reasoning dictates behaving in that way in the supposed circumstances. This does not, in any straightforward way, involve psychological generalizations or predictions.

Chapter 5
The Language of Thought

1. The Semantics of the Language of Thought

I have urged that a person is a physical structure having states whose interactions adequately mimic human rational architecture. Rational architecture itself dictates that a person must be capable of sensing some of its own internal states, and some of these internal states are thoughts. What determines what such a physical structure is thinking on any particular occasion? To say what thought a person has is to classify his thought, so the question "What determines what thought a person has?" must always be understood relative to some system of classification. Philosophers of mind often seem to suppose that a thought (or other mental state) has a unique correct classification. They talk about *the* type of a thought.[1] That is surely incoherent. Thoughts are of many types—evil thoughts and kind thoughts, thoughts of Jones and thoughts of Smith, confused thoughts and clear thoughts, and so on. Of course, no one would deny this. Perhaps what they have in mind is that thoughts have unique content-classifications. But even this turns out to be false. As we will see, there are four importantly different systems of content-classification for thoughts, and they are used for different purposes.

The problem of determining what a physical system is thinking when it has a thought is *the problem of intentionality*. I assume that thought involves a way of codifying information—a system of mental representation—and I bow to convention and follow Fodor [1975] in calling this 'the language of thought'.[2] But I want to insist from the outset that this system of mental representation may not be very language-like. In using the expression 'the language of thought', I do not mean to imply that

---

[1] They also talk about classifications *individuating* thoughts, which seems to involve a type/token confusion.

[2] Fodor takes the term from Harman [1973], who reports that he got it from Wilfrid Sellars.

there are close affinities between language and thought. I doubt that the affinities are nearly as great as is often supposed. For convenience, I will occasionally refer to this system of mental representation as 'Mentalese'. Our problem is then to describe the semantics of thought, or the semantics of Mentalese.

This chapter is basically a digression. It is not so much addressed at the task of building a person as it is at understanding our person once it is built. Making a system mimic rational architecture is a computational task. The computations involved in rational thought access thoughts in terms of those physical properties that might reasonably be called 'syntactical'. Semantics plays no role in computation. Insofar as there is a determinant answer to the question of what a physical system is thinking on a particular occasion, that must result from its rational architecture and its being wired into the world in the way it is. Speaking a bit loosely, semantics must supervene on syntax (or more accurately, on computation), and it is not something that we have to build explicitly into the system in order to make it a person.

2. Introspection

It is commonly supposed that we can introspect the contents of thoughts. I argued in chapter 1 that introspection is an essential aspect of defeasible reasoning. We talk loosely about being able to introspect whether one thought is the same as another, but what we introspect is not really the identity of thoughts. Thoughts are mental occurrences, and what we are introspecting is that two different mental occurrences (occurring at two different times) are alike along certain introspectible dimensions. For reasons that will become apparent shortly, I will say that such thoughts are *syntactically identical*.

What we can introspect are the qualitative characteristics of our thoughts. The conclusions of chapter 4 regarding qualia have the consequence that interpersonal judgments of syntactical identity are impossible. We cannot ascertain the qualitative characteristics of another person's mental states, and that applies to thoughts as well as other mental states. Thus I cannot know that someone else is having a thought syntactically identical to mine. This conclusion is less weighty than it might seem. Literally for years, I supposed that there must be an intrinsic connection between the syntactical classification of a thought and its content. This is the normal assumption made by philosophers of mind.[3] But the assumption is false, and the recognition of this fact is extremely important for understanding the nature of thought. It certainly must be the case that, within a single individual, content is normally the same for different thoughts that are syntactically identical. Otherwise, the ability to introspect the syntactic characteristics of our thoughts would be of no use in cognitive processing. However, it is only a contingent fact that thoughts of a particular syntactic type usually have the same contents and that they have the contents they do. This is illustrated by spectrum inversion. Consider baby Jones, who undergoes neurosurgery to have his spectrum inverted while still in the womb and before he acquires any kind of consciousness. He goes on to live a normal life. It would be preposterous to suppose that he is plagued by undetectable falsehoods every time he has thoughts about the colors or apparent colors of the objects around him. However, some of those thoughts are syntactically interchanged with others as a result of the neurosurgery. For instance, the sentence of Mentalese that is elicited in him by the presence of a red object would instead have been elicited by the presence of a blue object if it were not for the surgery. Given that he is not plagued by undetectable falsehoods, it follows that under the same external circumstances, he has thoughts about his surroundings that have the same truth conditions as if he had not had the surgery. Hence, a state that would have been the thought that there is a red ball before him (that is, it would have had that truth condition) becomes, as a result of the surgery, a thought that there is a blue ball before him. Thus the surgery had the effect of interchanging the truth conditions of syntactically characterized thoughts. It follows that the syntactical (introspectible) characteristics of a thought do not determine the content. It is for this reason that I call introspectible thought categories 'syntactical'. I would not suppose that 'syntax' has any clear initial meaning as applied to mental representations, so this is really a recommendation regarding how to understand it. The introspectible features of thoughts are those employed in the computational manipulations that constitute reasoning. This is analogous to the syntactical manipulations that comprise theorem proving in formal logic. Hence my use of the term 'syntax'. Notice that qualitative (noncomparative) classifications of appearance states are syntactical in exactly the same sense.

This has the consequence that we do not have direct introspective access to the contents of our thoughts. The only thing to which we have

---

[3] Fodor [1987] makes this assumption repeatedly but offers no argument for it.

direct introspective access is the syntactical characteristics of our thoughts, and that provides us with only indirect access to their contents, via the contingent fact that different thoughts that are syntactically the same usually have the same contents.   This can be understood by reflecting upon the computational rationale given in chapter 1 for building introspection into an intelligent machine.   Such introspection is computationally important, but computation is a syntactical matter. Semantics contributes nothing to computation.   Consequently, this is only a rationale for enabling the cognizer to introspect syntactical relations between thoughts.

Fodor [1987] takes the distinguishing feature of the language of thought hypothesis to be that mental representations have a syntax. Where we may disagree is about how that syntax is implemented in neurology.   In particular, I would not automatically assume that one mental representation being syntactically part of another consists of these mental representations being neurological items and the first being physically part of the second. I think it is dubious that mental representations are physical items at all.   The thoughts employing those representations are neurological events, but they need not have physical constituents corresponding to the representations. For instance, I gather that Fodor would suppose that what the states of *thinking that P* and *desiring that P* have in common is some physical constituent corresponding to the content expressed by *P*. But there are numerous alternative possibilities, and I doubt that we are in a position to choose between them at this time. To illustrate using a computer metaphor, each state might consist of there being a 1 rather than a 0 at a certain memory location, and the introspectible connection between the states (their having a common syntactical part corresponding to the English expression 'that *P*') may consist of nothing more than those addresses being related by some mapping employed by our reasoning processes. Similarly, generative structures (for example, Fodor's [1987] 'antianti-antimissile' example) can be implemented (and are on computers) by storing the addresses of constituents at the physical location representing the structure, not by storing the constituents themselves there. I am not proposing this as the true theory of mental syntax, but it illustrates my claim that we are not now in a position to do more than speculate about how syntax is implemented in neurology.   What is characteristic of syntactical relations is their introspectibility, not their physical implementation.

3. Narrow Content

If introspectible categories are syntactical rather than semantical, we need not be able to categorize someone else's thought in that way in order to determine the contents of his thought. The argument that led us to the conclusion that such categories are syntactical also suggests what is required for the semantical categorization of thoughts. A necessary condition for your thought and my thought to be the same semantically is that they occupy corresponding positions in our rational architectures. That is, it must be possible to map your rational architecture onto mine in a way that preserves all rationality relations and puts the two thoughts into correspondence. Let us call such mappings *rational isomorphisms*. Note that a rational homomorphism is just a rational isomorphism holding between a person and himself. That two thoughts are put into correspondence by a rational isomorphism is a necessary condition for them to have the same content.[4] This is not also a sufficient condition, however. Because there are rational homomorphisms that map my own thoughts onto one another in ways that preserve rationality relations, it follows that there are different rational isomorphisms mapping your thoughts onto mine in different ways. These different isomorphisms put one thought of yours into correspondence with several different thoughts of mine, and my thoughts have different contents, so your thought cannot have the same content as all of my corresponding thoughts.

The Baby Jones example suggests that what more is required to ensure sameness of content is that the rational isomorphism also preserves input correlations. What makes my thought the thought that there is something red before me is the way it is related in my rational architecture to the state of seeming to see something red, and what makes a state of me the state of seeming to see something red is a combination of the way it enters into my rational architecture and the fact that it tends to be elicited by the presence of red objects. In other words, it is the *comparative* classification of appearance states, not their qualitative (syntactical) classification, that is important in determining the semantical behavior of thoughts related to them in rational architecture.

Let us say that a mapping between the states of two individuals is a *rational input isomorphism* iff it is a rational isomorphism and it also

---

[4] Fodor [1987] observes that this has the consequence that cognizers with slightly different rational architectures cannot have thoughts with the same content. This is a consequence that I embrace. It only seems problematic because one is confusing narrow content with what is described using 'that' clauses. See section 5.

preserves the input correlations anchoring rational architecture to the world. The suggestion is then that your thought and my thought have the same content iff they are mapped onto one another by a rational input isomorphism.[5] This is a functionalist account of content.

We must be careful about what we take the preservation of input correlations to require. What makes a state α the state of *being appeared to φly* for some property φ has to do with input correlations, but this is a bit more complicated than it might seem at first. The natural first suggestion would be that α is the state of being appeared to φly iff α is correlated with the presence of an object with property φ more strongly than it is correlated with any other state of affairs. But several authors have noted, for example, that being appeared to redly is more strongly correlated with certain kinds of irradiation of the optic nerves than it is with the presence of red objects, and we do not want to conclude that what we are perceiving is the irradiation rather than red objects.[6]

A clue to seeing what is responsible for making α the state of being appeared to redly emerges from realizing that a cognizer could have a perceptual state β that *does* detect irradiation of the optic nerve rather than the presence of red objects. The difference between α and β would have to be the way in which they are plugged into the rest of rational architecture. In particular, perceptual judgments based upon α and β will be defeated by different considerations. For instance, my judgment on the basis of α that there is something red before me will be defeated by discovering that the lighting is peculiar, but that will be irrelevant to a judgment of irradiation based upon β. The result is that α and β will elicit different perceptual judgments in a cognizer, and the judgments elicited by α are more strongly correlated with the presence of red objects than they are with red irradiation of the optic nerve, while the converse is true of β. That, I propose, is what makes α and state of being appeared to redly and β the state of being appeared to "as if the optic nerve is undergoing red irradiation". It is the perceptual judgments that are based upon α that must be correlated with the presence of red objects rather than α itself being so correlated. As in figure 1, there are two sets of correlations relating mental states to the environment via perception. Correlation #1 correlates appearance states with

---

[5] This is a kind of "two-factor theory", but different from the familiar theories of Block [1986], Loar [1982], and McGinn [1982], which take the second factor to consist of the referents of mental terms. See Fodor [1987] for a criticism of those two-factor theories.

[6] For instance, Fodor [1987], Baker [1987], and Cummins [1989].

perceptual judgments

appearance states

states of the world

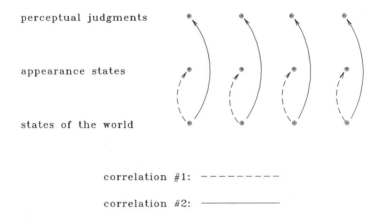

correlation #1: — — — — — — — —

correlation #2: ———————————

Figure 1. Perceptual input correlations

states of the world.   Correlation #2 correlates perceptual *judgments* with states of the world.   Correlation #1 cannot be used to determine the semantical characteristics of our thoughts, because appearance states are ever more closely correlated with states of the world comprising intermediate causal links in perception than they are with the perceived states of the world.   However, perceptual judgments strive to correct for deviations between perceived states of the world and states of our perceptual apparatus.   Accordingly, the perceptual judgments are more strongly correlated with the perceived state than they are with other states comprising causal links in perception, and that can be used to determine the content.

To make this precise, we have to talk about the nature of the judgments elicited by a state α.   Making a judgment consists of "endorsing" a sentence in the language of thought (where this is to be cashed out computationally).   Where P is a Mentalese sentence, *endorsing P* will be a mental state.   Perceptual judgments are those of the form ⌜There something present with the property P⌝ where P is a "perceptual predicate" of Mentalese.   Perceptual predicates are those for which sensory states are treated (computationally) as prima facie reasons (where sensory states are the output states of the sense organs).   This can be made precise in terms of rationally adequate mappings:

Relative to a physical structure S, state ξ of S is a *computational prima facie reason* for state θ iff there is a rationally adequate mapping f relative to S such that $f(\xi)$ is a prima facie reason for $f(\theta)$.

Relative to a physical structure S, a Mentalese predicate P is *perceptual* iff there is a sensory state α such that S's being in α is a computational prima facie reason for S to endorse $\exists P$ (the Mentalese sentence that there is something present that satisfies P), and there is a sensory state β such that S's being in β and not in α is a computational prima facie reason for S to endorse $\sim\exists P$.

My proposal is then that (1) P gets its content by virtue of that fact that perceptual judgments of the form $\exists P$ are more highly correlated with the presence of red objects than they are with anything else causally involved in perception, and (2) α is the state of being appeared to redly by virtue of the fact that it is a computational prima facie reason for endorsing $\exists P$. Where φ is a property, let $\exists\varphi$ be the state of affairs of there being something present with property φ. A necessary condition for P to express φ is that, in the structure S, endorsing $\exists P$ is positively relevant to the occurrence of the state of affairs $\exists\varphi$. More accurately, let us define:

P is *positively relevant* to φ relative to a physical structure S iff:

(1)   prob($\exists\varphi$ / S endorses $\exists P$) > prob($\exists\varphi$ / S does not endorse $\exists P$); and

(2)   prob($\sim\exists\varphi$ / S endorses $\sim\exists P$) > prob($\sim\exists\varphi$ / S does not endorse $\sim\exists P$).

The probabilities here are to be understood as *nomic probabilities*. That is, relevance requires that the laws of nature dictate that for anything having the physical structure S, endorsing $\exists P$ or $\sim\exists P$ is statistically relevant to whether $\exists\varphi$ or $\sim\exists\varphi$ obtains. The significance of these being nomic probabilities is that they are not sensitive to the possibly idiosyncratic circumstances of a particular cognizer. For instance, if the cognizer has been persuaded by a wandering philosopher that there are no red objects in the world, then his endorsing $\sim\exists P$ will not make $\sim\exists\varphi$ more likely. However, this improbable circumstance is, in effect, already factored into nomic probability.[7]

P must be positively relevant to φ in this sense, but that is not sufficient to make P express φ, because P may be positively relevant to more than one property. For instance, my Mentalese predicate 'red' is positively relevant both to the presence of red objects and to my optic

---

[7] For a general discussion of nomic probability, see my [1989a]. For a more detailed discussion, see my [1989].

nerves undergoing irradiation by red lights. What makes 'red' express the former rather than the latter is that the correlation is better. Let us define:

Relative to a physical structure S, P is *more relevant* to φ than to θ iff:
(1)   prob($\exists\varphi$ / S endorses $\exists P$) > prob($\exists\theta$ / S endorses $\exists P$); and
(2)   prob($\sim\exists\varphi$ / S endorses $\sim\exists P$) > prob($\sim\exists\theta$ / S endorses $\sim\exists P$).

Only those properties whose instantiation is a normal causal link in perception are candidates for being perceived. Let us say that such properties are *perceptually involved*. My proposal is then:

For any physical structure S, if P is a Mentalese perceptual predicate relative to S, then P expresses the property φ relative to S iff:
(1) φ is perceptually involved;
(2) P is positively relevant to φ relative to S; and
(2)   for any perceptually involved property θ distinct from φ, if P is positively relevant to θ relative to S then P is more relevant to φ relative to S.

The identity of a sensory state is determined by the perceptual predicate to which it is attached in rational architecture:

For any physical structure S, a sensory state α of S is the state of being appeared to φly iff there is a Mentalese predicate P relative to S for which:
(1) P expresses the property φ relative to S; and
(2) S's being in state α is a computational prima facie reason for S to endorse $\exists P$.

Finally, the contents of the states of a particular cognizer are determined by his having a physical structure relative to which his states have content:

A state ξ of a cognizer C is the state of believing that there is something φ present iff C has a physical structure S for which there is a Mentalese perceptual predicate P such that:
(1) P expresses the property φ relative to S; and
(2) ξ is the state of endorsing $\exists P$.

A sensory state α of a cognizer C is the state of being
appeared to φly iff C has a physical structure S relative to
which α is the state of being appeared to φly.

This proposal makes precise the sense in which the content of a belief
state is a function of both its place in rational architecture and perceptual input correlations.[8]

The kind of content that is shared by thoughts put in correspondence
by rational input isomorphisms is *narrow content*, in the official sense
that two people who are molecular duplicates ("twins") will automatically have thoughts with the same content. This does not mean, however,
that their thoughts will have the same truth conditions. Understanding
narrow content in this way requires us to recognize an indexical element
in our thoughts. For instance, if my twin and I have thoughts we would
each express by saying "I am tired", my thought is about myself, while
my twin's thought is about himself, and correspondingly our thoughts are
made true or false by different states of the world. I remarked in
chapter 2 that a person's language of thought contains a special way of
thinking of himself. This "first-person designator" plays a special role
in rational thought and can thus be characterized functionally by its
place in our rational architecture. For each person, this is a way of
thinking of himself. Thus the thoughts of different people that have the
same narrow content but involve first-person designators will have
different truth conditions simply by virtue of the fact that they are the
thoughts of different people. A second source of indexicality is the
Mentalese analogue of 'now', which is a primitive designator used to
think about the present time.

In light of indexicality, we must say that the truth conditions of a
thought are determined by a combination of its narrow content and the
context in which it occurs.[9] It is important to realize that the Mentalese
'I' and 'now' are not the only indexicals in our language of thought. The
indexicality of 'I' and 'now' infects other elements of the language of
thought. For instance, I have observed elsewhere that we often think of

---

[8] To avoid the kinds of difficulties raised by Lynne Baker [1987], these
correlations must be understood as nomically determined by a person's physical
structure. Such correlations are not altered, for example, by habitually wearing colored
glasses.

[9] This makes my view of narrow content similar in certain respects to that of
Fodor [1987]. Fodor takes narrow content to be a function from context to truth
conditions. An important difference between us, however, is that he denies that the
function has a functionalist specification. I, on the other hand, am proposing an
analysis of the function in terms of rational architecture and input correlations.

familiar objects in terms of mental representations that are phenomeno-logically (that is, syntactically) simple.[10] I called these *de re representations*. The way these work is that one begins by thinking of the object in some other way and then adopts the *de re* representation as a kind of shorthand. The referent of the *de re* representation is determined by the original representation from which it is derived, but thoughts involving the original representation and thoughts involving the *de re* representation are syntactically distinct. If the original representation was indexical, so is the *de re* representation. For instance, I may start off thinking of my mother as 'my mother', a description that is indexical. I subsequently come to think of her in a phenomenologically simple way. Someone else may employ a *de re* representation derived in the same way from the description 'my mother' in *his* language of thought, but it will be a way of thinking of *his* mother, so although our thoughts have the same narrow content, they are about different states of the world. They inherit the indexicality of the description 'my mother'.

A similar point must be made about Mentalese predicates. We *can* think of kinds in terms of syntactically complex descriptions, but we often think of kinds in syntactically simple ways that are derived psychologically from syntactically complex descriptions of the kinds. This is much like the way *de re* designators work. This can be illustrated by considering Putnam's Twin Earth example [1975]. $Adam_1$ lives on Earth, and his twin, $Adam_2$, lives on Twin Earth. Both have the thought they would express as "Water is wet", but these thoughts have different truth conditions because $Adam_1$ is thinking about H_2O while $Adam_2$ is thinking about XYZ. This is explained by noting that the way in which $Adam_1$ originally began thinking about water involved descriptions indexically tied to his actual situation and hence to H_2O. For instance, he probably began by thinking of water under some partially metalinguistic description like "that wet stuff people around here call 'water'". Similarly, $Adam_2$ originally began thinking about "water" in terms of descriptions indexically tied to *his* situation on Twin Earth and hence to XYZ. Thus their thoughts have the same narrow content, but due to indexicality they have distinct truth conditions. Notice that although $Adam_1$'s initial way of thinking of water is metalinguistic, once he comes to think of water in a syntactically simple way, his thought is no longer metalinguistic in any straightforward sense. This is because it has no syntactical element referring to language. There is a deep semantical connection but no surface connection.

---

[10] Pollock [1980], [1982]. See also Diana Ackerman [1979], [1979a], [1980].

A similar diagnosis can be given for Tyler Burge's 'arthritis' example ([1979], [1982]). Initially knowing little about arthritis, we are apt to begin by thinking of it in terms of an indexical description like "what is called 'arthritis' in my linguistic community". The kind picked out by the resulting syntactically simple representation is determined by the content picked out by the initial indexical description, although the thoughts are introspectibly (that is, syntactically) distinguishable. If, in accordance with Burge's thought experiment, we consider a counterfactually different world in which we have the same internal history but the word 'arthritis' is used differently in our linguistic community, then we will have a thought about a different syndrome. The reason people have been puzzled by this is that they have overlooked the fact that one of the important devices of our system of mental representation is one enabling us to substitute syntactically simple representations for complex ones. The new representations retain the deep logical characteristics of the originals but are introspectibly different and hence syntactically distinct. This has the consequence that the new representations need not, at least in a shallow sense, be "about" what the original representations were about; that is, they need not contain syntactical parts referring to everything to which syntactical parts of the original referred. In particular, they need not be metalinguistic.

4. Propositional Content

On an indexical view of narrow contents, the narrow contents of a thought do not have truth values. Two thoughts can have the same narrow content but differ in truth value because the indexical parameters have different values. This makes it a bit peculiar to think of narrow contents as contents at all. A somewhat more natural notion of the content of a thought is the "proposition" expressed by the thought. We can think of the proposition as being determined by the combination of the narrow content and the values of the indexical parameters.

Most philosophers of mind approach the problem of intentionality with a certain picture in mind. They think of thoughts as neurological events, and they think of propositions or truth conditions as "things out there in the world", in principle completely separable from thoughts, and then they ask how they can get connected. My inclination is to proceed in the opposite direction, taking narrow contents as more basic than either propositions or truth conditions. Narrow contents are characterized functionally, in terms of rational input isomorphisms, and then propositions can be regarded as pairs ⟨content,parameters⟩ consisting of narrow contents and values of indexical parameters. Furthermore, rather than taking truth conditions as somehow "ontologically given", I think of truth conditions *as* the conditions under which various propositions are true.

This contrasts with the prevailing view, according to which propositions are individuated by their truth conditions, and then thoughts are to be understood by relating them to propositions. I am suggesting instead that thought is basic, and truth conditions and propositions must both be understood in terms of thought. I have urged that propositions can be understood in terms of narrow contents, where narrow contents are characterized functionally, and I want to deny that propositions can be understood in terms of truth conditions. What I am contesting is the claim that it is informative to say that propositions (the contents of thoughts) are individuated by their truth conditions. What is the truth condition of a proposition like *the proposition that it is raining*? It is the condition of its being the case that it is raining. In general, the truth condition of a proposition consists of that proposition's being true. To propound this as a theory of the individuation of propositions is like saying: "I'm going to give you a theory of the individuation of physical objects. They are individuated by their *identity conditions*, where the identity condition of a physical object is the condition of *being that object*." Obviously, this is a vacuous criterion, and the individuation of propositions in terms of their truth conditions is equally vacuous. We can understand the identity conditions of an object only in terms of that object, and we can understand the truth conditions of a proposition only in terms of that proposition.

It *is* true that propositions are individuated by their truth conditions, in the sense that $P = Q$ iff the truth condition of $P =$ the truth condition of Q,[11] but it is equally true that objects are individuated by their identity conditions. What is objectionable about this is not that it is false but that it is trivial and uninformative. This is often overlooked because it is confused with the nonvacuous claim that propositions can always be characterized by giving informative truth condition analyses. But these are not at all the same claim, and if the last thirty years of analytic philosophy have taught us anything, it ought to be that this claim about the availability of truth condition analyses is false. It is the rare proposition that can be given an informative truth condition analysis.

---

[11] This assumes that we can employ a fine-grained notion of truth conditions so that logically equivalent truth conditions need not be identical.

5. 'That' Clauses

When we give third-person descriptions of mental contents, we normally describe thoughts and beliefs using 'that' clauses. We say things like "Jones thinks that *P*". This way of classifying mental contents works very differently from either first-person introspective (syntactical) classification, classification in terms of narrow content, or classification in terms of propositional content. This has generally been overlooked because of a common mistake in the philosophy of language that has pervaded most recent philosophy of mind. In its crudest form, this mistake consists of supposing that in belief ascriptions of the form ⌜Jones thinks that *P*⌝, the 'that' clause plays the role of a singular term that literally denotes the proposition thought by Jones. This strikes me as an egregious error, and I have spent large parts of two books trying to correct it ([1982], [1984b]). But nobody seems to have been listening, so perhaps it will not be inappropriate if I repeat myself.

The first thing to notice is that it is not a requirement of successful communication that the hearer come to entertain the very same proposition that the speaker was thinking when he made his statement. It is possible to think of one and the same object in different ways. If Jones says to Smith, "Reagan is in California", Jones will be thinking of Reagan in some particular way. If Smith understands Jones, he must also have a thought that is about Reagan, but there is no reason he has to think of Reagan in precisely the same way Jones is thinking of Reagan. That this is so is an absolutely essential feature of language and communication, because in a normal case Smith will not have the slightest clue as to precisely how Jones is thinking of Reagan. The use of the proper name in an appropriate context is enough to get Smith to think of the right person and know what Jones is attributing to that person, and that is enough to make the communication successful.

The same point is only slightly less obvious when applied to other parts of speech. For instance, as Putnam [1975] has observed, I think of aluminum quite differently from a metallurgist, but we can still communicate successfully about whether the pots and pans in my kitchen are made of aluminum.

My general point is that successful linguistic communication does not require the literal transmission of propositions or mental contents. The speaker and hearer do not have to have the same thought, either in the sense of "syntactically the same thought" or "thought with the same propositional content". Communication requires only that the hearer come to have thoughts "appropriately related" to those of the speaker. Spelling out the requisite relations generates interesting theories in the philosophy of language, and I have pursued that elsewhere, but the point I am making now is independent of any specific views on those matters. This point seems to me to be completely obvious, and it should be uncontroversial, but everyone seems to ignore it. Let us see what implications it has for understanding both language and mental contents.

We describe linguistic communication by talking about "statements", both in the sense of "the act of communicating" and "what was communicated". To avoid ambiguity, it is convenient to distinguish here between *statings* and *statements*. Statements are what are communicated by statings. In describing what is communicated in a particular case, we use 'that' clauses. We might say, "Jones said that Reagan is in California". The standard dogma in the philosophy of language is that the 'that' clause is used as a singular term to denote the proposition communicated. But I have just been urging that there is no proposition communicated. The speaker and hearer entertain related propositions (or have related thoughts), but there is no proposition that is "conveyed" by the stating. Accordingly, this must be an incorrect view of 'that' clauses.

The content of a communication is determined by what the relationship must be between the thoughts of the speaker and hearer for the communication to be successful. A convenient way to codify this is to take the *statement* made to be composed of a range of "possible sent propositions" and "acceptable received propositions".[12] Then the function of the 'that' clause in a sentence like "Jones said that Reagan is in California" is to pick out a statement so construed. The important thing to realize is that such statements are not propositions. Instead, they correspond to ranges of propositions.

'That' clauses are also used in reporting thoughts and beliefs. If I regard Jones's statement as in earnest, then I may also say, "Jones thought that Reagan is in California", and "Jones believes that Reagan is in California". If the 'that' clause in "Jones *said* that Reagan is in California" does not serve as a singular term designating a proposition that Jones is trying to convey, then it seems clear that the 'that' clause in "Jones *thought* that Reagan is in California" plays no such role either. After all, I might say the latter simply as a result of hearing Jones say, "Reagan is in California". I can understand this speech act without knowing precisely how Jones is thinking of Reagan, and hence without knowing just what proposition he is entertaining or what thought he is thinking, so it seems clear that when I report, "Jones thought that

---

[12] See my [1982] for a full formulation of a theory of statements along these lines. A summary description of the theory can be found in chapter 2 of my [1984b].

Reagan is in California", I am not using "that Reagan is in California" to designate any such proposition. Instead, I am using it to *describe* Jones's thought. I would think that this point is obvious. There is an important difference between describing something and uniquely identifying it. Obviously, belief ascriptions using 'that' clauses describe one's beliefs, but there is no reason to think they uniquely identify them, and in fact it seems apparent that they do not.

I think that the functioning of 'that' clauses in belief ascription can be understood as parallel to the functioning of 'that' clauses in statement ascriptions. When I say, "Jones said that Reagan is in California", I am describing the communication act by indirectly specifying the range of propositions that are possible sent propositions for the speaker and acceptable received propositions for the hearer. We can describe these as possible sent and acceptable received propositions for *the statement that Reagan is in California*. In a precisely similar fashion, if I say, "Jones thinks that Reagan is in California", what I say is true iff Jones is thinking a proposition that is a possible sent proposition for the statement that Reagan is in California. This is to classify Jones's thought as being a member of a certain class, that is, as being a certain kind of thought, but it does not say precisely which thought it is.[13] We might regard such content-classifications as describing *wide content*, because they are sensitive to all of the external social factors that affect the use of public language. Burge has urged the importance of these factors in content ascriptions, but they are relevant only to ascriptions of wide content.

This account has important implications for the philosophy of language. For instance, Kripke's [1979] case of puzzling Pierre is readily explicable in terms of this account of belief ascription.[14] Overlooking the statement/proposition distinction has resulted in the philosophy of language and the philosophy of mind growing together in unfortunate ways. On the assumption that what we say (a statement) is the same as what we believe (a proposition), theories of language and theories of belief must have much in common. But given the distinctness of statements and propositions, that need not be the case, and I do not believe that it is the case. For example, there may be something right

---

[13] For a precise theory of belief sentences along these lines, see my [1982], pp. 190-196.

[14] See my [1982], pp. 192-193. For a more recent endorsement of the same account, see Brian Loar [1987] and [1988]. Loar also attempts to handle Putnam's twin earth case and Burge's arthritis example using this machinery, but I do not think that can be done without the addition of "derived" syntactically simple kind terms of the sort I described in section 3.

about the historical connection theory of reference as applied to language,[15] but I doubt that it makes any sense at all when applied to mental representation. In particular, the familiar arguments in its favor bear *only* upon language.

The statement/proposition distinction can be used to defuse an objection to my earlier diagnosis of the Putnam twin earth examples and Burge's arthritis example. For instance, on that account, when one believes he has arthritis, he is typically thinking about arthritis in a syntactically simple way that is derived from an earlier syntactically complex description. I have not given a theory of precisely how this works, but it seems likely that a correct account will have the consequence that the truth values of different people's beliefs about arthritis will be determined by somewhat different features of their environment, and hence their beliefs have different propositional contents. If we thought that communication involved the literal transmission of propositions, this would prevent our talking to each other about arthritis, and that would be ridiculous. However, given the statement/proposition distinction, no such consequence ensues.

This account also explains why we find it as easy as we do to ascribe beliefs to other people. If we had to know precisely what proposition they are thinking, we would find it very difficult to ascribe beliefs. For instance, I do not usually know how Jones is thinking of Reagan when he says, "Reagan is in California", but this does not imply that I cannot know that Jones thinks that Reagan is in California. I do not have to know *which* proposition Jones is entertaining in order to know this. I need only know what kind of thought he is having.

To extend this account to belief ascriptions involving more complex 'that' clauses, we must have analyses of the different kinds of sentences that can go into the 'that' clauses, because it is their analyses that determine the ranges of possible sent propositions. I have discussed these questions at some length elsewhere [1982], and I will not pursue them further here, but they present no difficulties in principle.

6. Conclusions

To conclude then, our question was, "What determines the content of a thought?" This question gets its punch by being set against the background assumption that thoughts are internal physical occurrences. The answer I have proposed is that thoughts can be classified in four

---

[15] Kripke [1972], Donnellan [1972].

importantly different ways.   Introspection yields syntactic categories. These are important for cognitive processing, but they do not correspond to contents.   A second way of categorizing thoughts is in terms of narrow content. This is determined by the functional role of the thought in rational architecture together with the way in which that rational architecture is tied to the world through input correlations.   Narrow contents are indexical, so to get truth bearers we must augment the narrow contents with the values of the indexical parameters. Propositional content can be taken to consist of pairs of narrow contents and values for indexical parameters.   Finally, wide content is described by 'that' clauses.   This kind of classification does not uniquely determine propositional content but describes it in a more general way.   For purpose of cognitive processing, it is the syntactical properties of thoughts that are important. For social purposes, our interest is usually in wide content.   We rarely have any direct interest in either narrow content or propositional content.   However, we cannot dispense with narrow content because it is one of the determinants of wide content.

Chapter 6
Cognitive Carpentry

1. How to Build a Person

Having explored the question of how to build a person, I now propose to do it. I have defended the currently popular view that persons are physical objects and what makes an object a person is its functional organization. Where I differ from most philosophers of similar persuasion is in the details of the functional organization that I take to be necessary and sufficient for personhood. Philosophers use the word 'person' as a technical term. They are not just referring to biological organisms of the species *homo sapiens*. They use the term 'person' so that it would include Martians if there were any, sentient dolphins, and basically anything with a mental life that is enough like ours. Then they ask, "Could a machine be a person?" We come to this problem with only a vague idea of what we mean by 'person', and part of our task is to construct (not just analyze) a more precise concept. I have argued that if the concept of a person is to be such that it can in principle include creatures with different physiologies, then *the concept of a person must simply be the concept of a thing having states that can be mapped onto our own in such a way that if we suppose the corresponding states to be the same, then the thing is for the most part rational.* In other words, something is a person iff it has states whose interactions appropriately mimic our rational architecture. Obviously, on this criterion, a machine can be a person. To create such a machine, all we must do is make it behave in a way that can be regarded as rational. This is not just the Turing test (Turing [1950]), because the requisite "behavior" includes internal states. It follows from this account of personhood that if we can construct an accurate and complete computer model of rational architecture, a computer running the resulting program and connected to the world in an appropriate manner will thereby be a person. It will have precisely the same credentials for being a person as any member of the species *homo sapiens*. Of course, it will have a different physiology, but that is, by definition, not what is relevant in determining personhood.

It follows from this account that personhood admits of degrees. This is because there can be degrees to which the states of a system (either mechanical or biological) can be mapped onto rational architecture. For instance, chimps and dolphins might turn out to be "pretty person-like", and Alpha Centaurians even more so, without their states exactly mimicking human rational architecture. By the same score, advanced AI systems may someday be person-like without exactly modeling human rationality. They may actually improve upon human rationality.

My claim is that constructing a person is the same thing as construct-ing an accurate computer model of human rational architecture. An important segment of the artificial intelligence community is concerned with modeling rationality. It is a consequence of my view that they are actually in the business of building persons. This is the thesis of *strong AI*. It deserves to be emphasized just how much is required to achieve an accurate and complete computer model of rational architecture. Many different kinds of states can be assessed as to their rationality. These include thoughts, beliefs, desires, intentions, emotional states, actions, and so forth. The entire nexus of rationality relations relating these items to one another and also to sensory input constitutes human rational architecture. In modeling rational architecture, it is not sufficient to construct a system of mental representation and simple rules for reasoning with those mental representations in a nonreflective way, for three reasons. (1) Theoretical reasoning requires the ability to introspect one's own states, reason about them, and use these results in forming beliefs about the world. This is particularly important for defeasible reasoning. (2) Practical reasoning requires the system to have states identifiable as desires, intentions, emotional states like fear or embarrassment, and so forth, because all of these are subject to evaluations of rationality and they can affect the rationality of other states. (3) As I argued in chapter 2, both theoretical reasoning and practical reasoning require the cognitive agent to have a special way of thinking of itself (a *de se* designator) that is essentially a way of thinking of *itself* and not of anything else. The abilities to think about oneself and to introspect one's own states comprise important aspects of what we call 'consciousness'. All of this is part of rationality. The upshot of this is that a system adequately mimicing human rational architecture will have a very rich mental life. A corollary is that current AI systems do little more than scratch the surface of the problem of modeling rational architecture. For instance, a system that proves mathematical theorems in a mechanical and un-self-conscious way is modeling only a very small fraction of human rational architecture. On the other hand, it is a start.

I have urged that the abstract task of building a person consists of modeling human rational architecture. But to avoid misunderstanding, let me quickly acknowledge that much more is required for building a person that will function in the real world—a robot. That will also involve vision, or more generally, perception, and also motor control, language, and myriad special-purpose modules that shortcut reasoning to make information processing more efficient. These are the *Q&I systems* (quick and inflexible) discussed in chapter 1. In some ways, reasoning is the least important element of such a robot. A robot incorporating sophisticated subsystems for perception, motor control, and a variety of Q&I systems, could function very well in a cooperative environment without reasoning. It would be a mechanical analogue of a lower animal, some of which are extraordinarily good at what they do. But such a robot would lack any kind of self-awareness and would not be a person. On the other hand, a robot endowed with reasoning but lacking any Q&I systems would probably be too slow to function in real time.

It is not uncommon for philosophers to urge that personhood is determined by functional organization, wave their hands feebly about the nature of the functional organization required, and then move on to other topics. I have already been more specific about the general nature of the requisite functional organization than many philosophers. But I am not content with this. I want to construct an account of human rational architecture accurate in every detail, and model it on a computer. The overall enterprise is AI, but the theories driving the implementation are philosophical. I have a project underway at the University of Arizona whose ultimate objective is the construction and modeling of a general theory of rationality. This is the OSCAR Project. OSCAR is the system that will result. Of course, the general project of modeling rationality is an immense one, and it will occupy researchers for centuries. But we are in a position to make a good start on it right now. The rest of this chapter will be a kind of prolegomenon to building OSCAR.

The refining and the modeling of theories of reasoning go hand in hand in a way that philosophers have generally overlooked. I would urge that much work on reasoning in AI suffers from inadequate theoretical foundations. These foundations consist largely of epistemology and the theory of practical reasoning. Providing these foundations is a matter of doing philosophy. I find an increasing awareness of this within AI. But philosophers also need to learn more about AI and computer modeling. I recommend this as *the* proper way to do epistemology. It is probably the only way to get epistemological theories wholly right. One does not have to spend long constructing computer models of theories of reasoning to discover that they almost never do precisely what we expect them to do, and sorting out why leads to the discovery of subtle errors in the theories. From the comfort of his armchair, a philosopher will be able to discover some of the more obvious counterexamples to a flawed theory, but there are often subtle difficulties that do not emerge in simple cases and will generally be overlooked by mere reflection. When a computer model is applied to complicated cases, however, the difficulties become apparent. The computer thus becomes a mechanical aid in the discovery of counterexamples. I cannot emphasize too strongly how important this is. Computer modeling has led me to make profound changes in my own theories. Philosophers may not fully appreciate what a powerful technique this is until they try it, but once they try it they will never be content to do without it. I predict that this will become an indispensable tool for epistemology over the next twenty years. When that happens, philosophy and AI will have grown together, to the benefit of both.

2. A Naturalistic Theory of Rationality

The rules comprising rational architecture are normative.[1] They are not mere descriptions of what people do—they describe what people *ought* to do. This has often been taken to imply that epistemology and cognitive psychology are talking about entirely different matters and have little to do with one another. However, I believe that to be a mistake. In an important sense, epistemological theories *are* psychological theories. This turns upon there being different kinds of 'ought's. Every philosopher is familiar with the distinction between the 'ought' of moral reasoning and the 'ought' of prudential reasoning. What has often been overlooked is that there is another kind of 'ought' as well. This might be called *the procedural 'ought'*. This is used in formulating procedural knowledge. When you have procedural knowledge of how to do something, you have in some sense internalized rules for how to do it. The procedural 'ought' is used in formulating those rules. For instance, the rules we learn when we learn to ride a bicycle tell us to turn the handlebars clockwise when we feel ourselves falling to the right. This is just a rule of the system of rules that we internalize when we learn how to ride a bicycle. It has no moral or prudential status, but nevertheless we can express it by saying that when we feel ourselves falling to the right, we *should* turn the handlebars clockwise.

---

[1] What follows is a capsule description of the theory propounded in Pollock [1986]. See that source for more detail.

It is useful to compare rules of rationality with rules of grammar. Rules of grammar are naturally given a normative formulation. They tell us "how we should construct our utterances". But despite their apparent normativity, no one thinks that they are moral rules or rules for prudential reasoning. The use of normative language just reflects the fact that they are rules—in this case, rules internalized in our procedural knowledge of how to speak the language. Precisely the same thing should be said about the normativity of epistemology. Rules for reasoning make up a system whose internalization comprises our knowing how to reason. This is completely analogous to knowing how to speak the language, except that the rules for reasoning are probably hardwired into us to a greater extent than rules for language.

My claim is thus that the apparent normativity of epistemology is merely a reflection of the fact that epistemology is concerned with rules for how to do something, just like linguistics. This is no reason for thinking that you cannot derive epistemic 'ought's from psychological 'is's. It would be very surprising if we could not do that for linguistics, and I think it would be equally surprising if we could not do that for epistemology.

There is another strand to this story, however. Human beings do not always behave rationally. In particular, they do not always reason correctly. Thus epistemic rules cannot be regarded as mere descriptions of how people reason. On the other hand, that is what psychology gives us, doesn't it? So how can psychology be relevant to epistemology? But again, it is good to reflect on the parallel between epistemology and linguistics. People do not always conform to linguistic rules either, but that does not mean that linguistic rules cannot be the subject of psychological investigation. In either epistemology or linguistics, what we have is a system that, left to its own devices, would result in our always following the rules, but in each case the system is embedded in a larger system that can override it and result in "infractions" of the rules. In linguistics this gives rise to the competence/performance distinction. We need an analogous distinction in any case of procedural knowledge, and in particular we need such a distinction in epistemology. Epistemology is about reasoning competence. Theories of competence describe embedded systems that govern behavior when left alone but can be overridden. Epistemology is concerned with describing this embedded system. This kind of embedded system is perfectly understandable, and there is no reason it should not be subject to psychological investigation. However, the empirical investigation of such a system is difficult simply because the embedding system does not always conform to the rules of the embedded system.

Having decided that epistemological rules are a legitimate subject of psychological investigation, we might start worrying about philosophical methodology. After all, the way in which philosophers investigate these matters is very different from the way psychologists do it. Philosophers just sit and think. Their investigations are supposed to be *a priori*. How, then, can they be investigating psychological matters? Lest this be deemed a crushing objection to philosophical methodology, note that something very similar goes on in linguistics. At least a great deal of linguistic theory is based on linguists' "linguistic intuitions" rather than any kind of direct empirical investigation.

I think that the explanation for this has to do with a general feature of procedural knowledge. Procedural knowledge generally concerns ongoing processes rather than instantaneous performances. Furthermore, even when we have internalized the rules, they may be hard to follow. Think, for instance, of knowing how to swing a golf club. Even though we may know how to do it, it may be hard to do it right, and we may fail to do it right in specific cases. A built-in feature of procedural knowledge seems to be the ability to monitor ongoing performance and correct deviations from the internalized norm. In other words, we can "sense" or "introspect" whether we are conforming to the norm. It is this that allows us to tell whether a particular golf swing is done right, whether a particular utterance is linguistically correct, and whether a particular bit of reasoning is rationally correct. It is the ability to tell by introspection what we are thinking, together with this "judgmental" aspect of introspection, that enables us to formulate epistemological theories or grammatical theories just by reflecting. We do not have any direct introspective access to what our internalized rules are, but we do have introspective access to the correctness or incorrectness of individual performances, and that provides the data for constructing general theories about the nature of the rules. This, I suggest, is what goes in epistemology.

It is a contingent fact that humans possess the rational architecture they do. Insofar as epistemological theories are descriptions of our rational architecture, they are contingent. On the other hand, it follows from the account of the language of thought propounded in chapter 5 that the identity of a concept is determined by its place in rational architecture.[2] If we take this to describe the *conceptual role* of a concept, that conceptual role is an essential feature of the concept. It is a necessary truth that a concept has the conceptual role it does, but

---

[2] The identity of a concept is not determined by its place in the abstract uninterpreted structure of rational architecture, but it is determined by its place relative to other concepts whose identities are given.

it is not a necessary truth that we employ the conceptual framework we do.   It makes no sense to speculate about cognizers who reason differently about the concept *red*, because the way they reason determines what concept they are employing, but it makes perfectly good sense to speculate about cognizers who employ different concepts than we do and accordingly have different rational architectures.[3]

In conclusion, I am suggesting that the epistemological investigation of reasoning is an empirical investigation concerned with describing an embedded system that governs reasoning, and this makes it a psychological investigation of sorts. The methodology the epistemologist uses for his investigation can be understood by considering our ability to observe our own thought introspectively and assess it as we assess performance in connection with any procedural knowledge. So understood, the methodology is pretty much the same as the methodology of the linguist. More conventional techniques of empirical investigation are in principle applicable, but at this stage of development in cognitive psychology it is very hard to bring such techniques to bear on the problem.   The structures we are trying to elicit are extremely complex, and it is hard to see how we could ever formulate reasonable theories about them just by looking at the output of a human black box. We are, in effect, trying to describe the inner workings of one black box embedded within another black box. At this stage of investigation, it seems best to use traditional philosophical methodology for the formulation of theories of reasoning and then use empirical psychological techniques for trying to assess the consequences of the theories. Even the latter seems to me to be very difficult, but I imagine that cognitive psychologists will be sufficiently ingenious to find indirect ways of doing this. Eventually, I expect the work of the philosopher and the psychologist to merge and form one continuous body of theory. In an important sense, what I am arguing here is that there really is such a thing as cognitive science. There exists a range of problems concerning cognition with which we cannot deal adequately without making use of the knowledge and tools of all three of the disciplines of philosophy, AI, and cognitive psychology.

3. The Structure of Intellection

Rationality can be divided into *theoretical rationality* and *practical rationality*.   Theoretical rationality is concerned exclusively with the

---

[3] As I argued in chapter 5, their concepts would not have to be identical to ours in order for linguistic communication to be possible.

rationality of beliefs, and it comprises the subject matter of epistemology. Assessing the rationality of a belief amounts to determining whether it ought to be held in the present epistemological circumstances. So the issue is really one of belief updating. Belief updating is accomplished by reasoning, broadly construed. The kind of reasoning involved in belief updating is called *theoretical reasoning*.

Practical rationality encompasses all aspects of rationality other than theoretical rationality. This includes most centrally the rationality of actions, but it also includes the rationality of nondoxastic mental states like desires, intentions, emotions (for instance, a fear can be rational or irrational), and so on. The point of ascribing rationality or irrationality to nondoxastic states has to do with their role in reasoning about actions. Such reasoning is called *practical reasoning*.

I am identifying the theory of rationality with the theory of correct reasoning. The theory of epistemic rationality is thus the theory of theoretical reasoning, and the theory of practical rationality is the theory of practical reasoning. I will refer to the processes of theoretical and practical reasoning jointly as *intellection*. Rationality is thus identified with the operation of intellection. It must be recognized, however, that this involves a narrow construal of rationality, and there is no implication that the beliefs and actions of rational agents should always be the result of reasoning. The difficulty is that reasoning is slow. Many aspects of reasoning would seem to be essentially serial. Human beings gain speed by employing their inherently slow hardware for parallel processing. Much of reasoning cannot be done in parallel, so human processing includes many "nonintellectual" processes (processes that are not part of intellection) that also issue in beliefs and actions. These are the Q&I modules.

3.1   The Role of Q&I Modules

The simplest Q&I modules are closely related to motor skills like catching a baseball, but it must not be supposed that all Q&I modules are of that sort. Psychological evidence strongly suggests that most everyday inductive and probabilistic inference is carried out by Q&I modules.[4] In this case, the modules are not just inflexible but also inaccurate. Accurate probabilistic reasoning is in many cases computationally unfeasible. As the number of probabilities increases, the difficulty of making calculations in accord with the probability calculus increases exponentially. Even high-speed computers cannot keep up with this exponential explosion for long. Human beings deal with this by

---

[4] Kahneman, Slovic, and Tversky [1982].

relying upon processes like Tversky's "representativeness heuristic".[5] Tversky's proposal is that we often use stereotypes to estimate probabilities. Given a description of a bird, we may estimate the probability of its being a robin by judging how closely that description conforms to our stereotype of a robin. This may yield reasonable estimates, but it may also yield estimates that conflict with the probability calculus. Tversky and Kahneman cite the following example. Subjects were given the following task:

> Linda is 31 years old, single, outspoken, and very bright. She majored in philosophy. As a student she was deeply concerned with issues of discrimination and social justice, and also participated in anti-nuclear demonstrations.
>
> Please rank the following statements by their probability, using 1 for the most probable and 8 for the least probable:
>   Linda is an teacher in elementary school.
>   Linda works in a bookstore and takes Yoga classes.
>   Linda is active in the feminist movement. (F)
>   Linda is a psychiatric social worker.
>   Linda is a member of the League of Women Voters.
>   Linda is a bank teller. (T)
>   Linda is an insurance salesperson.
>   Linda is a bank teller and is active in the feminist movement. (T&F)

85% of the subjects rated (T&F) more probable than T alone, which conflicts with the probability calculus.[6]

That such approximation methods can yield inaccurate probability estimates does not imply that it is unreasonable to rely on them. It is very important for humans to be able to make rough probability judgments. Most of the generalizations that allow us to get around in the world are of this sort. But it is rarely important for our probability estimates to be very accurate. As the preceding two sentences illustrate, we normally require only probability information that can be formulated loosely using terms like 'most', 'rarely', or 'usually'. Thus the approximation methods serve us well, whereas the alternative of explicit reasoning is too slow for many practical purposes.

I would urge that much ordinary inductive inference is also the result of Q&I modules. Inductive inference *can* be carried out intellectually — by explicit reasoning from explicitly stated data — and scientists try to do that. But this requires the storage and processing of huge databases,

---

[5] Tversky [1977].

[6] Kahneman, Slovic, and Tverskey [1982], pp. 92ff.

which is exhaustive of system resources and computationally expensive. Only in science do we tend to accumulate an explicit body of data, peruse it, and then engage in explicit inductive reasoning about it. Instead, we normally employ procedures that allow us to use the data as we acquire them and then forget them, forming provisional generalizations that we modify as we go along. This is much more efficient, but it is subject to pitfalls having to do with the possibility of non-independent data that cannot be judged non-independent because they are no longer recalled. To illustrate with a simple example, suppose we are attempting to estimate the proportion of robins in the neighborhood that are male. After a number of observations, we estimate that approximately half are male. But suppose there is really only one male robin in the neighborhood, and he keeps flying around and around our house. This upsets the statistics, but if we cannot remember the earlier observations then there is no way we can correct them by discovering that it is the same male robin.

We do not want to require rational agents, human or otherwise, to make inductive inferences only by explicit inductive reasoning. That is too slow and computationally too difficult for many practical purposes. In this connection it is interesting to reflect upon much of the machine learning literature. Although I will not try to substantiate this here, I would suggest that many of the systems developed there are best viewed as Q&I systems. They are conclusion-drawers but not reasoners. Reasoning is a step-by-step sequential process, but many machine learning systems do nothing like that.[7] This does not make them any the less interesting. A general purpose automated cognizer with humanlike cognitive powers will have to be provided with potent Q&I modules to supplement explicit reasoning.

The advantage of Q&I modules is speed and efficiency. The advantage of intellection, on the other hand, is extreme flexibility. It seems that it can in principle deal with any kind of situation, but it is slow. In complicated situations we may have no applicable Q&I modules, in which case we have no choice but to undertake explicit reasoning about the situation. In other cases, human beings accept the output of the Q&I modules *unless* they have some explicit reason for not doing so. In sum, the role of intellection should be (1) to deal with cases to which built-in Q&I modules do not apply, and (2) to monitor and override the output of Q&I modules as necessary. The various information-processing modules that go into building a person are combined as in figure 1.

---

[7] For instance, think of Holland et al [1986].

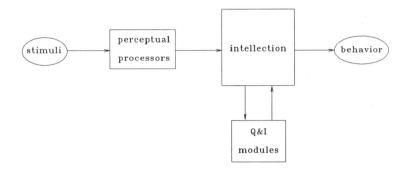

Figure 1. The place of intellection

3.2 Interactions between Theoretical and Practical Reasoning

Within philosophy, it tends to be the case that either theoretical reasoning is discussed in isolation from practical reasoning, or the attempt is made to reduce theoretical reasoning to practical reasoning by identifying it with practical reasoning about what to believe.[8] Neither strategy can be completely successful. The reduction of theoretical reasoning to practical reasoning cannot be successful because practical reasoning must be based upon knowledge of the agent's current situation. For instance, it may require a prior estimate of the likelihood of actions having different outcomes. Such knowledge must be the result of theoretical reasoning.[9] Thus any practical reasoning must presuppose prior theoretical reasoning. This has the immediate consequence that theoretical reasoning cannot be viewed as just a special kind of practical reasoning.[10]

By and large, epistemologists have tried to ignore practical reasoning

---

[8] The latter has also been urged in AI by Jon Doyle [1988] and [1988a].

[9] I assume that the Q&I modules are theoretically dispensable, giving us nothing that we could not have obtained more laboriously by engaging in theoretical reasoning.

[10] It might be objected that the theoretical knowledge required for practical reasoning could be obtained from the Q&I modules without engaging in any theoretical reasoning. However, I presume that the Q&I modules are "theoretically" expendable in the sense that if there were no time pressures or resource limitations, the agent could do without them and just rely upon intellection.

in their investigations of theoretical reasoning, but that cannot be entirely satisfactory either. The difficulty is that theoretical reasoning is often guided by practical reasoning about how best to reason. For instance, a mathematician addressing an unsolved problem may spend more time considering how to approach the problem than in actually constructing trial proofs. Similarly, an experimental scientist may spend more time considering what experiments to perform or what hypotheses to test than in evaluating the data resulting from the experiments. In each case the rational agent is conducting practical reasoning about what theoretical reasoning to perform.

In precisely what ways can practical reasoning affect the course of theoretical reasoning? At the very least, it can affect the strategies we employ in attempting to answer questions. We can learn that certain natural (default) strategies are unlikely to be effective in specific circumstances, and we can discover new strategies that are effective. The latter are often obtained by analogy from previous problem solving.

On the other hand, it is commonly asserted that practical reasoning cannot affect belief directly because belief is not under voluntary control. Theoretical reasoning is "directly causally efficacious" in belief formation in a sense in which practical reasoning is not. Notice that practical reasoning appears to be directly causally efficacious in the formation of intentions and desires in precisely the same way theoretical reasoning is directly causally efficacious in belief formation. Intentions and desires are not under voluntary control either. It is only actions that are under voluntary control.

Even in the case of actions the situation is a bit muddy. *Turning off the light* is an action, but it is not something that we can do infallibly. If we try to turn off the light, circumstances may intervene to prevent it. Perhaps we should say that, in a strict sense, *turning off the light* is not under voluntary control. Action theorists distinguish between *basic actions*, which need not be performed *by* performing other actions, and *nonbasic* actions, which can be performed only by doing something else. *Turning off the light* is a nonbasic action. Raising your arm is supposed to be a basic action. The observation that beliefs are not under the direct control of practical reasoning seems to amount to no more than that beliefs are not basic actions. Beliefs are, to some extent, under the control of practical reasoning. If one desires not to have a certain belief, one can take steps that affect one's beliefs indirectly. For instance, one can avoid thinking about the evidence supporting the belief. The only difference between beliefs and nonbasic actions seems to be that beliefs are somewhat more difficult to control—even indirectly.

It must be possible for the rational agent to use practical reasoning to direct the course of theoretical reasoning (and also to direct the course of practical reasoning itself). On the other hand, because practical reasoning presupposes theoretical reasoning, some theoretical reasoning must be possible without practical reasoning. To avoid an infinite regress, a rational agent must have built-in default reasoning strategies for both theoretical reasoning and practical reasoning. The agent must be able to employ these default strategies without engaging in practical reasoning about how to reason. The general architecture of rational thought can thus be diagrammed as in figure 2.

In order to perform practical reasoning about how to reason, an agent must be able to think about its own reasoning. I will refer to a reasoner with such capabilities as an *introspective reasoner*. An introspective reasoner must have the ability to reason, then "move up a level" to reason about what reasoning has occurred. An introspective reasoner must be built on top of a *planar reasoner* that lacks the ability to move up a level and observe itself. A planar reasoner can still reason about

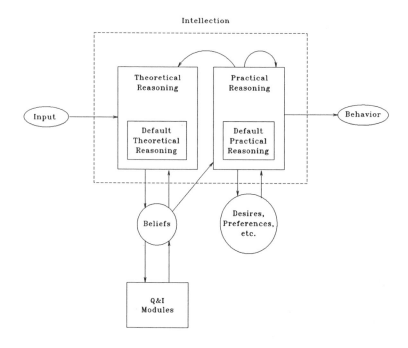

Figure 2. The architecture of rational thought

reasoning, in the same way it reasons about anything else, but it will have no special mechanisms for use in reasoning specifically about reasoning. The default planar reasoner is part of the default theoretical reasoner, and hence it engages exclusively in theoretical reasoning. The rest of this book will focus on theoretical reasoning to the exclusion of practical reasoning. This is not because I feel that one is more important than the other. It just reflects my conviction that we currently know more about theoretical reasoning than practical reasoning and are in a better position to develop that part of OSCAR. The next section will investigate the structure of the default planar reasoner, and the subsequent section will be concerned with the construction of an introspective reasoner based upon the planar reasoner.

4. The Default Planar Reasoner

4.1 Defeasibility

Theoretical reasoning can lead not only to the adoption of new beliefs but also to the retraction of old beliefs. Similarly, practical reasoning can lead to the formation of intentions but also to the retraction of intentions. In philosophy, reasoning is said to be *defeasible* in the sense that correct reasoning can lead first to the adoption of a conclusion and subsequently to its retraction. Both practical reasoning and theoretical reasoning are defeasible. This aspect of reasoning has been called "nonmonotonic" in AI work.[11]

In AI there is the common impression that defeasible reasoning consists of "jumping to conclusions" or making "tentative guesses".[12] It is supposed that defeasible reasoning is less secure than normal reasoning and should be countenanced only for the sake of computational efficiency. What is overlooked is that defeasible reasoning *is* normal reasoning. Its use is not just a matter of computational efficiency. It is logically impossible to reason successfully about the world around us using only deductive reasoning. All interesting reasoning outside of mathematics involves defeasible steps. For instance, our basic informa-

---

[11] The work on defeasible reasoning in philosophy stems mainly from the publications of Roderick Chisholm and myself. See Chisholm [1957], [1966], [1977], and Pollock [1967], [1970], [1974], [1986], [1987]. See also Kyburg [1974] and [1983]. For a sampling of the work in AI, see Delgrande [1988], Etherington [1987], Etherington and Reiter [1983], Loui [1987], McCarthy [1980] and [1984], McDermott and Doyle [1980], Moore [1985], Nute [1988], Pearl [1988], Pollock [1987], Poole [1985] and [1988], Reiter [1980], and Reiter and Criscuolo [1981].

[12] Doyle [1979].

tion about the world comes from sense perception. Things appear certain ways to us, and we take that to be a reason for believing that they are that way. Clearly, this reason is defeasible, but our reasoning in this way is no mere matter of convenience. As years of work in epistemology has made clear, there is in principle no way to logically deduce the state of the world from the way it appears.[13] Moving on up the epistemic ladder, we use induction to form general beliefs summarizing observed regularities. If a regularity has been observed to hold in every case, that gives us a reason for thinking that it holds in general. If it has been observed to hold only in most cases, that gives us a reason for thinking it will continue to hold in most cases. Such inductive reasoning is defeasible, and it cannot be replaced by deductive reasoning. There is no way to deduce general conclusions from finitely many observations. Given that a generalization holds most of the time, we can use that to infer that it will hold in further unobserved cases. This inference is also defeasible. It takes ⌜Most A's are B's, and this is an A⌝ to be a defeasible reason for ⌜This is a B⌝. The upshot of all this is that defeasible reasoning is not just common; it is thoroughly pervasive and absolutely essential. Almost everything we believe is believed at least indirectly on the basis of defeasible reasoning, and things could not have been any other way.[14]

Reasoning proceeds in terms of reasons. A reason can be represented as an ordered pair $\langle X, P \rangle$ where X is the set of premises and P is the conclusion. In most cases, X consists of a single proposition Q, in which case we say that Q rather than $\{Q\}$ is a reason for P. Within theoretical reasoning, some reasons are *conclusive reasons*, in the sense that they logically entail their conclusions. Others support their conclusions only defeasibly. The latter are *prima facie reasons*, and the considerations that can lead to the retraction of conclusions based upon prima facie reasons are *defeaters*. Notice that prima facie reasons and defeaters make theoretical reasoning defeasible already at the level of the default planar reasoner. We do not require an introspective reasoner for defeasibility (although introspection is required for the acquisition of some important kinds of defeaters).[15]

---

[13] For further discussion of this point, see my [1986], pp. 39ff.

[14] It was argued in chapter 1 that there is a purely computational reason why a sophisticated cognizer will function better with an appearance/reality distinction and a merely defeasible connection between appearance and reality. This provides a deeper reason for the necessity of defeasible reasoning.

[15] I have in mind reliability defeaters, which defeat a prima facie reason by noting that it is an unreliable indicator of the truth of the conclusion under circumstances of the sort in which the system currently finds itself.

What makes reasoning defeasible is that prima facie reasons can be defeated. Considerations that defeat prima facie reasons are *defeaters*. There are two importantly different kinds of defeaters. Where P is a prima facie reason for Q, R is a *rebutting defeater* iff R is a reason for denying Q. All work on nonmonotonic logic and defeasible reasoning has recognized the existence of rebutting defeaters, but it has often been overlooked that there are other defeaters as well. For instance, suppose x looks red to me, but I know that x is illuminated by red lights and red lights can make things look red when they are not. This defeats the prima facie reason, but it is not a reason for thinking that x is *not* red. After all, red objects look red in red light too. This is an *undercutting defeater*. Undercutting defeaters attack the connection between the reason and the conclusion rather than attacking the conclusion directly. Where P is a prima facie reason for Q, R is an undercutting defeater if and only if R is a reason for denying that P would not be true unless Q were true. ⌜P would not be true unless Q were true⌝ is a kind of conditional, and I will symbolize it as ⌜$P \gg Q$⌝. Taking ΠX to be the conjunction of the members of a set X of propositions, if X is a prima facie reason for Q, then an undercutting defeater is a reason for $\sim(\Pi X \gg Q)$.

4.2 Justification and Warrant

Theories of reasoning are basically procedural theories. They are concerned with what a reasoner should do next when it finds itself in any particular epistemological situation. Correct reasoning can involve numerous false starts, wherein a belief is adopted, retracted, reinstated, retracted again, and so forth. At each stage of reasoning, if the reasoning is correct then a belief held on the basis of that reasoning is justified, even if subsequent reasoning will mandate its retraction. *Epistemic justification*, in this sense, is a procedural notion consisting of the correct rules for belief updating having been followed by the system up to the present time in connection with the belief being evaluated. Justified belief is a dynamic notion having to do with the present state of the reasoning system. The justification of a belief can vary not just as a result of further perceptual input but also as one's reasoning progresses without further input. For instance, a person can be perfectly justified in holding beliefs that are logically inconsistent with one another, provided he has good reasons for believing them and his reasoning has not exposed the inconsistency. If he later discovers the inconsistency, then he becomes unjustified in continuing to hold both beliefs, and this change occurs without any new perceptual input.

For this reason, the set of justified beliefs has few interesting logical properties. Consequently, most abstract work on justified belief has focused on the idealized notion of *warrant*. A proposition is warranted in a particular epistemic situation iff, starting from that epistemic situation, an ideal reasoner unconstrained by time or resource limitations, would ultimately be led to adopt belief in the proposition. Warranted propositions are those that would be justified "in the long run" if the system were able to do all possible relevant reasoning. A proposition can be justified without being warranted, because although the system has done everything correctly up to the present time and that has led to the adoption of the belief, there may be further reasoning waiting to be done that will mandate the retraction of the belief. Similarly, a proposition can be warranted without being justified, because although reasoning up to the present time may have failed to turn up adequate reasons for adopting the proposition, further reasoning may provide such reasons. Similarly, reasoning up to the present may mandate the adoption of defeaters which, upon further reasoning, will be retracted. So justification and warrant are two importantly different notions, although they are closely related.

Two schools of thought are represented in current work on non-monotonic logic and defeasible reasoning. Most theorists are members of the *semantical school*, according to which an adequate theory must be based upon a formal semantics.[16] The *procedural school*, on the other hand, proposes to analyze defeasible reasoning by giving a straightforward description of "how it works", in a procedural sense, and holds semantical questions in abeyance.[17] The semantical/procedural distinction is related to, but not quite the same as, the warrant/justification distinction. Procedural theories are typically about justification rather than warrant, and semantical theories are typically about warrant rather than justification. However, if one understands 'semantical' in a fairly narrow sense so that it includes only model theoretic semantics, then there can be theories of warrant that are not semantical. The theory of warrant presented below will not be semantical in this narrow sense.[18]

This is not the place to survey the AI literature on nonmonotonic logic, but to illustrate some of my points it will useful to sketch one of

---

[16] See, for example, McCarthy [1980] and [1984], McDermott and Doyle [1980], Moore [1985], and Reiter [1978] and [1980].

[17] The most noteworthy representative of this school is Jon Doyle [1979]. A more recent proponent is Ron Loui [1987].

[18] Two other theories that are not semantical in this narrow sense are Delgrande [1988] and Pearl [1988].

the simpler theories of nonmonotonic logic. This is *default logic*, due to Raymond Reiter [1980]. Default logic is based upon *defaults*, which are written in the form $\ulcorner P : Q\ /\ R \urcorner$ and can be regarded roughly as telling us that P is a prima facie reason for R, with $\sim Q$ being the only defeater. So-called *normal defaults* have the form $\ulcorner P : R\ /\ R \urcorner$. These correspond to prima facie reasons for which the only defeaters are rebutting defeaters.[19] Most work on default logic has focused on normal defaults. Relative to a set $\Re$ of defaults, an *extension* of a set X of formulas is a set Y such that (1) $X \subseteq Y$, (2) Y is closed under entailment (i.e., if a formula S is true in every model of Y then $S \in Y$), and (3) for each $\ulcorner P : Q\ /\ R \urcorner$ in $\Re$, if $P \in Y$ and $\ulcorner \sim Q \urcorner \notin Y$ then $R \in Y$. A *minimal extension* is an extension not properly contained in any other extension. On the orthodox formulation of default logic, given a set of defaults and a set X of inputs, a set Y is a rationally acceptable set of beliefs iff Y is a minimal extension of X. There can be more than one minimal extension, so this has the consequence that there can be more than one rationally acceptable set of beliefs. This has come to be called 'the multiple extension problem'.

The multiple extension problem is easily illustrated by supposing $\Re$ to consist of the pair of normal defaults $\ulcorner P : R\ /\ R \urcorner$ and $\ulcorner Q : \sim R\ /\ \sim R \urcorner$, and $X = \{P, Q\}$. In this case there are two minimal extensions of X, one containing R and the other containing $\sim R$. The orthodox formulation of default logic would tell us that we can take our choice and believe either R or $\sim R$. But if we consider concrete examples, this seems wrong. Suppose Jones tells me that P is true and Smith tells me that P is false. I regard Jones and Smith as equally reliable, and I have no other evidence regarding P. What should I believe? A theory telling me that I can take my choice and believe either P or $\sim P$ is *credulous* in the sense of Horty *et al* [1987].[20] But surely, in the face of such conflicting evidence, I should believe neither. I should *withhold belief* rather than randomly choose what to believe. Responding to a related criticism by Touretzky [1984], Etherington [1987] writes, "These criticisms suggest that a (common) misapprehension about default logic has occurred. ... In fact, while extensions are all acceptable, the logic says nothing about preference of one to another. It has always been assumed

---

[19] Experience in epistemology strongly suggests that there are no such prima facie reasons. What gives specific varieties of defeasible reasoning their unique flavors tends to be the undercutting defeaters associated with the prima facie reasons.

[20] The nonmonotonic logic of McDermott and Doyle [1980] is not credulous, but this seems to have been overlooked in the subsequent literature, and in recent conversation Jon Doyle disavows that aspect of the 1980 theory.

that an agent would 'choose' one extension or another, but nothing has been said about how such choices should be made."[21] If all extensions are acceptable but rationality can dictate preference of one extension over its competitors, then what notion of 'acceptable' can default logic possibly be analyzing? Certainly not 'warrant', which is my target.

I have heard credulous theories defended on the grounds that if we are building a system to give us practical advice, it is better to tell us something rather than nothing.[22] Sometimes this seems right. For instance, if the system is deciding where to have the staff picnic and the considerations favoring two sites are tied, it seems reasonable to choose at random.[23] But there are other situations in which such a policy could be disastrous. If we are designing a system to perform medical diagnosis, and the evidence favoring two diseases is tied, we do not want the system to decide randomly to treat the patient for one disease rather than the other. It could happen that the diseases are not serious if left untreated, but if the patient is treated for the wrong disease, that treatment will gravely exacerbate his condition and perhaps even be fatal. In such a case we want the system to reserve judgment on the matter and not proceed blindly.

The preceding defense of credulous reasoning systems seems to confuse theoretical reasoning and practical reasoning. A system making practical decisions must first decide what to believe and then use that to decide what to do, but these are two different matters. If the evidence favoring two alternative hypotheses is equally good, the system should record that fact and withhold belief. The practical reasoning module can then decide what to do given that epistemic conclusion. In some cases it may be reasonable to choose one of the hypotheses at random and act as if it is known to be true, and in other cases more caution will be prescribed. But what must be recognized is that the design of this practical reasoning module is a separate question from the design of the theoretical reasoning module that feeds it epistemic conclusions. The theory of defeasible reasoning is a theory of theoretical reasoning and accordingly should not be credulous. In the taxonomy of Horty et al [1987], a non-credulous system is *skeptical*. The simplest way to produce a skeptical default logic is to say that a proposition is warranted iff it is contained in every minimal extension. Then in the preceding example,

---

[21] See also Doyle [1988a].

[22] Both Jon Doyle and Richmond Thomason have argued this way in recent conversations.

[23] This example is due to Jon Doyle (in conversation).

neither R nor $\sim R$ is warranted.   This strikes me as a much more reasonable theory.

Default logic is just one variety of nonmonotonic logic. I mentioned it here because it is the easiest to formulate. It is characteristic of most nonmonotonic logics in that it attempts to characterize the set (or sets) of reasonable beliefs model theoretically. My own opinion is that the importance of model theoretic semantics is vastly overrated.[24] Experience in formal logic has indicated that it is possible to construct model theoretic semantics for even the most outlandish logical theories. The mere existence of a model theoretic semantics shows nothing at all about the correctness of the theory. If a theory is already known to be correct, then the discovery of a formal semantics for it can be a useful technical tool in its investigation. But the formal semantics is not itself an argument for the correctness of the theory unless there is some independent reason for thinking that the semantics is correct. The systems of formal semantics that define various species of nonmonotonic logic do indeed have initial plausibility, but I would urge that their authors have sometimes been driven more by considerations of formal elegance than by an appreciation of the subtleties required of defeasible reasoning for a full-blown epistemology. Before getting carried away with a semantical investigation, we should be sure that the theory described by the semantics is epistemologically realistic, and that requires attending to the nuts and bolts of how defeasible reasoning actually works. This quickly reveals that standard theories of nonmonotonic reasoning are unable to accommodate even some quite elementary defeasible reasoning. For instance, suppose we know that there is a small animal in the next room and we are trying to identify it by the sounds it makes. Knowing that most birds can fly, we may reason that if it is a bird then it can fly. Surprisingly, no AI system of nonmonotonic reasoning can accommodate this simple inference. Our actual reasoning is very simple. We *suppose* that the animal is a bird, infer defeasibly that it can fly, and then discharge the supposition (use conditionalization) to conclude that if it is a bird then it can fly. The reason standard systems of nonmonotonic reasoning cannot accommodate this reasoning is that they are unable to combine defeasible reasoning with conditionalization.

Linear arguments are arguments that do nothing but draw new conclusions from previous conclusions in accordance with reasons.

---

[24] I hold this opinion in general, not just for nonmonotonic logic. See chapter 6 of my [1984] for a discussion of the significance (or lack thereof) of model theoretic semantics for standard logical theories, including the predicate calculus and modal logic.

Linear reasoning is reasoning that instantiates linear arguments. An important feature of human reasoning is that not all reasoning is linear. Instead, we engage in various kinds of *suppositional reasoning* wherein we "suppose" things that have not been established, draw conclusions from the suppositions, and then "discharge" the suppositions to draw conclusions that are no longer dependent upon them. Conditionalization is one form of suppositional reasoning. Other forms include reasoning by cases and *reductio ad absurdum.*   The preceding example is a problem for AI systems of nonmonotonic reasoning because none of them incorporates suppositional reasoning. As the example illustrates, this prevents their drawing conclusions that ought to be drawn.

Our epistemological intuitions are about reasoning, and that suggests that the best we can do is build a system that mimics human reasoning. I think that that is overly restrictive, however. We do not necessarily want an automated reasoner to reason exactly the way human beings do. Resource differences may make it possible to construct automated reasoners that improve upon human reasoning. The sense in which they improve upon it must be that they update their beliefs in ways that are more efficient at bringing the set of their beliefs into conformance with the set of warranted propositions.   This suggests that the target of analysis should be *warrant* rather than *justification.* Our intuitions about reasoning are equally about warrant, because given a general description of an epistemological situation replete with a description of all the relevant arguments, our intuitions can inform us about what beliefs ought to be adopted and what beliefs ought to be retracted. A characterization of what ought to be believed given all possible relevant arguments is a characterization of the set of warranted propositions.   Such an account can be given fairly easily if we take as primitive the notion of one argument defeating another. Merely having an argument for a proposition does not guarantee that the proposition is warranted, because one might also have arguments for defeaters for some of the steps in the first argument.   Iterating this, one argument might be defeated by a second, but then the second argument could be defeated by a third thus reinstating the first, and so on.   A proposition is warranted only if it ultimately emerges from this process undefeated. To illustrate, suppose we have the three arguments diagrammed in figure 3. Here β defeats α, and γ defeats β. It is assumed that nothing defeats γ. Thus γ is ultimately undefeated. This should have the effect of reinstating α, leading to V being warranted. We can capture this kind of interplay between arguments by defining:

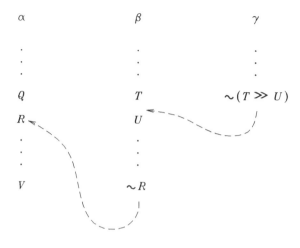

Figure 3. Interacting arguments

All arguments are *in at level 0.*
An argument is *in at level n+1* iff it is not defeated by any argument in at level *n*.

Let us also define:

An argument is *ultimately undefeated* iff there is an *m* such that for every *n > m*, the argument is in at level *n*.

My proposal is then that a proposition is warranted iff it is supported by some ultimately undefeated argument.[25] This is illustrated by the three arguments in figure 3. Neither α nor β is in at level 1, because both are defeated by arguments in at level 0 . As γ is in at level *n* for

---

[25] This characterization of warrant is presented in my [1986] and [1987]. A similar proposal is contained in Horty, Thomason, and Touretzky [1987].

every n, β is defeated at every level greater than 0, so β is out at level n for $n > 0$. As a result α is reinstated at level 2 and is in at level n for every $n > 1$. Hence α is ultimately undefeated, and V is warranted.

It is of interest to see how this analysis handles the multiple extension problem. Suppose we have a prima facie reason P for R and a prima facie reason Q for $\sim R$. This generates an argument supporting R and an argument supporting $\sim R$. Both arguments are in at level 0, but as each defeats the other, they are both out at level 1. Then they are in again at level 2, and out again at level 3, and so on. As a result, neither is ultimately undefeated, and hence neither R nor $\sim R$ is warranted. This illustrates a general phenomenon, which I call *collective defeat*. Collective defeat operates in accordance with the following general principle:

The Principle of Collective Defeat
> If Σ is a set of arguments such that (1) each argument in Σ is defeated by some other argument in Σ and (2) no argument in Σ is defeated by any argument not in Σ, then no argument in Σ is ultimately undefeated.

This is because each argument in Σ will be in at every even level, but then it follows that each will be out at every odd level. We can define:

> An argument σ is *defeated outright* iff there is a level n such that σ is out at all higher levels.

> An argument σ is *collectively defeated* iff there is no level n such that σ is in at all higher levels or out at all higher levels.

> A proposition *undergoes collective defeat* iff some arguments supporting it are collectively defeated and any other arguments supporting it are defeated outright.

Collective defeat can arise in either of two ways: collective undercutting defeat or collective rebutting defeat. Collective undercutting defeat arises as follows:

The Principle of Collective Undercutting Defeat
> If R is warranted and there is a set Γ of propositions such that:
> (1)   we have equally good defeasible arguments for each member of Γ;

(2)   for each P in Γ, the supporting argument involves a
        defeasible step proceeding from some premises $S_1,\ldots,S_n$
        to a conclusion T, and there is a finite subset Γ_p of Γ
        such that the conjunction of R with the members of Γ_p
        provides a deductive argument for $\sim[(S_1\&\ldots\&S_n) \gg
        T]$; and
(3)   none of these arguments is defeated except possibly by
        their interactions with one another;
then none of the propositions in Γ is warranted on the basis
of these defeasible arguments.

A simple example of this is diagrammed in figure 4. For instance, R
might be 'People generally tell the truth'. Suppose P is 'Jones says
Smith is unreliable' and Q is 'Smith says Jones is unreliable'. $(P \& R)$
is a prima facie reason for believing S: 'Smith is unreliable'; and $(Q \&
R)$ is a prima facie reason for believing T: 'Jones is unreliable'. But S
is an undercutting defeater for the reasoning from $(Q \& R)$ to T, and
T is an undercutting defeater for the reasoning from $(P \& R)$ to S.
Presented with this situation, what should we believe about Smith and
Jones?   The intuitive answer is, "Nothing".   We have no basis for
deciding that one rather than the other is unreliable. Under the circumstances, we should withhold belief regarding their reliability.

Collective rebutting defeat works analogously, although here we must
attend to the relative strengths of the arguments.   Uniform collective
rebutting defeat arises when all of the arguments involved have the same
strength, and it proceeds in accordance with the following principle:

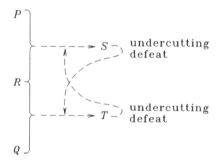

Figure 4. Collective undercutting defeat

The Principle of Uniform Collective Rebutting Defeat

If R is warranted and there is a set Γ of propositions such that:

(1)   we have equally good defeasible arguments for each member of Γ;

(2)   for each P in Γ there is a finite subset Γ_P of Γ such that the conjunction of R with the members of Γ_P provides a deductive argument for $\sim P$ that is as strong as our initial argument for P; and

(3)   none of these arguments is defeated except possibly by their interactions with one another;

then none of the propositions in Γ is warranted on the basis of these defeasible arguments.

The most common instances of collective rebutting defeat occur when Γ is a minimal finite set of propositions deductively inconsistent with R. In that case, for each P in Γ, $(\Gamma - \{P\}) \cup \{R\}$ gives us a deductive reason for $\sim P$. This is illustrated by an example that has played an important role in the philosophical foundations of probability theory—the *lottery paradox* (due to Kyburg [1961]). Suppose the proposition that we have a fair lottery with one million tickets is warranted. Let this be R. Then the probability of the ith ticket being drawn in such a lottery is .000001. This gives us a prima facie reason for believing that the ith ticket will not be drawn. Let the latter be P_i. But we have an analogous argument supporting each P_j. Furthermore, R entails that some ticket will be drawn, so these conclusions conflict with one another. Intuitively, there is no reason to prefer some of the P_i's over others, so none of them can be warranted unless they are all warranted. But they cannot all be warranted because the set $\{R, P_1, \ldots, P_{1000000}\}$ is deductively inconsistent. Hence by the principle of uniform collective rebutting defeat, none of the P_i's is warranted.[26]

4.3   A Criterion of Correctness for a Defeasible Reasoner

In an important sense, our ultimate interest in AI is in justification rather than warrant. We want to know how to build a system that reasons correctly, and that is a procedural matter. As I have just urged, the desideratum is not necessarily to build a system that replicates human reasoning in all respects because there may be more efficient ways of doing it. However, before we can decide whether a particular procedure is a more efficient way of doing it, we have to determine what the "it" is that we want the system to do. What exactly is the

---

[26] For a more extended discussion of the lottery paradox, see Pollock [1989].

connection between warrant and what we want a system of reasoning to accomplish? The simple answer, "We want the system to compute warrant", is demonstrably unsatisfiable if we understand 'compute' in an effective way. This is because, as has been observed by numerous authors,[27] on any theory of defeasible reasoning, the ultimate correctness of a piece of reasoning (that is, whether the conclusion of the reasoning will survive an indefinite amount of further reasoning and hence be warranted) may turn upon something's being unprovable, and if our resources for proof
include at least the full predicate calculus, then there is no effective test for unprovability. More precisely, by Church's theorem, the set of invalid formulas of the predicate calculus is not r.e. (recursively enumerable). It follows that, for example, in default logic, a first-order theory with normal defaults may have a set of theorems that is not r.e., and hence there can be no effective procedure for computing that set of theorems. The analogous conclusion applies to all theories of defeasible reasoning and to all nonmonotonic logics.

A consequence of the noncomputability of warrant is that we cannot expect an automated reasoning system ever to stop reasoning. It can inform us that "so far" a certain conclusion is justified, but it may have to continue forever in a possibly fruitless search for defeating arguments. This, of course, is just the way people work. It is not as crippling as it sounds, because once a conclusion becomes justified, it is reasonable to accept it provisionally and act upon it. That is what defeasible reasoning is all about.

If the desideratum for an automated reasoning system is not that of computing warrant, what is it? We want the system to modify its belief set systematically so that it comes to approximate the set of warranted propositions more and more closely. We want the set of beliefs to "approach the set of warranted propositions in the limit". I propose that we understand this on analogy to the standard ϵ/δ definition of limits in mathematical analysis. The precise desideratum for an automated reasoner is that justification should come to approximate warrant in the following sense:

The rules for reasoning should be such that:
(1)   if a proposition p is warranted then the system will eventually reach a point where p is adopted and stays adopted;

---

[27] I think that the first was David Israel [1980].

(2)   if p is unwarranted then the system will eventually reach
         a point where p is not adopted and stays unadopted.

So the task of a reasoner is not to compute warrant. It is to generate
successive sets of beliefs that approximate warrant more and more
closely, in the above sense. We can make this mathematically precise
as follows. Define:

A set A is *defeasibly enumerable* (d.e.) iff there is an effectively
computable set function f and a recursive set A_0 such that if
we define $A_{i+1} = f(A_i)$ then:
(1) $(\forall x)$ if $x \in A$ then $(\exists n)(\forall m > n)$ $x \in A_m$;
(2) $(\forall x)$ if $x \notin A$ then $(\exists n)(\forall m > n)$ $x \notin A_m$.

I will say that the pair $\langle A_0, f \rangle$ is a *d.e. approximation* of A. The intuitive
difference between r.e. sets and d.e. sets is that r.e. sets can be
"systematically approximated from below", while d.e. sets can be
systematically approximated from above and below simultaneously.
More precisely, if A is r.e., then there is an effectively computable
sequence of sets A_i such that

(1) $(\forall x)$ if $x \in A$ then $(\exists n)(\forall m > n)$ $x \in A_m$;
(2) $(\forall x)$ if $x \notin A$ then $(\forall m)x \notin A_m$.

The sets A_i approximate A from below in the sense that they are all
subsets of A and they grow monotonically, approximating A in the limit.
If A is defeasibly enumerable, however, the sets A_i need not be subsets
of A. They may approximate A only from above and below simultaneously, in the sense that they may contain elements not contained in
A. Every such element must eventually be taken out of the A_i's, but
there need not be any point at which they have all been removed. The
process of d.e. approximation can be pictured by thinking of A as a
spherical region of space and the A_i as representing successive stages of
a reverberating elastic ball whose center coincides with the center A.
As the reverberations dampen out, the outer surface of the ball will
come to approximate that of the spherical surface more and more
closely, but there will never be a point at which the ball is contained
entirely within the spherical surface.

To illustrate that d.e. sets need not be r.e., choose a pair of symbols
'□' and '◊' and define:

$A = \{\Box\varphi \mid \varphi$ is a valid formula of the predicate calculus$\}$
    $\cup \{\Diamond\varphi \mid \sim\varphi$ is an invalid formula of the predicate calculus$\}$.

By Church's theorem, A is not r.e., but it can be shown to be d.e. as follows. By the completeness theorem, there is an enumeration φ_i $(i\in\omega)$ of the valid formulas of the predicate calculus. If for some θ, $\varphi = \sim\theta$, let $\neg\varphi = \theta$, and let $\neg\varphi = \sim\varphi$ otherwise. Then define:

$A_0 = \{\Diamond\varphi \mid \varphi$ is a formula$\}$
$A_{i+1} = f(A_i) = (A_i \cup \{\Box\varphi_i\}) - \{\Diamond\neg\varphi_i\}$.

Then despite the fact that A is not r.e., $\langle A_0, f \rangle$ is a d.e. approximation of A. The d.e. approximation in this example has a particularly simple form in which once an element is added to or removed from some A_i (for $i > 0$), its status never changes. The general form of a d.e. approximation allows items to be repeatedly added and deleted. Notice that human reasoning works in the latter way. As our reasoning develops, beliefs may be repeatedly retracted and reinstated.

The proposal regarding reasoning and warrant is that the set of warranted propositions is defeasibly enumerable, and the rules for reasoning are rules for successively approximating warrant in this way, that is, they are rules for constructing a d.e. approximation. More accurately, we can think of a reasoner as a belief updater that operates repeatedly on a set of beliefs to generate a new set of beliefs. The reasoner starts with the set *input*, and each cycle of the reasoner constitutes the application of an effective set function f to the previous set of beliefs. I will say that the reasoner *provides a d.e. approximation to warrant* iff $\langle input, f \rangle$ is a d.e. approximation to the set of propositions that are warranted given that set of inputs. This is the criterion of correctness for a reasoner. This characterization of reasoning enables us to exploit differences between people and machines with regard to resource limitations. A rational machine need not reason in precisely the same way people do because it may be better at some tasks. Thus the construction of an automated reasoner divides into two parts. We must begin with a theory of warrant, and then given that characterization of warrant, we can look for rules for belief updating that provide a d.e. approximation to warrant.

4.4 Interest-Driven Reasoning

We can think of reasoning as consisting of three processes: (1) constructing arguments supporting conclusions in which we are interested, and the subsequent adoption of beliefs on the basis of the arguments we find; (2) retracting arguments and beliefs in the face of defeaters; and (3) the reinstatement of arguments and the readoption of beliefs when defeaters are themselves defeated or retracted. The first process is familiar from the AI literature on automated deduction, but the other two processes are unique to defeasible reasoning.

In searching for arguments, an introspective reasoner can bring to bear the full power of its practical reasoning, as informed by all of its prior experience. This would seem to be the only reason that an experienced mathematician is better at finding proofs than an equally intelligent math student. However, as we have seen, an introspective reasoner must be built on top of a non-introspective reasoner, and the searches of the latter are guided exclusively by the built-in procedures that constitute the default strategies for the introspective reasoner. The default reasoner may be quite good at constructing proofs that are not too difficult, but it is unlikely to provide any real competition for a human mathematician. On the other hand, a full-blown introspective reasoner might turn out to be capable of anything that a human mathematician can do.

It is of interest to reflect upon how work on automated theorem proving fits into the present scheme. Automated theorem provers have been able to prove some very difficult theorems, but it is noteworthy that they do so by employing what are called 'domain specific heuristics'. These are reasoning strategies tailored specifically for a particular subject matter, and not of general applicability. In fact, the most difficult theorems to be proved by automated theorem provers have generally been proved by tailoring the proof procedures to the specific problem in ways that are chosen by a human operator rather than by the program itself.[28] This is not unreasonable if, as has usually been the case, the automated theorem prover is intended to serve as an electronic assistant to a human mathematician, but it does detract from the theoretical significance of the system's being able to do the proof. I would suggest that such a system is best viewed as an approximation to part of an introspective reasoner, with the human operator providing the introspection and practical deliberation that alters the default reasoning strategies of the automated reasoner. Accordingly, such results show little about the unaided powers of a default non-introspective reasoner.

The first step in constructing OSCAR concerns the default strategies the system will employ in searching for arguments. Although there is a massive literature on searching for arguments, I have not found it very helpful in the present context. This is for two reasons. First, most of

---

[28] For an overview, see Wos [1988].

the literature on automated deduction is concerned with what are called 'resolution-based systems'. Resolution is a particular form of argument, about which I will say more below. Although resolution refutation is complete for first-order logic, it is not at all obvious how to extend it to encompass defeasible reasoning. In particular, resolution-based systems are unable to do any kind of suppositional reasoning (for instance, conditionalization or reasoning by cases). Such a narrow view of arguments is provably unproblematic for deductive reasoning in the predicate calculus because the resulting system is still complete, but at this time we have no reason to expect it to be equally unproblematic for reasoning in general. Second, as I have indicated, the more impressive results in automated reasoning have been achieved by systems working under the direction of human operators, and as such they do not model default non-introspective reasoning.

The process of searching for arguments seems to be generally the same whether the arguments are deductive or defeasible. Accordingly, it has proven expedient to begin the construction of OSCAR by building a purely deductive reasoner. The deductive reasoner carries out the first of the three processes (searching for arguments) that comprise default theoretical reasoning. I will sketch the structure of the deductive reasoner and then discuss how it is modified to incorporate defeat and reinstatement, thus creating a general purpose default reasoner that does both deductive and defeasible reasoning.

An important feature of human reasoning that has often been overlooked by philosophers is that our rules for reasoning do not mandate the adoption of every belief for which we have good reasons. For instance, for any propositions P and Q, P is a good reason for $(P \lor Q)$, but we do not automatically adopt belief in every disjunction one of whose disjuncts we already believe. Gilbert Harman [1986] calls this 'clutter avoidance'. Our epistemic rules must honor the fact that we are information processors with a limited capacity for processing and storage. If belief adoption is not mandated simply by the possession of good reasons, what more is required? It seems clear that it has something to do with interests (in the sense of 'what interests us' rather than 'what is in our interest'). If we are interested in knowing the value of $23+57$, we reason differently than if we are interested in knowing what time it is in Moscow. We do not just reason randomly until we happen upon the answers to our questions. In short, our rules for belief formation involve interest-driven reasoning.

Once you begin computer modeling of theories of reasoning, it is obvious that reasoning must be constrained by interests, and this is at least implicit in all AI work on automated reasoning. No automated reasoning system could possibly work unless its behavior was affected by what it was trying to establish. I believe, however, that the work that has actually been done on automated reasoning suffers from inadequate theoretical foundations. A *theory* of interest-driven reasoning should precede construction of automated reasoning systems. I will sketch such a theory. I will begin by confining my attention to deductive reasoning, but the general framework of interest-driven reasoning will remain unchanged when we turn to non-deductive reasoning.

In trying to prove a theorem in mathematics or trying to construct a derivation in logic, we sometimes cast about more or less at random, drawing whatever conclusions we can until we eventually see some way to put them together to get to our desired conclusion. At other times we proceed in a much more deliberate fashion, in effect reasoning backward from our desired conclusion. Such backward reasoning is interest-driven *par excellence*. Our reasoning usually involves a combination of backward reasoning and random forward reasoning. So far this is unsurprising. AI theorists will recognize this as the distinction between forward chaining and backward chaining. The surprise comes next. It is natural to suppose that backward reasoning is just forward reasoning done in reverse and that in any given instance we could just reason in one direction or the other without combining the two. I was astonished to stumble upon considerations that show that this view of reasoning is fundamentally mistaken. There are profound differences between random forward reasoning and backward reasoning, and neither is replaceable by the other. They are both absolutely essential for reasoning, and there is a definite logic governing when to use one and when to use the other. The choice is not just a matter of convenience. We literally could not arrive at our conclusions in any but the simplest cases without using both kinds of reasoning. This point becomes obvious when we look at concrete examples of reasons. For instance, if we are investigating deductive reasoning in the propositional calculus, we might propose that the following are among the reasons we employ:

Backward reasons:

adjunction:	$\{p,q\}$ is a reason for $(p \mathbin{\&} q)$
addition:	p is a reason for $(p \vee q)$
	q is a reason for $(p \vee q)$
~~ introduction:	p is a reason for $\sim\sim p$

Forward reasons:

simplification:	$(p \mathbin{\&} q)$ is a reason for p
	$(p \mathbin{\&} q)$ is a reason for q
~~ elimination:	$\sim\sim p$ is a reason for p
modus ponens:	$\{(\sim p \vee q),p\}$ is a reason for q

It takes only a moment's reflection to realize that the reasons listed under 'backward reasons' are of use only in backward reasoning, and those listed under 'forward reasons' are of use only in random forward reasoning. For instance, consider addition. Suppose we could use addition in random forward reasoning. Then if we adopted p, we would be led to adopt every disjunction containing p as one disjunct. But there are infinitely many such disjunctions, and most are useless in any given problem. In point of fact, we only use addition when we have some reason to be interested in the resulting disjunction. Much the same point can be made about adjunction. Suppose we could use it in random forward reasoning, and we adopted p and q. Then we would be led to adopt $(p \& q)$. That does not seem so bad, but it would not stop there. We would go on to adopt $[(p \& q) \& p]$, $(q \& p)$, $[(q \& p) \& (p \& q)]$, $[(q \& p) \& [(p \& q) \& p]]$, $(p \& [(q \& p) \& [(p \& q) \& p]])$, and so on without limit. Obviously, we do not do that, and a reasoning system that performed in this way would be crippled. This largely useless reasoning would continually get in its way, taking up its resources and preventing it from making more useful inferences.

The use of simplification in backward reasoning would be even more catastrophic. Suppose we are interested in q. Backward reasoning with simplification would lead us to adopt interest in $(p \& q)$, for *every* p, and then backward reasoning with adjunction (which is presumably acceptable) would lead us to adopt interest in p. Thus interest in anything would automatically lead to interest in everything, which would completely vitiate the interest restrictions in interest-driven reasoning. Similar reflection on the other reasons indicates that in each case, they can function only in the category in which they are listed.

The somewhat surprising conclusion to be drawn from this is that some reasons are of use in backward reasoning, and others are of use in random forward reasoning, and individual reasons may not play both roles. In fact, I have yet to find any reason that can play both roles (although I would stop short of affirming that as a general principle). Reasons can be classified as *forward reasons*, which can be used in a forward direction for deriving beliefs from beliefs, and *backward reasons*, which can be used in a backward direction for deriving interests from interests. Given the distinction between these two kinds of reasons, linear reasoning proceeds in terms of the following rules:

R-DEDUCE:

If X is a forward reason for q, and you adopt some member of X and already believe the others, then adopt q.

INTEREST-ADOPTION:

If you are interested in q, and X is a backward reason for q, then become interested in the members of X. If you already believe all the members of X then adopt q.

DISCHARGE-INTEREST:

If you are interested in the members of X as a way of getting q, and you adopt some member of X and already believe the others, then adopt q.

These rules form the basis for a simple automated reasoning system.[29] It is not yet a very good reasoning system, however, for reasons that I will explain next.

4.5 Suppositional Reasoning

A point that has often been overlooked by epistemologists, and to a large extent by AI theorists as well, but not by logicians, is that reasoning is *suppositional*. Epistemologists have tended to adopt a linear model of reasoning according to which all arguments are linear arguments. Recall that linear arguments do nothing but infer new conclusions from previously established conclusions that constitute reasons for them. The simplest way to see that this is inadequate is to note that deductive reasoning can lead to *a priori* knowledge of "truths of reason". For instance, we can obtain conclusions like $[(p \& q) \supset q]$ or $(p \lor \sim p)$ that do not depend upon any premises. Linear reasoning can draw conclusions only from previously adopted beliefs, so such *a priori* knowledge cannot be obtained by linear reasoning. Instead, we employ several kinds of rules enabling us to embed "subsidiary arguments" within the main arguments and draw conclusions within the main argument that are related to conclusions drawn in the subsidiary arguments. Familiar examples are rules governing conditionalization, *reductio ad absurdum*, reasoning by cases (dilemma), and some form of universal generalization.

The use of subsidiary arguments constitutes *suppositional reasoning*, wherein we suppose something "for the sake of argument", reason using the supposition in the same way we reason about beliefs and interests nonsuppositionally, and then on the basis of conclusions drawn using the

---

[29] Harman [1986] (p. 26) suggests that there should be a general constraint to the effect that a belief should be adopted only if an agent is interested in it. That is to assimilate all reasoning to backward reasoning and it ignores random forward reasoning. That makes the proposal unworkable, because both kinds of reasoning are essential in actually being able to draw conclusions.

supposition we draw further conclusions that do not depend upon the supposition. For instance, in conditionalization, in order to establish a conditional $(p \supset q)$, we "suppose" the antecedent, try to derive the consequent from that supposition, and then "discharge" the supposition to infer the conditional. Similarly, in *reductio ad absurdum*, if we are trying to establish p, we may suppose $\sim p$, show that that leads to a contradiction, and then discharge the supposition to infer p. In both of these kinds of reasoning, what is crucial is the use of suppositions to get conclusions related to our desired conclusions and their subsequent discharge. Within the supposition, we reason as if the supposed propositions were believed, using all the rules for adoption and interest adoption that are used in connection with linear reasoning. It is fairly straightforward to build an automated reasoning system for the predicate calculus that does interest-driven suppositional reasoning of the sort I have been describing.[30] This is incorporated into OSCAR.

It is extremely interesting to compare OSCAR with more conventional work on automated reasoning in AI. OSCAR is based upon some very simple ideas. There is nothing particularly tricky about the way OSCAR is built. And yet OSCAR bears almost no similarity to other automated reasoning systems.[31] Most of those systems are based upon what is called 'resolution refutation'. *Resolution* is the following inference rule:

If for some $i \leq n$ and $j \leq m$, $p_i = \ulcorner \sim q_j \urcorner$, then from $(p_1 \vee \ldots \vee p_n)$ and $(q_1 \vee \ldots \vee q_m)$, infer $(p_1 \vee \ldots \vee p_{i-1} \vee p_{i+1} \vee \ldots \vee p_n \vee q_1 \vee \ldots \vee q_{j-1} \vee q_{j+1} \vee \ldots \vee q_m)$.

Resolution refutation is a form of *reductio ad absurdum* that proceeds by first reducing the premises and the negation of the desired conclusion to prenex conjunctive normal form and then repeatedly applying resolution to the result until a contradiction is obtained.[32] Resolution refutation was introduced by J. A. Robinson [1965], and is provably

---

[30] This system is described in my [1988c]

[31] The only major exception is Pelletier's THINKER [1985]. It is probably significant that Pelletier is a philosopher. OSCAR stands in stark contrast with, for instance, the systems of Lusk and Overbeek [1984], Lusk, McCune and Overbeek [1985], Stickel [1985], [1986], Wos and Winker [1983], and others too numerous to mention. Systems to which OSCAR bears a distant resemblance are HARP (Oppacher and Suen [1985]), TPS (Andrews et al [1983], [1985]), and the UT Natural Deduction Prover (Bledsoe [1977] and [1983], Bledsoe and Tyson [1975]), and the systems of Murray [1982] and Nevins [1974].

[32] For a more detailed description, see Genesereth and Nilson [1987], or any other contemporary text in AI.

complete for the predicate calculus. I think it is clear to everyone, however, that resolution refutation is not descriptive of human reasoning. That was never the intent of the AI systems based upon it. Instead, they were designed with the idea that computers are better at certain kinds of "symbol crunching" than human beings, and automated reasoning systems can take advantage of that. This always struck me as reasonable, and so my expectation was that OSCAR would be slow compared to other automated reasoning systems. Thus I have been surprised to find that OSCAR is actually quite fast.

There are no established standards for comparing reasoning systems, but there are a few problems that have been run on a wide variety of reasoning systems and provide at least rough comparisons. I have tested OSCAR on (a corrected version of) Pelletier's [1986] problems. OSCAR is written in COMMON LISP, and running on a Symbolics 3600, OSCAR takes only a few seconds (on the average) to do each of Pelletier's propositional and predicate calculus problems. Many of these are too easy to be indicative of much, but one of the harder problems is the Schubert steamroller problem. That is the following problem in the predicate calculus:

$(\forall x)(Wx \supset Ax)$ $(\forall x)(\forall y)[(Cx \ \& \ By) \supset Mxy]$

$(\forall x)(Fx \supset Ax)$ $(\forall x)(\forall y)[(Sx \ \& \ By) \supset Mxy]$

$(\forall x)(Bx \supset Ax)$ $(\forall x)(\forall y)[(Bx \ \& \ Fy) \supset Mxy]$

$(\forall x)(Cx \supset Ax)$ $(\forall x)(\forall y)[(Fx \ \& \ Wy) \supset Mxy]$

$(\forall x)(Sx \supset Ax)$ $(\forall x)(\forall y)[(Wx \ \& \ Fy) \supset \sim Exy]$

$(\exists w)Ww$ $(\forall x)(\forall y)[(Wx \ \& \ Gy) \supset \sim Exy]$

$(\exists f)Ff$ $(\forall x)(\forall y)[(Bx \ \& \ Cy) \supset Exy]$

$(\exists b)Bb$ $(\forall x)(\forall y)[(Bx \ \& \ Sy) \supset \sim Exy]$

$(\exists c)Cc$ $(\forall x)[Cx \supset (\exists y)(Py \ \& \ Exy)]$

$(\exists s)Ss$ $(\forall x)[Sx \supset (\exists y)(Py \ \& \ Exy)]$

$(\exists g)Gg$ $(\forall x)(Gx \supset Px)$

$(\forall x)[Ax \supset [(\forall w)(Pw \supset Exw) \lor (\forall y)((Ay \ \& \ (Myx \ \& \ (\exists z)(Pz \ \& \ Eyz))) \supset Exy)]]$

$$(\exists x)(\exists y)[(Ax \ \& \ Ay) \ \& \ (\exists z)[Exy \ \& \ (Gz \ \& \ Eyz)]]$$

This is a slightly whimsical symbolization of the following:

Wolves, foxes, birds, caterpillars, and snails are animals, and there are some of each of them. Also, there are some grains, and grains are plants. Every animal either likes to eat all plants or all animals much smaller than itself that like to eat some plants. Caterpillars and snails are much smaller than birds, which are much smaller than foxes, which in turn are much smaller than wolves. Wolves do not like to eat foxes or grains, while birds like to eat caterpillars but not snails. Caterpillars and snails like to eat some

plants. Therefore, there is an animal that likes to eat a grain-eating
animal.[33]

Many respected automated reasoning systems that are considered fast
take a long time to do this problem. A system due to Mark Stickel (not
his latest system) was reported to do this problem in 2 hours 53 minutes
on a Symbolics 3600 computer, and the well-known ITP theorem prover,
operating on a much faster computer and written in Pascal (faster than
LISP), was reported to do the problem in 11 minutes.[34] The fastest
published time is attributed to a current system of Stickel, which does
the problem in 6 seconds on a Symbolics 3600.[35] It is noteworthy that
this time was obtained by using the system interactively in a way that
allowed the human operator to tailor the reasoning strategies to this
particular problem. Stickel notes that a more natural initial choice of
strategy resulted in the system's taking 1 hour 35 minutes. By way of
contrast, OSCAR does this problem in 13 seconds on a Symbolics 3600
and does this while operating in a completely automatic way. OSCAR
seems equally fast on other problems.

As I have noted, most theorem provers are designed to be used
somewhat interactively, allowing the human operator to choose different
proof strategies for different problems. That is desirable if they are to
be used as tools, but it detracts from the theoretical significance of
speed results. After all, given any valid formula P, we could adopt a
rule saying ⌜Infer P⌝. Of course, no one would actually incorporate a
rule like this into a theorem prover, but this represents just the extreme
end of a continuum. Fast times using strategies chosen especially for a
particular problem may show little unless some theoretical rationale can
be provided for the choice of strategy and the rationale built into the
theorem prover itself so that it can choose its own strategies. In this
connection it should be noted that OSCAR is a purely automatic
theorem prover, using the same strategies on all problems. After all,
the intent of OSCAR is to model the deductive fragment of the default
theoretical reasoner.

It is interesting to inquire into the source of OSCAR's surprising
speed. It seems that OSCAR is fast because it is efficient. OSCAR's
proof of the Steamroller problem is 42 lines long. In searching for the
proof, OSCAR performs only 5 unnecessary inferences. By contrast,
even on Stickel's fastest time his theorem prover performed 479

---

[33] Pelletier [1986], p. 203.

[34] These times are reported in Cohn [1985].

[35] Stickel [1986].

inferences, and when his theorem prover was used non-interactively, it performed 245,820 inferences. Stickel also provides data on some other theorem provers doing the Schubert steamroller problem, according to which they performed between 1,106 and 26,190 inference steps. This means that between 91% and 99.98% of the inferences performed by these theorem provers were unnecessary, as opposed to a real measure of 11% for OSCAR.

To take another example, a problem of moderate difficulty that has been run on a number of theorem provers is that of showing that a group is commutative if the square of every element is the identity element. This problem is from Chang and Lee [1973]. Letting '$Pxyz$' symbolize '$x \cdot y = z$', this problem can be formulated as follows:

given: $(\forall x)Pxex$
$(\forall x)Pexx$
$(\forall x)(\forall y)(\forall z)(\forall u)(\forall v)(\forall w)[(Pxyu \ \& \ (Pyzv \ \& \ Puzw)) \supset Pxvw]$
$(\forall x)(\forall y)(\forall z)(\forall u)(\forall v)(\forall w)[(Pxyu \ \& \ (Pyzv \ \& \ Pxvw)) \supset Puzw]$
$(\forall x)Pxxe$
$Pabc$
prove: $Pbac$

OSCAR's proof of this theorem is 15 lines long. In searching for the proof, OSCAR performs only 4 unnecessary inferences. By contrast, Wilson and Minker [1988] give performance data for this problem on four theorem provers (this is the problem they call 'Group2'). Where 21% of OSCAR's inferences are unnecessary, those theorems provers performed 79%, 87%, 96%, and 96% unnecessary inferences. Furthermore, these were presumably the results after tailoring the theorem provers to the problem to get the best performance. Stickel's new PTTP (*Prolog technology theorem prover*) solves this problem in a startling .284 seconds (OSCAR requires 8 seconds), but performs 1,136 inferences in the process. In terms of sheer speed, nothing can hold a candle to Stickel's PTTP on this problem, and I do not mean for these remarks to detract from its significance, but the percentage of unnecessary inferences is perhaps indicative of what can be expected from a resolution theorem prover that does not use strategies carefully tailored to the individual problem.

These redundancy figures hold up across a wide variety of problems. In solving Pelletier's propositional calculus problems (numbers 1-17), OSCAR's average percentage of unnecessary inferences is only 8%, and on the pure predicate calculus problems (numbers 18-47), the redundancy figure only goes up to 26%. It appears that OSCAR's interest constraints are extremely effective in eliminating unnecessary inferences. This would seem to be the key to OSCAR's surprising speed.

OSCAR was not constructed with speed in mind and is not even written very efficiently. A sustained effort at optimization would accelerate the system appreciably. OSCAR's speed does not result from fancy programming but from the general architecture of the system. This suggests that that architecture may have an inherent advantage over resolution theorem provers. As this is the architecture of human reasoning, this would seem to show something very interesting about human beings.

The rules for interest-driven reasoning comprise the reasoning strategies built into the default theoretical reasoning module. These are strategies available to the reasoner without his having to engage in practical reasoning about how to reason. They are part of the makeup of a non-introspective reasoner. Of course, a human being is an introspective reasoner, so humans often reason in more sophisticated ways than the system just described. However, an introspective reasoner must be built on top of a non-introspective reasoner, so the present system represents the starting point for the construction of a more general reasoner.

4.6 Defeasible Reasoning

A great deal of work in AI has tried to reduce all reasoning to deductive reasoning.[36] It is important to emphasize that that is not the intent of OSCAR. In the previous section, I focused on deductive reasoning only as a convenience. The general theory of interest-driven reasoning is intended to be applicable to all reasoning, deductive or nondeductive. Let us turn then to nondeductive reasoning.

The first success of the OSCAR project was the construction of an automated reasoning system that does reasonably sophisticated defeasible reasoning.[37] It was not a total success, however, because it was based upon some simplifying assumptions. It had three main shortcomings. First, it was not interest-driven. It drew every conclusion it could draw given its input. Second, it did not do suppositional reasoning and accordingly could not accommodate much purely deductive reasoning. Third, it ignored variations in strength between reasons, taking all reasons to be equally good. The present version of OSCAR overcomes all of these shortcomings. It is constructed by extending the deductive reasoner described above. The details are too complex to present here, but I will briefly sketch how the deductive reasoner must be modified to accommodate defeasible reasoning.

---

[36] The *locus classicus* of this is McCarthy [1977].

[37] This is described in Pollock [1987].

Undercutting Defeat

Defeasible reasoning is based upon three kinds of procedures: (a) those governing argument construction and belief adoption, (b) those governing belief retraction in the face of defeat, and (c) those governing reinstatement when defeaters are themselves retracted. It is convenient to separate the treatment of undercutting defeaters and rebutting defeaters. The adoption of an undercutting defeater affects these three processes in two ways: (1) it can block a new inference that employs the defeated prima facie reason; (2) it can defeat an inference already made, necessitating the retraction of propositions already adopted. Case (1) will be handled by building qualifications into the adoption rules, requiring OSCAR to check for the presence of defeaters before making an inference. Case (2) is handled by telling OSCAR that whenever it adopts $\sim(\Pi X \gg q)$ where X is a prima facie reason for q, it must check to see whether it believes q on the basis of X, and if so OSCAR must retract q. Both kinds of defeat must be recorded in such a way that if OSCAR subsequently retracts belief in $\sim(\Pi X \gg q)$ then it can reinstate q and continue any reasoning based upon q that was interrupted as a result of the adoption of the defeater.

Backward reasoning can also be defeated. If a prima facie reason is defeated, we do not want it used in subsequent backward reasoning, because this may lead to endless useless backward reasoning that can never lead to belief adoption. Accordingly, the rule of INTEREST-ADOPTION must be sensitive to the presence of defeaters. For the same reason, if OSCAR acquires a defeater for a prima facie reason already used in backward reasoning, OSCAR must retract interests derived from that prima facie reason in order to prevent further useless backward reasoning. This must be done in such a way that interests can be reinstated if the defeater is subsequently retracted.

Circular Reasoning

In defeasible reasoning, the possibility of circular reasoning creates difficulties of a sort not encountered in deductive reasoning. For instance, suppose the system engages in circular reasoning as in figure 5. Having already adopted P on the basis of R, inferring it again on the basis of $(P\&Q)$ does not itself lead to the system's having beliefs it should not have, but if OSCAR subsequently retracted R, this would not result in P being retracted because OSCAR would still have a reason for P, namely, $(P\&Q)$. Such circular reasoning is blocked by precluding OSCAR from adopting p if it is already believed. Notice, however, that if OSCAR could have gotten a conclusion in more than one way, and the way it actually got the conclusion is defeated or retracted, then we

Figure 5. Circular reasoning

want to make sure that the other reasoning chains "reawaken" and the conclusion is readopted on another basis.

Rebutting Defeat

Rebutting defeat occurs when we have a reason for p but also have a reason for $\neg p$. If we take account of the strengths of reasons, the reason for p may be significantly stronger than the reason for $\neg p$, in which case we should believe p and reject $\neg p$. But if the reasons are of roughly similar strength, then we should not believe either p or $\neg p$; that is, we have a case of collective rebutting defeat. For expository purposes, I will make the simplifying assumption that all reasons are of the same strength. Consequently, all cases of rebutting defeat become cases of collective defeat.

It turns out that the most difficult task in the construction of a defeasible reasoner is to handle collective defeat properly. Collective rebutting defeat arises when an inference to a proposition p would otherwise be performed but $\neg p$ has already been adopted. In that case we must make three kinds of adjustments: (1) withdraw belief in $\neg p$; (2) withdraw belief in anything used deductively in obtaining $\neg p$; (3) withdraw belief in anything depending upon $\neg p$ or something withdrawn in (2). The propositions withdrawn in (2) and those withdrawn in (3) have a different status because those in (3) can be reinstated by acquiring a new reason for them, but new reasons for the propositions in (2) just expand the collective defeat. We might say that $\neg p$ and those propositions in category (2) are *rebutted* (*simpliciter*), while those in category (3) are *indirectly rebutted*.

Collective defeat occurs initially when we acquire a reason for the negation of a proposition that has previously been adopted. A simple example is diagrammed in figure 6. Defeasible inferences are indicated by broken arrows and nondefeasible inferences by solid arrows. Given a case of collective defeat having this structure, neither q nor $\neg q$ should be believed. q is a deductive consequence of P_{13} and P_{14}, so they

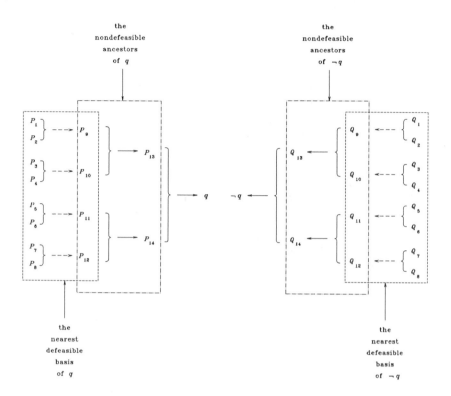

Figure 6. A simple case of collective defeat

cannot both be believed either. As the assumption is being made that all reasons are of the same strength, there is no basis for choosing between P_{13} and P_{14}, so neither should be believed. Similarly, P_{13} is a deductive consequence of P_9 and P_{10}, so they must both be withdrawn. In this manner we work backward from q and $\neg q$ withdrawing each proposition used deductively in getting q or $\neg q$ until we reach the nearest defeasible inferences underlying the contradiction. The prima facie reasons involved in these nearest defeasible inferences have thus undergone rebutting defeat. Their antecedents are not withdrawn, but their conclusions are. The propositions withdrawn in this way comprise *the nondefeasible ancestors of q* and $\neg q$, and the defeasible steps comprise their *nearest defeasible bases*.

It may seem odd that we withdraw all of the nondefeasible ancestors of q and $\neg q$. Why not just withdraw some of them? If we had better reasons for some than for others, that would be the reasonable course, but on the simplifying assumption that all reasons are equally good, there is no nonarbitrary way of choosing which nondefeasible ancestors to withdraw. Furthermore, that a case like this is structured as a conflict between q and $\neg q$ is largely an historical accident. Given any non-defeasible ancestor p of either q or $\neg q$, the argument can be restructured as a conflict between p and $\neg p$. For instance, from P_{13} and P_{14} we can deduce q, but then it follows that we can also deduce $\neg P_{13}$ from $\neg q$ and P_{14}. Thus we could just as well restructure the argument as in figure 7.

Expanding Collective Defeat

A proposition can undergo collective rebutting defeat for more than one reason at the same time. Multiple sources of collective rebutting defeat arise from the fact that if q is collectively rebutted then acquiring a new reason for q does not reinstate it. Instead, it just leads to new arguments for the same inconsistent conclusions and hence it leads to

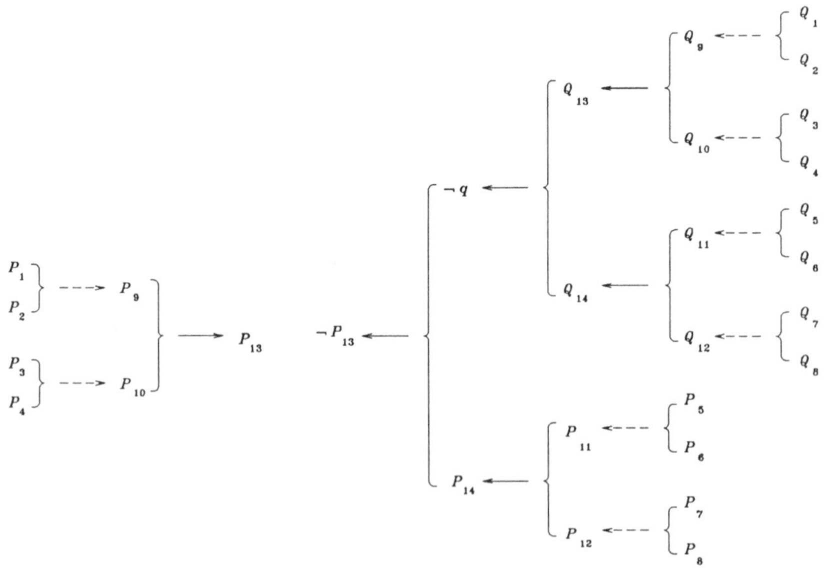

Figure 7. Restructing collective defeat

further collective defeat. For instance, if we modify figure 6 as in figure 8 by adding a new argument for P_9, we then have two separate (but overlapping) arguments arg_1 and arg_3 for $\neg q$, each of which conflicts with the original argument arg_2 for q and constitutes a separate source of collective rebutting defeat. To handle this we need a rule POS-REBUT which retracts the new contingent nondefeasible ancestors of P_9 and records the new collective defeat.

A similar, although simpler, situation arises when we acquire a new argument for the negation of a collectively rebutted proposition, as in figure 9. In this case arg_1 and arg_2 enter into collective defeat. This situation is handled by adding a rule NEG-REBUT which retracts the contingent nondefeasible ancestors of $\neg P_{13}$ and records the new collective defeat.

Reinstatement from Collective Rebutting Defeat

Propositions defeated by collective rebutting defeat can be reinstated by removing the source of that defeat. Such defeat results from having a collection of prima facie reasons whose conclusions are jointly deductively inconsistent. If one of those prima facie reasons is removed, that has the effect of reinstating reasoning based upon the others. Where X is a prima facie reason for p and it enters into collective defeat with some other prima facie reasons, this reason can be removed either by adopting an undercutting defeater for it or by retracting some proposition in X. In either case, the other prima facie reasons are reinstated.

This has been just a rough sketch of how the interest-driven deductive reasoner is modified to turn OSCAR into a defeasible reasoner. It gives little more than the flavor of the defeasible reasoner. The actual reasoner is made considerably more complicated by the fact that it allows reasons to vary in strength. This has the consequence that rebutting defeat is not automatically a case of collective defeat. The details of this are too complex to be pursued here. They will be presented in full in a future book. The final result is a general-purpose interest-driven suppositional deductive and defeasible reasoner. This will eventually provide the inference engine for the implementation of more specific kinds of reasoning of the sorts that will be described in section 6.[38]

---

[38] For a more detailed account of this inference engine, see Pollock [1988].

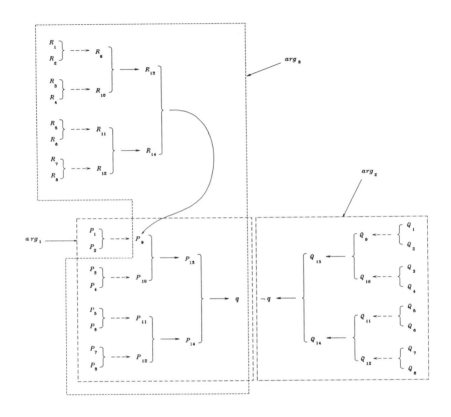

Figure 8. Operation of POS-REBUT

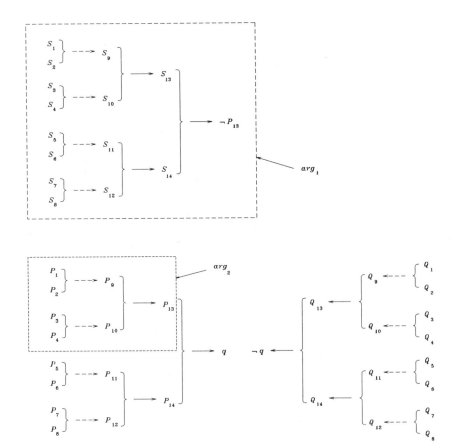

Figure 9. Operation of NEG-REBUT

5. Introspective Reasoners

Both defeasible reasoning and practical reasoning about problem-solving strategies require the reasoner to think about its own thoughts. For instance, in defeasible reasoning a pervasive kind of defeater is a *reliability defeater*. If X is a prima facie reason for p, a reliability defeater arises from discovering that in circumstances of the present sort, X is not a reliable indicator of the truth of p. For instance, ⌐x is illuminated by red lights, and something's looking red is not a reliable indicator of its being red when it is so illuminated⌐ is a reliability defeater for ⌐x looks red to me⌐ as a prima facie reason for ⌐x is red⌐. The establishment of reliability defeaters requires us to be able to conclude inductively that reasoning of a certain sort tends to be unreliable under specifiable circumstances, and that requires that we are able to monitor our own reasoning and discover that beliefs we adopted at some earlier point are false. We must have a system of mental representation that makes this kind of reasoning possible. We can distinguish between low-level reasoning, which is not about thought, and higher-level reasoning, which is. Ordinarily, we engage in only low-level reasoning, but special circumstances can require higher-level reasoning. Similarly, practical reasoning normally proceeds in terms of desires without involving thought about desires, but sometimes we must think about our desires (for instance, when we become critical of them). So the ability to think about thoughts is essential for sophisticated reasoning. A reasoner with this capability is an *introspective reasoner*. It was argued in chapter 5 that introspection involves thinking about thoughts syntactically rather than semantically. Introspection apprises us of the occurrence of thoughts with recognizable "qualitative" characteristics, but those qualitative characteristics are connected only contingently with semantical features of the thoughts. Only an introspective reasoner will be capable of using practical reasoning to override its own default strategies for theoretical reasoning.

An introspective reasoning system must incorporate rules that determine when to engage in higher-level thought, and it must incorporate rules concerning how to go about it. The former are rules prescribing when the system should attend to its thoughts. Such attention is interest-driven. The general phenomenon of attention is of considerable interest to cognitive psychologists, but there is no commonly accepted theory of what attention involves.[39] My suggestion is that we

---

[39] For a review of contemporary theories of attention in cognitive psychology, see Cowin [1988].

should distinguish between *intellectually driven* attention and *nonintellectual* attention. The former is a part of interest-driven reasoning.

An introspective reasoner must be able to (1) monitor its own reasoning, forming beliefs about what it is thinking and the basis for those thoughts, and (2) evaluate thoughts as true or false. The latter is not just a matter of revising the earlier beliefs but of forming beliefs *about* whether the earlier beliefs are true. Only in that way can the reasoner inductively generalize about what kinds of reasoning are apt to be reliable or unreliable in yielding true conclusions under particular circumstances. Monitoring and evaluating thoughts are two distinct operations. Both require some way to think about thoughts—something analogous to quotation names of sentences in the language of thought. Without trying to say just what this involves, if p is a sentence in the language of thought, let «p» be its quotation name. Introspective monitoring will then proceed in terms of interest-driven rules something like the following:

If you adopt belief in p on the basis of the reason $\{q_1,\ldots,q_n\}$,
then:
(1)   if you are interested in whether you believe p, adopt
       the belief $\ulcorner$I believe «p»$\urcorner$;
(2)   if you are interested in the basis on which you believe
       p, adopt the belief $\ulcorner$I believe «p» on the basis of
       «q_1»,$\ldots$,«q_n»$\urcorner$.[40]

Whatever the precise form for these rules should be, I will take them to comprise the *introspective monitoring module*. Notice that on this account, introspective monitoring is a purely computational matter. It does not involve the addition of a new sense organ but just rules "moving up a level" and forming beliefs *about* beliefs. Most reasoning involves no such level shifting, and I will call it *planar reasoning*. Planar reasoning can still involve beliefs about beliefs, but it is distinguished by the fact that it does not involve any such moving up and down of levels. In planar reasoning, we reason about beliefs just as we reason about anything else.

Introspective reasoning involves thinking about thoughts (using

---

[40] In light of the results of Nisbett and Wilson [1977], discussed in chapter 1, it might seem dubious that we can introspect the basis upon which we believe something. This must not be construed as introspecting a cause, however. In order for defeasible reasoning to work, the system must keep track of the bases upon which it believes something. These are stored in a data structure, and what we are introspecting is the contents of that data structure.

quotation names) and judging them to be true or false. I will call such reasoning *T-reasoning*, and the computational module comprising T-reasoning will be the *T-module*. The default theoretical reasoning module can be viewed as consisting of a planar reasoning module, the introspective monitoring module, and the T-module combined as in figure 10. This is all part of default theoretical reasoning, because the system must perform this much reasoning *before* it can apply practical reasoning to the question of how to reason.

The obvious candidate for the rules for T-reasoning involves an interest-driven analogue of Tarski's T-schema:[41]

(1) p is a backward reason for $\ulcorner «p» \text{ is true}\urcorner$.
(2) $\ulcorner «p» \text{ is true}\urcorner$ is a forward reason for p.

The problem is that incorporating these rules into a reasoner will lead immediately to the liar paradox. The resulting inconsistency will be catastrophic in any reasoner that is able to draw all possible deductive consequences from its beliefs. There is a massive literature in philosophical logic regarding how to avoid the liar paradox, and that all becomes relevant here.[42] Thus the liar paradox, which initially appears to

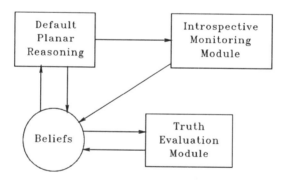

Figure 10. The structure of default theoretical reasoning

---

[41] Tarski [1956].

[42] For a sampling of the literature on the liar paradox, see Martin [1970], [1984].

be a purely logical puzzle, becomes resurrected as an obstacle to AI. I think that this will not be unusual. A great many familiar philosophical problems arise in a new guise when we start modeling actual reasoning.

Within the context of describing an introspective reasoner, I am tempted by a radical solution to the liar paradox. I am inclined to think that, despite the inconsistency, the T-schema is an accurate description of our rules for reasoning about truth. Any attempt to avoid the liar paradox by restricting the T-schema seems *ad hoc* and unmotivated. My suggestion is that the solution to building an introspective reasoner that does not collapse in the face of the liar paradox lies in damage control rather than damage avoidance. When an introspective reasoner gets into trouble, it is able to apply practical reasoning to the situation and back out gracefully without necessarily solving the problem that led to the difficulty. This is a general phenomenon of considerable importance. It is illustrated by a number of phenomena. For instance, mathematicians tend to be very cautious about accepting the results of complicated proofs. But the proof, if correct, is simply an exercise in deductive reasoning. How is such caution possible? Why doesn't their rational architecture force them to accept the conclusion automatically? The answer seems to be that they have learned from experience that complicated deductive reasoning is error prone. Practical reasoning about theoretical reasoning has the power to intervene and prevent acceptance of the conclusion until the proof is adequately checked. That practical reasoning has this power is just a brute fact about our rational architecture.

The gambler's fallacy provides another illustration of this phenomenon. Contrary to popular opinion, reasoning in accordance with the gambler's fallacy is not automatically irrational. Such reasoning proceeds in terms of a perfectly good defeasible reason of the form ⌜Most A's are B's, and this is an A, so (defeasibly) this is a B⌝. In the case of the gambler's fallacy, there is a defeater for this prima facie reason, but it is surprisingly difficult to say precisely what the defeater is.[43] Most people who consciously refrain from reasoning in accordance with the gambler's fallacy do so not because they understand precisely what is wrong with it but because they know from experience that they get into trouble when they reason that way. Again, it is practical reasoning that intervenes to prevent the theoretical reasoning.

---

[43] For a detailed discussion of the reasoning involved in the gambler's fallacy and defeater responsible for making the reasoning ultimately incorrect, see chapter 9 of my [1989].

A related phenomenon is common in any intellectual discipline. A researcher formulating a theory will frequently encounter difficulties that he cannot answer in the early stages of the investigation, but this does not automatically move him to give up his investigation. He may suspect that there is a way for the theory to handle the difficulty even if he cannot initially see what it is. This can be a perfectly reasonable attitude based upon the observation that the theory has been successful in avoiding many other difficulties whose solutions were not initially obvious. If the theorist were constrained to follow the canons of theoretical reasoning blindly, he would have to give up the theory until he is able to resolve the difficulty, but because he anticipates that he will eventually be able to resolve it, he instead retains the theory and continues to look for a solution to the problem while developing the theory in other ways. This example is particularly interesting because the theorist may literally have inconsistent beliefs but postpone retracting any of them. Instead of retracting the beliefs, he retains them but does not draw any conclusions from the resulting contradiction. Practical reasoning imposes a kind of damage control that encapsulates the problem until a solution is found.

My suggestion is that precisely the same phenomenon is involved in the liar paradox. Reasoning about the liar sentence gets us into cognitive difficulties. We do not immediately see our way out of them, but we do not simply go crazy as a result. Instead, practical reasoning intervenes to encapsulate the problem until we find a solution. The difference between this case and the previous case is that there may be no solution to the liar paradox. If the T-schema is an accurate description of part of our rational architecture, then our rational architecture is logically inconsistent, and there is nothing we can do about it. However, for an introspective reasoner, that need not be catastrophic.

All of these examples illustrate that in an introspective reasoner, practical reasoning can intervene to prevent theoretical reasoning that would otherwise occur. Such intervention does not result from the mere fact that we would prefer not to adopt certain conclusions that are repugnant to us for one reason or another. The intervention results from the threat of *purely cognitive* difficulties. At this stage it is not clear how to give a precise formulation of the rules of practical reasoning that are involved.

6. Some Substantive Reasons

The preceding sections have addressed the abstract structure of reasoning. In an actual cognizer, this abstract structure is filled out with an array of substantive reasons and defeaters, thus enabling the cognizer to reason about concrete situations. These substantive reasons govern reasoning about the perceivable properties of objects, reasoning with beliefs supplied by memory, inductive and probabilistic reasoning, spatio-temporal reasoning, mathematical reasoning, and so forth. Some of these reasons have been the subject of extensive epistemological investigation, and we can make use of the results of that investigation in building a person. In my [1986] and [1989], I have given a general account of much of human epistemology, and I propose to model the construction of OSCAR on that account. The details are not always uncontroversial, but they are defended in those works, so I will not try to defend them here. In this section, I will sketch, largely without defense, a general account of some of the substantive reasons that play a central role in human reasoning about the world.

6.1 Perception
Perception begins with stimuli impinging on the sense organs and culminates in introspectible sensory states. Intellection then takes over and makes inferences about the cognizer's surroundings. The epistemologist (*qua* epistemologist) confines his attention to the last step, although it now seems apparent that the hardest part of the task of endowing a machine with sense perception must already have been accomplished by that point. Current theories of vision involve a great deal of complicated non-introspectible processing preceding the production of the introspectible sensory state.[44] The nature of this processing can be discovered only by empirical investigation.

The philosopher's task begins when the hardest part is completed. Reasoning begins with the introspectible output of our perceptual system. This provides the "data" from which the system reasons. There is a problem regarding exactly what form the data take. Epistemologists have traditionally adopted the *doxastic assumption*, according to which the justifiedness of a belief is a function exclusively of one's overall set of beliefs. The rationale for this assumption is that in deciding what to believe, we can take account of something only insofar as we have a belief about it. Thus all that can rationally affect our deliberations are other beliefs. Given the doxastic assumption, it follows that we must

---

[44] For instance, see Marr [1982].

regard perception as outputting beliefs, because only they can provide the input to our reasoning system. This leads inevitably to some kind of foundationalist theory according to which reasoning begins from *self-justifying* perceptual beliefs. These are supposed to be beliefs that are justified simply by virtue of our having them, and then they provide the basis for all other justified belief. Unfortunately, this view of perception is subject to a very simple objection. First, the only beliefs that could be self-justifying in this sense are "appearance beliefs"—beliefs about how things appear to us—rather than beliefs about the objective physical properties of our surroundings.[45] But second, in normal perception, we form no beliefs about how things appear to us. We just form beliefs about how things are. For instance, if you look out the window at the campus, you will come to believe that there are buildings, trees, and people walking around, but you will not acquire beliefs on the order of "Something looks red to me". Such thoughts rarely cross your mind unless something about the situation makes you distrust your senses and turn your attention inward to reflect upon how things appear to you. For this reason, foundationalist theories cannot possibly be right. Reasoning does not start from beliefs about how things appear to us.[46] On the other hand, the output of perception must be instrumental in determining what we ought to believe about our surroundings. It follows that it must be the perceptual states themselves (that is, things appearing to us in certain ways) rather than our beliefs about the perceptual states that determine what we ought to believe. This would seem unexceptionable were it not that it conflicts with the doxastic assumption.

The solution to this problem is to reject the doxastic assumption. The rationale for the doxastic assumption was that in deciding what to believe, we can take account of something only insofar as we have beliefs about it, and so in particular we can only take account of perceptual states insofar as we have beliefs about them. This reasoning has been very influential, and virtually every epistemologist has succumbed to it, but there is a simple response to it. This is that belief is not under voluntary control, and we do not literally decide what to believe. That is not what epistemic justification is all about. The rules describing what we "ought to do" in belief formation are not rules of practical reasoning guiding deliberate behavior. Instead, they are rules describing the operation of an embedded system of intellection which, although it operates automatically, is subject to interference from other cognitive systems. As I urged in section 2, the use of normative

---

[45] If this seems doubtful, see my [1986], pp. 59ff.

[46] For a more detailed discussion of this point, see my [1986], pp. 61ff.

language in describing reasoning gets its point from the fact that intellection can be overridden.[47]

Having rejected the doxastic assumption, we are free to suppose that intellection appeals directly to perceptual states in determining what beliefs to adopt about our surroundings. In other words, the starting point for reasoning is nondoxastic perceptual states, not beliefs. This allows us to accommodate perception as a source of belief by adopting principles like the following:

(1) x's looking red to S is a prima facie reason for S to think that
      x is red.

This must be augmented with an account of the defeaters for this prima facie reason. The most important defeater is probably the "reliability defeater":

⌈I am viewing x under circumstances of type C, and something looking red to me under circumstances of type C is an unreliable indication of its actually being red⌉ is an undercutting defeater for (1).

This provides only the bare beginnings of an account of perceptual reasoning. There are many important details to be worked out, but this gives the flavor of the system that I propose to build.[48]

6.2 Memory

There is a temptation for epistemologists to regard memory as a mere technicality. It is just a device for storing our beliefs, and plays no epistemological role itself. But such a view is profoundly mistaken. To see this, let us begin with the distinction between occurrent thoughts and stored beliefs. Epistemologists often ignore this distinction, but it will be of paramount importance in getting the structure of our rational architecture right.   Occurrent thoughts are introspectible *events*. Reasoning proceeds in terms of occurrent thoughts. Stored beliefs can be used in reasoning only by first retrieving them and making them occurrent. I take it that this is obvious, but it creates the following difficulty. It seems to be the case that beliefs and their reasons are stored separately, and the latter are much harder to retrieve and may not be retrievable at all. This is presumably for the sake of efficient

---

[47] The doxastic assumption is discussed in more detail in Pollock [1986].

[48] Some of these details are worked out in chapter 5 of my [1974].

retrieval of beliefs. The most natural rules for belief maintenance would require us to reject a belief when we reject other beliefs on the basis of which the first belief is held. But if we cannot remember our reasons for beliefs, then how can we update our system of beliefs in the light of new beliefs?

The inescapable answer is that memory itself plays a certifying role for the retrieved beliefs. Memory serves as a source of nondoxastic input to intellection in much the same way perception does. Let *recalling P* be the state of retrieving *P* (possibly mistakenly) from memory. Then we have the following prima facie reason:

(2)   *S*'s recalling *P* is a prima facie reason for *S* to believe *P*.

There are two distinct considerations that indicate this must be at most a prima facie reason. First, memory itself is fallible. We sometimes have "false memories". But second, even if our memory were infallible, our original reason for believing what we now remember will typically involve defeasible reasoning. Accordingly, we must be able to reject memory beliefs when they conflict with other information.

Of course, we do not always forget our reasons for beliefs, and when we can recall them we must be able to take them into account in belief updating. At a first approximation, this can be accommodated by adopting the following defeater for (2):

> *S* now recalls *P* because he originally believed it on the basis of a set of beliefs one of which is false.[49]

In other words, even though our current reason for a belief held on the basis of memory is the state of recollection and not our original reason for adopting the belief, insofar as we remember the original reason it remains relevant just as it would have been if the current belief were held on that basis rather than on the basis of memory. But if we do not remember our reason, we can still deal with the memory belief in a defeasible way.

There are some intriguing problems concerning how memory interacts with interest-driven reasoning. For instance, we have seen that we do not want a reasoning system to infer $(P \lor Q)$ whenever it infers P. The

---

[49] As I argued in my [1986], we actually need defeaters that are a bit more sophisticated than this. Any beliefs for the original reasoning supporting *P* must be a potential defeater for the memory belief if we also remember enough about the original reasoning.

interest constraints prevent that—addition is not a forward reason. However, *modus ponens* is a forward reason. Suppose that on some past occasion the system has adopted belief in the conditional $[P \supset (P \lor Q)]$. If that conditional is stored in memory and the system now recalls it, then by *modus ponens* it will infer $(P \lor Q)$. We do not want it to make that inference randomly, but it seems that the only way to block the inference is to prevent the system from recalling the conditional. What we recall is influenced in part by nonintellectual psychological processes, but the present considerations suggest that recollection must also be intellectually driven. Our rational architecture must regulate what memory searches are undertaken. It is not at all obvious just how this should work. Notice, however, that this constitutes a purely computational reason for there being a difference between working memory and long-term memory. We do not want the contents of long-term memory to play the same computational role as the contents of working memory. Just how far we can push this explanation of the difference between working memory and long-term memory remains to be seen.

6.3 Induction and Probability

Perception and memory provides the basic data from which reasoning begins, but after perception or recollection has occurred, most of the epistemological burden is carried by probabilistic reasoning and induction.[50] Induction leads to the adoption of general beliefs. Some of these are exceptionless generalizations of the form ⌜All *A*'s are *B*'s⌝, but more frequently they are probabilistic generalizations of the form ⌜Most *A*'s are *B*'s⌝. In scientific contexts these probabilistic generalizations may be given numerical values, yielding conclusions of the form ⌜prob(*B*/*A*) = *r*⌝. The *statistical syllogism* then licenses inferences to particular facts on the basis of these probabilistic generalizations. I will say a brief word about each of these forms of inference.

General beliefs about the world are produced by inductive reasoning. There are a number of different kinds of inductive reasoning. The simplest is enumerative induction, which proceeds in terms of a prima facie reason of the following form:

(3) If *G* is projectible with respect to *F* then ⌜*X* is a sample of *F*'s all of which are *G*'s⌝ is a prima facie reason for ⌜$(\forall x)(Fx \supset Gx)$⌝.

---

[50] This is a sketch of the theory that is presented in full in my [1989]. A more extensive sketch can be found in my [1989a].

The projectibility constraint is essential here. As Goodman [1955] showed, without it any bit of inductive reasoning could be made to conflict with some other inductive reasoning based upon the same sample, with the result that all inductive reasoning would be defeated. It has, however, proven quite difficult to give a general account of projectibility. I will say more about this below.

It is hard to find true exceptionless generalizations outside of the physical sciences. Many of our most useful generalizations are of the form ⌜Most A's are B's⌝. These are probabilistic generalizations. They tell us that the probability is high of an arbitrary A being a B. To accommodate reasoning with such probabilities, we need a principle of *statistical induction*, which enables us to discover the values of these probabilities, and we need a principle of *statistical syllogism* enabling us to draw conclusions about individual A's from the fact that most A's are B's. Statistical induction proceeds in terms of a rule of roughly the form:

(4)   If B is projectible with respect to A, then ⌜X is a sample of n A's r of which are B's⌝ is a prima facie reason for ⌜$prob(B/A)$ is approximately r/n⌝.

More generally, we may use a qualitative version of statistical induction to reason as follows:

(5)   If B is projectible with respect to A, then ⌜X is a sample of A's most of which are B's⌝ is a prima facie reason for ⌜Most A's are B's⌝.

The probability beliefs obtained by statistical induction are used to infer non-probability beliefs in accordance with the statistical syllogism, which can be formulated as follows:

(6)   If B is projectible with respect to A and $r > .5$, then ⌜Ac & $prob(B/A) \geq r$⌝ is a prima facie reason for ⌜Bc⌝, the strength of the reason being a function of r.

When reasoning from probabilities, inferences based upon more information take precedence. This can be captured by augmenting (6) with the following defeater:

(7)   If C is projectible with respect to A then $\ulcorner Cc$ & $\mathrm{prob}(B/A\&C)$ < $\mathrm{prob}(B/A)\urcorner$ is an undercutting defeater for (6).[51]

To illustrate this with an example familiar in the AI literature, if we know that Tweety is a bird and most birds can fly, (6) gives us a prima facie reason for believing that Tweety can fly. But suppose we also know that Tweety is a penguin, and most penguins are unable to fly. This gives us a prima facie reason for the conflicting conclusion that Tweety cannot fly. Because being a penguin entails being a bird, (7) resolves the conflict by defeating our reason for thinking that Tweety can fly and leaving our reason for thinking Tweety cannot fly undefeated.[52]

As I remarked above, outside of science we rarely attach numerical values to probabilities. Accordingly, rather than employing (6), we usually employ the following qualitative version of the statistical syllogism:

(8)   If B is projectible with respect to A then $\ulcorner Ac$ & most A's are B's$\urcorner$ is a prima facie reason for $\ulcorner Bc\urcorner$.

There is a defeater for (8) that is analogous to (7).

The role of projectibility in probabilistic reasoning and induction is puzzling. First, it can be argued persuasively that it is the same notion of projectibility that occurs in each of these prima facie reasons.[53] In each case it turns out that without the projectibility constraint, any application of one of these rules will be defeated by another convoluted instance of the same rule, so the projectibility constraint is required to make the rules nonvacuous. Goodman [1955] introduced the notion of projectibility using contrived predicates like 'grue' and 'bleen',[54] and the impression has remained that most concepts are projectible with just a few "funny" ones being nonprojectible. However, the opposite is the case. I showed in Pollock [1972] that most concepts fail to be projec-

---

[51] This account of the statistical syllogism was first given in Pollock [1983]. A somewhat similar account was first proposed in the AI literature by Touretzky [1984], although the latter account is a bit less general.

[52] The complete account of reasoning by statistical induction and the statistical syllogism is much more complicated than this. Some of the details can be found in my [1983], [1983a], [1984], [1984a], [1986a], [1987a], [1988d], [1989a], and a full theory of probabilistic reasoning and induction will be presented in my [1989].

[53] See Pollock [1989] and [1989a].

[54] An object is grue iff it is first examined before the year 2000 and is green, or is not first examined before the year 2000 and is blue. 'bleen' is defined analogously.

tible, projectibility being the exception rather than the rule. Roughly, conjunctions of "simple" concepts and their negations are projectible, but most logical compounds are nonprojectible. This much can be argued on the grounds that it is required to make (3)−(7) work, but no successful general analysis of projectibility has ever been given.[55]

There are other kinds of reasoning that can properly be called 'inductive'. The most important of these is inference to the best explanation. For instance, I may infer that my cat has been sitting on my chair because it is covered with white hair. I do not believe this because I believe that my cat has been sitting on my chair whenever it is covered with white hair. Rather, I believe it because this is the best explanation for the presence of the hair. I would urge that it is a variant of this that is involved in the confirmation of scientific theories. In that case, inference to the best explanation is called *abduction*. Abduction is generally more interesting than either enumerative or statistical induction. However, there is at present no reasonable theory of precisely how this works. A fair amount of work has been done on abduction in AI, but it tends either to take the notion of an explanation as primitive and unanalyzed, or more commonly it adopts a simplistic view according to which P explains Q if P entails Q.[56] The latter has the unfortunate consequence for abduction that if one hypothesis is confirmed by the data, so is any stronger hypothesis.

OSCAR must eventually be able to reason inductively in all of these ways. The implementation of these various species of induction subsumes the general topic of 'machine learning' in AI. There is a large literature on this that must be reconciled with the corresponding philosophical literature. Once OSCAR's inference engine (the general-purpose interest-driven suppositional deductive and defeasible reasoner) is complete, one of the first tasks that will be undertaken is the implementation of the theories of probabilistic and inductive reasoning formulated in Pollock [1989]. This will simultaneously be a test of those theories and a foray into machine learning.

To put this enterprise in the proper perspective, it deserves to be emphasized again how important the Q&I systems are for probabilistic and inductive reasoning in human beings. The reasoning I have sketched is part of intellection, but it is very expensive computationally. This is particularly true of the probabilistic reasoning. Scientists reason

---

[55] A number of analyses have been proposed, but they are all based upon the misconception that most concepts are projectible. They overlook the problem of logical compounds.

[56] For example, see Charniak and McDermott [1985], pp. 453ff.

in this way when they are being careful, but ordinary people rarely do, and even technical people do not reason in this way outside the context of explicit scientific investigation.[57]   Instead, they form beliefs in ways that are more efficient but yield only approximately correct conclusions.[58]   This is probably essential in any real world system.   It is also of interest to consider AI systems of machine learning in this light. No extant system can be regarded as anything but a very crude approximation to those aspects of intellection that govern inductive reasoning, but such systems are much more plausible when viewed as first approximations to Q&I systems of induction.[59]

6.4 Deductive Reasoning and A Priori Knowledge

Deductive reasoning is any reasoning that is mediated exclusively by conclusive reasons. Deductive reasoning can proceed from other beliefs or suppositions, or it can generate conclusions that do not depend upon any antecedent beliefs. The latter is made possible by suppositional reasoning. For instance, we can deduce $[(P\&Q) \supset Q]$ by supposing $(P\&Q)$, inferring Q, and then conditionalizing. This is connected in interesting ways with the epistemological problem of *a priori* knowledge. A once popular view was that *a priori* truths expressed linguistic conventions. This view withered in the face of Gödel's theorem,[60] but it was not obvious what to put in its place. It seemed to many philosophers, including me, that the only alternative was a kind of "logical intuitionism" according to which we simply "intuit" that certain propositions are true—these are *self-evident* propositions—and then others are derived logically from the self-evident ones.[61]   The problem with this view was that it never seemed plausible that we have such a faculty of logical intuition.

The observation that suppositional reasoning can lead to conclusions that do not depend upon any premises and are thus *a priori* suggests the "no theory theory" of *a priori* knowledge. According to this theory, *a*

---

[57] For instance, Kuipers, Moskowitz, and Kassirer [1988] argue persuasively that even when numerical probabilities are available, expert physicians do not make use of them in diagnosing illness.

[58] This is well documented in Kahneman, Slovic, and Tversky [1982]. Tversky and Kahneman [1974] propose an account of some of this reasoning in terms of what is called *the representativeness heuristic.*

[59] A good sampling of work in machine learning can be found in Michalski, Carbonell, and Mitchell [1983] and [1986]. See also current issues of the journal *Machine Learning.*

[60] See Pollock [1974] for an argument against conventionalism.

[61] Pollock [1974].

priori knowledge does not have any special source; it is just a side effect of the structure of reasoning. Some propositions are *a priori* certifiable by virtue of various kinds of suppositional reasoning, and then others can be deduced from them. Whether this can provide an adequate account of all *a priori* knowledge remains to be seen, but it is an intriguing idea. It will be investigated further in the course of the OSCAR project.

7. Mental Representations

Reasoning manipulates thoughts, and thoughts require a system of mental representation. So far, I have been able to pursue the OSCAR project without getting involved in problems of mental representation. At the abstract level at which development of the inference engine has proceeded, the system is neutral regarding issues of representation. I expect that to change, however, when an attempt is made to implement real world reasoning with huge knowledge bases. At that point, all of the AI work and psychological work on frames, schemes, scripts, and the like will become pressingly relevant. The philosopher *qua* philosopher has little to contribute to much of this. There are a few places, however, in which the nature of reasoning itself dictates certain features of the system of representation. I will just touch upon two aspects of mental representation to which the philosopher can make contributions specifically by examining what is required by his theories of reasoning.

7.1 De Se Thought
David Hume wrote, "Reason is and ought to be a slave of the passions". In more modern terminology, the point of incorporating theoretical reasoning into a cognizer is to help it achieve practical goals. More generally, theoretical reasoning provides factual input for practical reasoning, and practical reasoning in turn can provide higher level guidance for theoretical reasoning. This requires that the systems of mental representation used in theoretical reasoning and practical reasoning mesh properly. That, in turn, requires the agent to have beliefs and desires specifically about his own situation, and as I argued in chapter 2, that requires the agent to have a mental representation that is *essentially* a representation of himself. This must be a logically primitive element in a cognizer's system of mental representation. Thought involving this representation is *de se* thought. A number of philosophers have taken note of the fact that we seem to have such a

logically primitive way of thinking about ourselves.[62]   My proposal is that *de se* thought is required for the proper meshing of practical reasoning and theoretical reasoning.   This amounts to a computational explanation of the phenomenon, and indicates that it must be included in any adequate model of rational architecture.

7.2 Kinds

Thought involves the categorization of objects.   These mental categories are concepts.   An adequate theory of reasoning must include a theory of concepts.   It was once the prevailing view in philosophy that some concepts are logically primitive, getting their content directly from their role in perception, and all the rest have definitions in terms of those logically primitive concepts.   It is now generally recognized that such a theory is inadequate.   It seems that very few concepts have definitions (in the sense of logically necessary and sufficient conditions for satisfaction).   But it is much less clear what sort of theory should be put in the place of the traditional theory.   Many philosophers give lip service to the Kripke/Putnam theory of natural kinds,[63] but it is unclear what that theory amounts to.   It has never been worked out with any precision, and I have argued elsewhere[64] that many aspects of the theory are indefensible.   The psychological literature on concept formation is interesting and should not be ignored by philosophers,[65] although the psychological literature tends sometimes to be a bit naive from a philosophical point of view.[66]   I have no solutions to offer here. I just want to urge that the practitioners of the various subdisciplines of cognitive science should work together on this.

8. A Road Map for Future Research

I envisage the task of modeling human reasoning in OSCAR as progressing through a number of stages, each stage associated with a certain group of problems, and it seems a useful exercise to list these

---

[62] See Castaneda [1966], [1967], and [1968], Chisholm [1981a], Lewis [1979], Perry [1977] and [1979], and my [1982].

[63] See Kripke [1972], Putnam [1973], [1975].

[64] Pollock [1982], pp. 136ff.

[65] See, for example, Smith and Medlin [1981].

[66] For instance, one standard view in psychology takes an agent's concept of a kind to consist of all of his beliefs about the kind.   But that has the untoward consequence that every time your beliefs change, so do your concepts.

problems in the tentative order in which I propose to undertake them. Some parts of some of these problems have already been addressed and tentative solutions implemented.

1. The first task is the construction of a system doing non-introspective interest-driven suppositional deductive defeasible reasoning. This has already been accomplished, although some aspects of the system require further investigation.

2. Integrating defeasible reasoning into a more general system requires us to investigate the conditionals that are connected with undercutting defeaters. That may turn out to be logically quite complicated. At this point all of the contemporary philosophical literature on conditionals becomes potentially relevant.

3. Perception provides defeasible justification for beliefs about the physical world, and it does so without our forming beliefs about how things appear to us. We must consider just how to work "nondoxastic reasons" into the theory of reasoning. The implementation of perceptual reasoning also requires investigation of the role of interest in attention. Of course, to really implement perception, we must have much more than a theory of reasoning from sensory images to beliefs about the world. A considerably more difficult problem is that of understanding the production of the sensory images themselves. However, this process is not part of rational architecture. Image formation is not subject to evaluations of rationality. Instead, it provides the input to rational architecture. In modeling rational architecture we must take image formation as given and then build a system of reasoning on top of that. The intent would be that modules implementing different psychological theories of perception could be incorporated into the system without changing the theory of reasoning.

4. We must investigate the intellectually driven aspects of the use of memory in general purpose reasoning. Memory must provide defeasible certification for remembered thoughts. This is another example of a nondoxastic reason. There are two interconnected problems regarding the role of memory in reasoning. First, there is the problem of integrating memory use with interest-driven reasoning. A deductive reasoner cannot be expected to prove everything from scratch. It must be able to prove simple theorems first and then use those in the proofs of more complicated theorems. But this must be done in a way that does not vitiate the interest constraints. Second, when and what we try to remember is an interest-driven phenomenon. As in the case of perception, however, the most difficult problems concerning memory are not

about the intellectually driven aspects of it. They concern the management of very large databases and are the subject of intense investigation in AI.[67]

5.   The default theoretical reasoning module of OSCAR will provide the inference engine for the implementation of epistemological theories regarding concrete areas of knowledge. The first logically complex case of reasoning that will be implemented in OSCAR is the statistical syllogism.

6.   The implementation of statistical and enumerative induction will be next. We must get the logic of this right before we can hope to implement it in an automated reasoner. That is the subject of Pollock [1989]. That book will appear at the same time as this book, and although it is primarily concerned with the logical aspects of probabilistic reasoning, it was written with implementation explicitly in mind. It is hoped that the theory propounded in that book will provide the jumping-off point for the construction of a reasoner capable of performing the same kinds of inductive reasoning as human beings.

7.   Once the system can deal with perception (of course, it will not really have perceptual processors) and reason inductively, it will be in a position to try to get around in the world and reason about the causal structure of the world. At that point we will encounter the frame problem.[68] AI theorists have tried to solve this problem by tampering with the structure of nonmonotonic reasoning.[69] I think that more is required. My diagnosis of the frame problem is that it has to do with reasoning about counterfactuals. I will try to handle it in part using the analysis I have previously given of counterfactuals, which is explicitly causal.[70] That must be supplemented by an epistemological account of how we learn the truth of counterfactuals, and that will involve defeasible reasoning.

8.   Further progress in the construction of an introspective reasoner requires it to do practical reasoning. The first step must be the construction of a non-introspective practical reasoner. This is an immense topic on which I have done very little. My feeling is that the structure of practical reasoning is much more like the structure of theoretical reasoning than has usually been acknowledged. The reasoning is defeasible, intentions play a role analogous to stored

---

[67] See, for instance, Stonebraker [1988] and Mylopoulos [1988].

[68] See Plyshyn [1987], and also Hanks and McDermott [1987].

[69] See Hanks and McDermott [1987], Shoham [1986].

[70] Pollock [1984b].

beliefs, and so forth.   Contrary to the prevailing opinion in philosophy, I doubt that the maximization of expectation value plays much role at all.   This is partly because of logical incoherences in the way the notion of maximizing expectation value is usually formulated.[71]   In addition, we rarely know the values of the requisite probabilities, and even if we did know the values, making heavy use of numerical probabilities in reasoning is computationally too difficult for any system (human or robot) that must operate in real time.

9.   All of the preceding steps concern the construction of a non-introspective reasoner. The system will next be given the ability to observe and think about its own thoughts. This involves adding the introspective monitoring module to the system of default planar reasoning. By combining step 8 with such introspective monitoring and the ability of the system to generalize inductively about its own thoughts, we can construct an introspective reasoner that is capable of the deliberate adoption of problem-solving strategies.   The control structure governing general intellection must be such that this high level deliberation can override its default reasoning strategies.

10.   At this stage, the system will also be able to engage in practical reasoning about practical reasoning.   Such high level practical reasoning will include such things as the self-criticism of desires in terms of other desires.

11.   The system must be given the ability to evaluate the truth values of its own thoughts.   This involves adding a T-module to the system. This will make it possible for OSCAR to discover reliability defeaters. At this point we will also become involved with the liar paradox.

---

[71] See Pollock [1983b].

Bibliography

Ackerman, Diana
1979   Proper names, propositional attitudes and non-descriptive connotations. *Philosophical Studies 35*, 55–70.
1979a Proper names, essences, and intuitive beliefs. *Theory and Decision* 11, 5-26.
1980   Thinking about an object: comments on Pollock. *Midwest Studies in Philosophy 5*, 501–508.
Andrews, P. B., Pfenning, F., Issar, S., and Klapper, C. P.
1985   The TPS Theorem Proving System. In *8th International Conference on Automated Deduction*, ed. J. H. Siekman. New York: Springer.
Andrews, P. B., Miller, D. A., Cohen, E. L., and Pfenning, F.
1983   Automating higher order logic. In *Automated Theorem Proving: After 25 Years*, ed W. W. Bledsoe and D. W. Loveland. Providence, RI: American Mathematical Society.
Armstrong, David
1968   *A Materialist Theory of Mind*. London: Routledge & Kegan Paul.
1980   *The Nature of Mind and Other Essays*. Ithaca: Cornell University Press.
Baker, Lynne
1987   Contents by courtesy. *Journal of Philosophy 84*, 197–213.
Bealer, George
1984   Mind and anti-mind: why thinking has no functional definition. *Midwest Studies in Philosophy 9*, 283–328.
Bledsoe, W.
1977   Non-reduction theorem proving. *Artificial Intelligence 9*, 1–35.
1983   Some automatic proofs in analysis. *Automated Theorem Proving: After 25 Years*, ed W. W. Bledsoe and D. W. Loveland. Providence RI: American Mathematical Society.
Bledsoe, W., and Tyson, M.
1975   The UT interactive theorem prover. University of Texas at Austin Math Dept. Memo ATP-17.

Block, Ned
1978   Troubles with functionalism. C. W. Savage (ed.), *Perception and Cognition. Issues in the Foundations of Psychology. Minnesota Studies in the Philosophy of Science 9*, 261-325. Reprinted with revisions in Block [1980]. Page references are to this reprinting.
1980   *Readings in Philosophy of Psychology*, vol. 1. Cambridge: Harvard University Press.
1986   Advertisement for a semantics for psychology. *Midwest Studies in Philosophy 10.*

Block, N. and Fodor, J.
1972   What psychological states are not. *Philosophical Review 81*, 159–181. Reprinted in Block [1980]. Page references are to this reprinting.

Boyer, R., and Moore, J.
1979   *A Computational Logic.* New York: Academic Press.

Burge, Tyler
1979   Individualism and the Mental. *Midwest Studies in Philosophy 4* (1979), 73–121.
1982   Other Bodies. In *Thought and Object*, ed. Andrew Woodfield. New York: Oxford.

Campion, J., Latto, R. and Smith, Y. M.
1983   Is blindsight an effect of scattered light, spared cortex, and near-threshold? *Behavioral and Brain Sciences 6*, 423–486.

Carnap, Rudolph
1928   *Der logische Aufbau der Welt.* Hamburg: Felix Meiner.

Cartwright, Nancy
1983   *How the Laws of Physics Lie.* Oxford.

Castaneda, Hector N.
1966   He*: A study in the logic of self-consciousness. *Ratio 8*, 130–157.
1967   Indicators and quasi-indicators. *American Philosophical Quarterly 4*, 85–100.
1968   On the logic of attributions of self-knowledge to others. *Journal of Philosophy 65*, 439–456.
1975   Identity and sameness. *Philosophia 5*, 121–150.

Chang, C., and Lee, R.
1973   *Symbolic Logic and Mechanical Theorem Proving.* New York: Academic Press.

Charniak, Eugene, and McDermott, Drew
1985   *An Introduction to Artificial Intelligence.* Reading, Mass: Addison Wesley.

Chisholm, Roderick
1957   *Perceiving*. Ithaca: Cornell University Press.
1966   *Theory of Knowledge*. Englewood Cliffs, NJ: Prentice-Hall.
1967   The loose and popular and the strict and the philosophical senses of identity.   In *Perception and Personal Identity: Proceedings of the 1967 Oberlin Colloquium in Philosophy*, ed. Norman Care and Robert Grimm.   Cleveland: Case Western Reserve, 82–106.
1976   *Person and Object*. London: Allen & Unwin.
1977   *Theory of Knowledge*, 2d edition. Englewood Cliffs, NJ: Prentice-Hall.
1981   A version of foundationalism. *Midwest Studies in Philosophy 5*, 543–564.
1981a   *The First Person*. Minneapolis: University of Minnesota Press.
Churchland, Paul
1979   *Scientific Realism and the Plasticity of the Mind*.   Cambridge: Cambridge University Press.
Cohn, A.
1985   On the solution of Schubert's steamroller in many sorted logic. *IJCAI85*.
Cowin, Nelson
1988   Evolving conceptions of memory storage, selective attention, and their mutual constraints within the human information-processing system. *Psychological Bulletin 104*, 163–191.
Creary, L. G., and Pollard, C. J.
1985   A computational semantics for natural language. *Proceedings of the Association for Computational Linguistics*.
Cummins, Robert
1983   *The Nature of Psychological Explanation*.   Cambrdige: Bradford/MIT Press.
1989   *Meaning and Mental Representation*. Cambridge: Bradford/MIT Press.
Davidson, Donald
1970   Mental events. In *Experience and Theory*, ed. Lawrence Foster and J. W. Swanson. Amherst: University of Massachusetts Press.
1973   Radical interpretation. *Dialecticos 27*, 313–328.
1974   Belief and the basis of meaning. *Synthese 27*, 309–323.
1975   Thought and talk. *Mind and Language*, ed. S. Guttenplan. New York: Oxford University Press.
Delgrande, J. P.
1988   An approach to default reasoning based on a first–order conditional logic: revised report. *Artificial Intelligence 36*, 63–90.

Dennett, Daniel
1971   Intentional systems. *Journal of Philosophy 68*, 87–106.
1978   Toward a cognitive theory of consciousness. *Minnesota Studies in the Philosophy of Science 9*, 201–228.
1978a   *Brainstorms*. Cambridge: Bradford/MIT Press.
1981   Making sense of ourselves. *Philosophical Topics 12*, 63–81.
1987   *The Intentional Stance*. Bradford/MIT Press.
Donnellan, Keith
1972   Proper names and identifying descriptions. In *Semantics of Natural Language*, ed. Donald Davidson and Gilbert Harman. Dordrecht: Reidel.
Doyle, Jon
1979   A truth maintenance system. *Artificial Intelligence 12*, 231–272.
1988   On universal theories of default. Carnegie Mellon Computer Science Department, technical report CMU-CS-88-111.
1988a   Artificial intelligence and rational self-government. Carnegie Mellon Computer Science Department, technical report CMU-CS-88-124.
Etherington, D.
1987   Formalizing non-monotonic reasoning systems. *Artificial Intelligence 31*, 41–86.
Etherington, D., and Reiter, R.
1983   On inheritance hierarchies with exceptions. *Proceedings of AAAI-83*.
Fodor, Jerry
1975   *The Language of Thought*. New York: Thomas Y. Crowell.
1987   *Psychosemantics*. Cambridge: Bradford/MIT Press.
Frege, Gottlob
1956   The thought: a logical inquiry. *Mind 65.*
Geach, Peter
1968   Identity. *Review of Metaphysics 21*, 3–21.
1980   *Reference and Generality*, 3d edition. Ithaca: Cornell University Press.
Genesereth, M., and Nilsson, N.
1987   *Logical Foundations of Artificial Intelligence*. Los Altos: Morgan Kaufmann.
Gibbard, Alan
1975   Contingent identity. *Journal of Philosophical Logic 4*, 187–221.
Goodman, N.
1955   *Fact, Fiction, and Forecast*. Cambridge: Harvard University Press.

Grice, H. P.
1941   Personal identity. *Mind 50.*

Hanks, S., and McDermott, D.
1987   Nonmonotonic logic and temporal projection.   *Artificial Intelligence 33*, 379–412.

Harman, Gilbert
1973   *Thought.* Princeton University Press.
1986   *Change in View.* Cambridge: Bradford/MIT Press.

Holland, J., Holyoak, K., Nisbett, R., and Thagard, P.
1986   *Induction: Processes of Inference, Learning, and Discovery.* Cambridge: MIT Press/Bradford Books.

Horty, J., Thomason, R., and Touretzky, D.
1987   A skeptical theory of inheritance in non-monotonic semantic nets. *Proceedings of AAAI-87.*

Hume, David
1888   *A Treatise of Human Nature*, ed. L. A. Selby-Bigge, Oxford: Oxford University Press.

Israel, David
1980   What's wrong with non-monotonic logic? *Proceedings of the First Annual National Conference on Artificial Intelligence.* 99–101.

Jackson, Frank
1982   Epiphenomenal qualia. *Philosophical Quarterly 32.*
1986   What Mary didn't know. *Journal of Philosophy 83*, 291–295.

Kahneman, Daniel, Slovic, Paul, and Tversky, Amos.
1982   *Judgment under Uncertainty: Heuristics and Biases.* Cambridge: Cambridge University Press.

Kim, Jaegwon
1978   Supervenience and nomological incommensurables. *American Philosophical Quarterly 15*, 149–156.
1984   Concepts of supervenience. *Philosophy and Phenomenological Research 45*, 153–176.

Kripke, Saul
1972   Naming and necessity. In *Semantics of Natural Language*, ed. Donald Davidson and Gilbert Harman. Dordrecht: Reidel.
1979   A puzzle about belief. In *Meaning and Use*, ed. Avishai Margalit. Dordrecht: Reidel.

Kuipers, Benjamin, Moskowitz, Alan J., and Kassirer, Jerome P.
1988   Critical decisions under uncertainty: representation and structure. *Cognitive Science 12*, 177–210.

Kyburg, Henry, Jr.
1974   *The Logical Foundations of Statistical Inference.* Dordrecht: Reidel.

1983   The reference class. *Philosophy of Science 50*, 374–397.

Lackner, J. R. and Garrett, M. F.
1972   Resolving ambiguity: effects of biasing context in the unattended ear. *Cognition 1*, 359–372.

Langley, Pat
1987   *Proceedings of the Fourth International Workshop on Machine Learning*. Los Altos: Morgan Kaufmann.

Lehrer, Keith
1974   *Knowledge*. Oxford: Oxford University Press.

Lewis, Clarence Irving
1946   *An Analysis of Knowledge and Valuation*. LaSalle, Ill.: Open Court.

Lewis, David
1970   How to define theoretical terms. *Journal of Philosophy 67*, 427–444.
1972   Psychophysical and theoretical identifications. *Australasian Journal of Philosophy 50*, 249–258. Reprinted in Block [1980]. Page references are to this reprinting.
1979   Attitudes de dicto and de se. *Philosophical Review 87*, 513–543.
1980   Mad pain and Martian pain. In *Readings in the Philosophy of Psychology* I, ed. Ned Block. Cambridge: Cambridge University Press.

Loar, Brian
1982   *Mind and Meaning*. Cambridge: Cambridge University Press.
1987   Names in thought. *Philosophical Studies 51*, 169–186.
1988   Social content and psychological content. In *Contents of Thought*, ed. Daniel Merril and Robert Grimm. Tucson: University of Arizona Press.

Loui, R.
1987   Defeat among arguments: a system of defeasible inference. *Computational Intelligence 3*.

Lusk, E., and Overbeek, R.
1984   The automated reasoning system ITP. ANL-84-27, Argonne National Laboratory.

Lusk, E., McCune, W., Overbeek, R.
1985   ITP at Argonne National Laboratory. *8th International Conference on Automated Deduction*, ed. J. H. Siekman. New York: Springer.

Marr, David
1982   *Vision*. New York: W. H. Freeman.

Martin, Robert L.
1970   *The Paradox of the Liar*. New Haven: Yale University press.

1984   *Recent Essays on Truth and the Liar Paradox.* New York: Oxford University Press.

McCarthy, J.

1977   Epistemological problems of artificial intelligence. *Proc. IJCAI-77.* 1038–1044.

1980   Circumscription–a form of non-monotonic reasoning. *Artificial Intelligence 13,* 27–39.

1984   Applications of circumscription to formalizing common sense knowledge. *Proceedings of the Workshop on Nonmonotonic Reasoning, 1984.*

McDermott, D., and Doyle, J.

1980   Non-monotonic logic I. *Artificial Intelligence 13.*

McGinn, Colin

1982   The structure of content. In *Thought and Object,* ed. A. Woodfield. Oxford: Oxford University Press.

Michalski, Ryzsard, Carbonell, Jaime, and Mitchell, Tom M.

1983   *Machine Learning: an Artificial Intelligence Approach.* Los Altos: Morgan Kaufmann.

1986   *Machine Learning: an Artificial Intelligence Approach, Volume 2.* Los Altos: Morgan Kaufmann.

Moore, R.

1985   Semantical considerations on nonmonotonic logic. *Artificial Intelligence 25,* 75–94.

Murray, N. V.

1982   Completely non-clausal theorem proving. *Artificial Intelligence 18,* 67–85.

Mylopoulos, John

1988   *Readings in Artificial Intelligence and Databases.* Morgan Kaufmann.

Nagel, Thomas

1965   Physicalism. *Philosophical Review 74,* 339–356.

1974   What is it like to be a bat? *Philosophical Review 83,* 435–450.

1979   Brain bisection and the unity of consciousness. *Mortal Questions.* Cambridge: Cambridge University Press.

Nevins, A.

1974   A human oriented logic for automatic theorem proving. *Journal of the Association for Computing Machinery 21,* 603–621.

Nisbett, Richard E., and Wilson, Timothy DeCamp

1977   Telling more than we can know: verbal reports on mental processes. *Psychological Review 84,* 231–259.

Nute, D.
1988   Defeasible reasoning: a philosophical analysis in PROLOG. *Aspects of AI*, ed. J. Fetzer. Dordrecht: Reidel.

Oppacher, F., Suen, E.
1985   Controlling Deduction with Proof Condensation and Heuristics. *8th International Conference on Automated Deduction*, ed. J. H. Siekman. New York: Springer.

Pearl, Judea
1988   *Probabilistic Reasoning in Intelligent Systems: Networks of Plausible Inference*. Los Altos: Morgan Kaufmann.

Pelletier, F. J.
1985   THINKER. *8th International Conference on Automated Deduction*, ed. J. H. Siekman. New York: Springer.
1986   Seventy-five problems for testing automatic theorem provers. *Journal of Automated Reasoning 2*, 191–216.

Perry, John
1975   *Personal Identity*. Berkely: University of California Press.
1977   Frege's theory of demonstratives. *Philosophical Review 86*, 474–497.
1979   The problem of the essential indexical. *Nous 13*, 3–22.

Place, U. T.
1956   Is consciousness a brain process?. *British Journal of Psychology 47*, 44–50.

Plyshyn, Zenon
1987   *The Robot's Dilemma*. Norwood, NJ: Ablex Publishing Co.

Pollock, John
1967   Criteria and our knowledge of the material world. *Philosophical Review 76*, 28–62.
1970   The structure of epistemic justification. *American Philosophical Quarterly*, monograph series 4, 62–78.
1972   The logic of projectibility. *Philosophy of Science 39*, 302–314.
1974   *Knowledge and Justification*. Princeton: Princeton University Press.
1979   A Plethora of Epistemological Theories. *Justification and Knowledge*, ed. George Pappas, Dordrecht: Reidel.
1980   Thinking about an object. *Midwest Studies in Philosophy 5*, 487–500.
1981   Statements and propositions. *Pacific Philosophical Quarterly 62*, 3–16.
1982   *Language and Thought*. Princeton: Princeton University Press.
1983   Epistemology and probability. *Synthese 55*, 231–252.
1983a   A theory of direct inference. *Theory and Decision 15*, 29–96.

1983b How do you maximize expectation value? *Nous 17*, 409–422.
1984   A solution to the problem of induction. *Nous 18*, 423–462.
1984a Foundations for direct inference. *Theory and Decision 17*, 221–256.
1984b *The Foundatinos of Philosophical Semantics.* Princeton: Princeton University Press.
1986   *Contemporary Theories of Knowledge.* Totowa, NJ: Rowman and Littlefield.
1986a The paradox of the preface. *Philosophy of Science 53*, 246–258.
1987   Defeasible reasoning. *Cognitive Science 11*, 481–518.
1987a Probability and proportions. *Theory and Decision: Essays in Honor of Werner Leinfellner*, ed. H. Berghel and G. Eberlein. Dordrecht: Reidel.
1987b How to build a person. *Philosophical Perspectives 1*, 109–154.
1988   *OSCAR: A General Theory of Reasoning.* Working paper.
1988a Interest driven reasoning. *Synthese 74*, 369–390.
1988b My brother, the machine. *Nous 22*, 173–212.
1988c Interest driven suppositional reasoning. Working paper.
1988d Defeasible reasoning and the statistical syllogism. working paper.
1989   *Nomic Probability and the Foundations of Induction.* New York: Oxford University Press.
1989a The theory of nomic probability. *Synthese*, forthcoming.
1989b Philosophy and artificial intelligence. *Philosophical Perspectives 4*, forthcoming.
1989c Understanding the language of thought. *Philosophical Studies*, forthcoming.
1989d OSCAR: a general theory of rationality. *Journal of Experimental and Theoretical Artificial Intelligence 1*.
1990   A theory of defeasible reasoning. *International Journal of Intelligent Systems*.
1990a Interest driven suppositional reasoning. *Journal of Automated Reasoning 7*.
Poole, D.
1985   On the comparison of theories: preferring the most specific explanation. *Proceedings of IJCAI-85*.
1988   A logical framework for default reasoning. *Artificial Intelligence 36*, 27–48.
Putnam, Hilary
1960   Minds and machines. In Sidney Hook, ed., *Dimensions of Mind*, New York: New York University Press.

1967   The nature of mental states (originally published under the title "Psychological predicates"). Reprinted in *Mind, Language and Reality: Philosophical Papers*, vol. 2.   London: Cambridge University Press, 1975.

1973   Explanation and reference. *Conceptual Change*, ed. G. Pearce and P. Maynard. Dordrecht: Reidel.

1975   The meaning of 'meaning'. *Minnesota Studies in the Philosophy of Science 7*, 131–193.

Quine, W. V.
1960   *Word and Object*. Cambridge: MIT Press.

Quinton, Anthony
1962   The Soul. *Journal of Philosophy 59*.

Rapaport, W. J.
1984   Quasi-indexical reference in propositional semantic networks. *Proc. COLING-84*.

1984a   Belief representation and quasi-indicators.   Technical Report 215, SUNY Buffalo Department of Computer Science.

Reiter, R.
1980   On reasoning by default. *Artificial Intelligence 13*.

Reiter, R., and Criscuolo, G.
1978   On closed world data bases. In H. Gallaire and J. Minker, ed., *Logic and data bases*, Plenum.

1981   On interacting defaults. *Proceedings IJCAI-81*, 270–276.

Robinson, J. A.
1965   A machine-oriented logic based on the resolution principle. *Journal of the Association for Computing Machinery 12*, 23–41.

Ross, L., Lepper, M. R., and Hubbard, M.
1975   Perseverance in self-perception and social perception: biased attributional processes in the debriefing paradigm. *Journal of Personality and Social Psychology 32*, 880–892.

Rumelhart, David, McClelland, James, and the PDP Research Group
1986   *Parallel Distributed Processing*. Cambridge: MIT Press.

Russell, Bertrand
1912   *The Problems of Philosophy*, Oxford: Oxford University Press.

Schiffer, Stephen
1987   *Remnants of Meaning*. Cambridge: Bradford/MIT.

Schlick, Moritz
1959   Positivism and Realism. In A. J. Ayer, ed., *Logical Positivism*. Glencoe, Ill: Free Press.

Schwartz, E. L.
1977   Spatial mapping in the primate sensory projection: analytic structure and the relevance to perception. *Biological Cybernetics 25*, 181–194.
1980   Computational anatomy and functional architecture of striate cortex: a spatial mapping approach to perceptual coding. *Visual Research 20*, 645–669.

Searle, John
1981   Minds, brains and programs. In John Haugeland, ed., *Mind Design*. Cambridge: MIT Press.
1983   *Intentionality*. Cambridge: Cambridge University Press.

Shoemaker, Sydney
1963   *Self-Knowledge and Self-Identity*, Ithaca: Cornell University Press.
1969   Critical notice: *Myself and Others* by Don Locke. *Philosophical Quarterly 19*, 276–278.
1975   Functionalism and qualia. *Philosophical Studies 27*, 291–315.
1982   The inverted spectrum. *Journal of Philosophy 79*, 357–381.

Shoham, Y.
1986   Time and causation from the standpoint of artificial intelligence. Computer Science Research Report No. 507, Yale University, New Haven.

Smart, J. J. C.
1959   Sensations and brain processes.   *Philosophical Review 68*, 141–156.

Smith, E. E., and Medlin, D. L.
1981   *Categories and Concepts*. Cambridge: Harvard University Press.

Stickel, M. E.
1985   The KLAUS Automated Theorem Proving System.   *8th International Conference on Automated Deduction*, ed. J. H. Siekman. New York: Springer.
1986   Schubert's steamroller problem: formulations and solutions. *Journal of Automated Reasoning 2*, 89–101.

Stitch, Stephen
1983   *From Folk Psychology to Cognitive Science*.   Cambridge: Bradford/MIT Press.

Stonebraker, Michael
1988   *Readings in Database Systems*. Los Altos: Morgan Kaufmann.

Strawson, P. F.
1958   Persons. *Minnesota Studies in the Philosophy of Science II*, ed. Herbert Feigl, Michael Scriven, and Grover Maxwell, Minneapolis: University of Minnesota Press.

Tarski, Alfred
1956   The concept of truth in formalized languages. *Logic, Semantics, and Metamathematics, Papers from 1923 to 1938, by Alfred Tarski*. London.

Thagard, Paul
1988   *Computational Philosophy of Science*. Cambridge: Bradford/MIT.

Touretzky, D.
1984   Implicit orderings of defaults in inheritance systems. *Proceedings of AAAI-84*.

Turing, Alan
1950   Computing machinery and intelligence. *Mind 59*, 434–460.

Tversky, A.,
1977   Features of similarity. *Psychological Review 84*, 327–352.

Tversky, A., and Kahneman, D.
1974   Judgment under uncertainty: heuristics and biases. *Science 185*, 1124–1131.

Uhr, Leonard
1978   Tryouts toward the production of thought. *Minnesota Studies in the Philosophy of Science 9*, 327–364.

Weiskrantz, L., Warrington, E. K., Sanders, M., and Marshall, J.
1974   Visual capacity in the menianopic field followed by a restricted occipital ablation. *Brain 97*, 709–728.

Wiggins, David
1967   *Identity and Spatio-Temporal Continuity*. Oxford: Blackwells.

Williams, Bernard
1970   The self and the future. *Philosophical Review 79*, 161–180.

Wilson, G., and Minker, J.
1976   Resolution, refinements, and search strategies: a comparative study. *IEEE Transactions on Computers C-25*, 782-801.

Wittgenstein, Ludwig
1953   *Philosophical Investigations*. trans. G. E. M. Anscombe, 3d edition. New York: Macmillan.

Wos, L.
1988   *Automated Reasoning: 33 Basic Research Problems*. Englewood Cliffs, NJ: Prentice-Hall.

Wos, L., and Winker, S.
1983   Open questions solved with the assistance of AURA. In *Automated Theorem Proving: After 25 Years*, ed. W. W. Bledsoe and D. W. Loveland. Providence RI: American Mathematical Society.

Index